A CULTURAL HISTORY OF WESTERN EMPIRES IN THE AGE OF EMPIRE

A Cultural History of Western Empires
General Editor: Antoinette Burton

Volume 1
A Cultural History of Western Empires in Antiquity
Edited by Carlos F. Noreña

Volume 2
A Cultural History of Western Empires in the Middle Ages
Edited by Matthew Gabriele

Volume 3
A Cultural History of Western Empires in the Renaissance
Edited by Ania Loomba

Volume 4
A Cultural History of Western Empires in the Age of Enlightenment
Edited by Ian Coller

Volume 5
A Cultural History of Western Empires in the Age of Empire
Edited by Kirsten McKenzie

Volume 6
A Cultural History of Western Empires in the Modern Age
Edited by Patricia Lorcin

A CULTURAL HISTORY OF WESTERN EMPIRES IN THE AGE OF EMPIRE

Edited by Kirsten McKenzie

BLOOMSBURY ACADEMIC
LONDON • NEW YORK • OXFORD • NEW DELHI • SYDNEY

BLOOMSBURY ACADEMIC
Bloomsbury Publishing Plc
50 Bedford Square, London, WC1B 3DP, UK
1385 Broadway, New York, NY 10018, USA
29 Earlsfort Terrace, Dublin 2, Ireland

BLOOMSBURY, BLOOMSBURY ACADEMIC and the Diana logo are trademarks of Bloomsbury Publishing Plc

First published in Great Britain 2018
Paperback edition published 2023

Copyright © Kirsten McKenzie and Contributors, 2018

Kirsten McKenzie and Contributors have asserted their right under the Copyright, Designs and Patents Act, 1988, to be identified as Author of this work.

Cover design: Raven Design
Cover image: British officer and wife seated on chairs on terrace
© Ashmolean Museum/Mary Evans Picture Library

All rights reserved. No part of this publication may be reproduced or transmitted in any form or by any means, electronic or mechanical, including photocopying, recording, or any information storage or retrieval system, without prior permission in writing from the publishers.

Bloomsbury Publishing Plc does not have any control over, or responsibility for, any third-party websites referred to or in this book. All internet addresses given in this book were correct at the time of going to press. The author and publisher regret any inconvenience caused if addresses have changed or sites have ceased to exist, but can accept no responsibility for any such changes.

A catalogue record for this book is available from the British Library.

A catalog record for this book is available from the Library of Congress

ISBN: HB: 978-1-4742-4261-5
PB: 978-1-3503-5825-6
ePDF: 978-1-3502-9041-9
eBook: 978-1-3502-9040-2

Series: The Cultural Histories Series

Typeset by RefineCatch Limited, Bungay, Suffolk
Printed and bound in Great Britain

To find out more about our authors and books visit www.bloomsbury.com and sign up for our newsletters.

CONTENTS

ILLUSTRATIONS		vii
GENERAL EDITOR'S PREFACE		xi
	Introduction *Kirsten McKenzie*	1
1	War *Susan Kingsley Kent*	19
2	Trade *Robert Aldrich*	43
3	Natural Worlds *Ruth A. Morgan*	67
4	Labor *Utathya Chattopadhyaya*	87
5	Mobility *Miranda Spieler*	109
6	Sexuality *Esme Cleall*	131
7	Resistance *Jennifer E. Sessions*	151

8 Race	175
Matthew P. Fitzpatrick	
NOTES	197
FURTHER READING	201
NOTES ON CONTRIBUTORS	235
INDEX	239

ILLUSTRATIONS

CHAPTER 1

1.1 Poster celebrating French African and Colonial forces fighting on the Western Front. Lucien Jones, 1917. — 25

1.2 *Danse de Guerre des Maoris*, Émile-Antoine Bayard, 1860, after Arthur Saunders Thompson. Credit: Photo12/UIG via Getty Images. — 26

1.3 Bengal sepoys. *Magasin Pittoresque*, 1857. — 27

1.4 Female Warriors of King Gezu of Dohomey, 1870. Credit: Lanmas/Alamy Stock Photo. — 29

1.5 General Piet Cronje and Boer Combatants, Mafeking, Second Anglo-Boer War. Credit: Popperfoto/Getty Images. — 32

1.6 Salvation Army making Doughnuts under bombardment of German Guns. Front Line—France. Postcard, *c.* 1914–18. — 38

CHAPTER 2

2.1 Colonialwaren in Germany. Postcard, Private Collection. — 45

2.2 Indian shop in Vietnam. Postcard, Private Collection. — 53

2.3 Department store in Hanoi. Postcard, Private Collection. — 56

2.4 Colonial produce stand. Postcard, Private Collection. — 57

2.5 Algerian sewing machine. Postcard, Private Collection. 59

2.6 Ceylon tea. Printed advertisement, Private Collection. 63

CHAPTER 3

3.1 Map of part of the environs of Madras, showing the relative positions of the Observatory House Station, and the guns, used in the experiments by John Goldingham, FRS, for ascertaining the velocity of sound. John Goldingham, *Madras Observatory Papers* (Madras: College Press, 1826), Courtesy: University of Cambridge, Institute of Astronomy Library. 70

3.2 An 1838 map based on Alexander von Humboldt's concept of isotherms. Heinrich Berghaus (1849), *Alexander von Humboldt's System Der Isotherm-Kurven*, 2nd edn, Gotha: Justus Perthes. Courtesy of the David Rumsey Map Collection. 71

3.3 Planten van suikerriet bij Tegal, *c.* 1890 (Sugarcane plantation, Tegal, Central Java). Courtesy of the University Library, Leiden, KITLV 10735. 75

3.4 Storm track of the hurricane of August and September 1848. Elisee Recluse, *The Ocean, Atmosphere and Life* (New York: Harper, 1873). Courtesy of the National Oceanic and Atmospheric Administration and US Department of Commerce. 83

CHAPTER 4

4.1 Chinese coolies in Cuba, 1860. Credit: Oldtime/Alamy Stock Photo. 91

4.2 Coolie Hut, Jamaica, *c.* 1890, by A. Duperly & Sons. Credit: Archive Farms Inc/Alamy Stock Photo. 94

4.3 December 1928: Lascars at the Opening of the Tower Hill Memorial. Credit: Fox Photos/Getty Images. 97

4.4 Coolie Woman, Martinique. Credit: Archive Farms Inc/Alamy Stock Photo. 100

4.5 East African Ngoma dancers with painted faces, headgear, and jewelry *c.* 1910. Credit: ullstein bild via Getty Images. 105

CHAPTER 5

5.1 Cutaway diagram by William Elford of the *Brooks*, a Liverpool slave ship. First published by The Society for Effecting the Abolition of the Slave Trade in November 1788. Public domain. — 113

5.2 Relégués (recidivists) at the Camp Saint Jean du Maroni in French Guiana (early twentieth century). Public domain. — 119

5.3 Photograph of tirailleurs sénégalais first published in *Les colonies françaises: petite encyclopédie coloniale*, vol. 1, edited by M. Maxime Petit. Paris: Larousse, 1902. Courtesy The New York Public Library. — 118

5.4 Lahore Railway Station. Photographed by William Henry Jackson (1843–1942). Courtesy Prints & Photographs Division, Library of Congress. — 124

5.5 Postcard of fortified train station at Ben Zireg, Algeria (*c.* 1906). Public domain. — 125

CHAPTER 6

6.1 Jean-Léon Gérôme, *The Snake Charmer*, *c.* 1879. Credit: Universal History Archive/Getty Images. — 134

6.2 Poster advertising the "Hottentot Venus." Courtesy of Wellcome Images under Creative Commons licence CC BY 4.0: https://creativecommons.org/licenses/by/4.0/ — 135

6.3 Hawaiian missionary family, 1878. Card from A.A. Montano's New Photographic Gallery, Honolulu. Public domain. — 138

6.4 The British Lion's Vengeance on the Bengal Tiger, *Punch* cartoon 1857. By John Tenniel, 1820–1914. Credit: Universal History Archive/UIG via Getty images. — 144

6.5 Josephine Butler, *c.* 1885. Credit: London Stereoscopic Company/Getty Images. — 147

CHAPTER 7

7.1 Commemorative panel depicting Abd al-Qadir in Aïn Torki, Algeria, in 2016. Credit: Jennifer Sessions. — 152

7.2 Colonial Patriots dressed as "Mohawks" dumping tea into
Boston Harbor, engraving *c.* 1846. Courtesy Prints &
Photographs Division, Library of Congress.   157

7.3 Father Miguel Hidalgo proclaiming the independence of
Mexico in 1810, engraving based on an 1830 lithograph.
Courtesy New York Public Library.   158

7.4 Toussaint Louverture, engraving by Marcus Rainsford, 1805.
Courtesy Schomburg Center for Research in Black Culture,
Manuscripts, Archives and Rare Books Division, The New York
Public Library.   165

7.5 Religious ceremony celebrating the abolition of slavery in
Martinique in 1850. Courtesy J. Paul Getty Museum Open
Content Program.   167

7.6 Two Kiowa women at the 1898 Trans-Mississippi and
International Exhibition in Omaha, Nebraska, photographed
by Frank Rinehart. Courtesy Boston Public Library.   172

CHAPTER 8

8.1 "Racial types" as per Josiah Nott and George Glidden's work
Types of Mankind, 1854. Courtesy University of Michigan
library.   179

8.2 Pacific Islanders on Pineapple Plantation, Queensland, Australia.
Photo courtesy of the National Library of Australia.   187

8.3 Governor Hahl of German New Guinea with his Tolai partner
and child, 1910. Credit: bpk/Ethnologisches Museum, SMB.   190

8.4 Indigenous Australian Prisoners in Neck Chains, Wyndham,
Western Australia. Photo courtesy of the State Library of Victoria.   191

8.5 Askari with the flag of the German Empire. German East Africa.
Photo courtesy of the Bundesarchiv.   192

Every effort has been made to trace copyright holders and to obtain their permission for the use of copyright material. The publisher apologizes for any errors or omissions and would be grateful if notified of any corrections that should be incorporated in future reprints or editions of this book.

GENERAL EDITOR'S PREFACE

Histories of empire have been transformed in the last three decades by a combination of new methods, new archives, and a new generation of scholars who have come of age in a postcolonial world. The impact of these historical forces on how imperialism is understood has been remarkable. For decades the province of geopolitics, diplomacy and the "official mind," imperial history is now just as likely to be told from the bottom up as from the top down. The rise of cultural history has played a significant role in how we think about and narrate imperialism from the ancient world to the twentieth century. With an emphasis on evidence drawn from literature, the arts, life-writing, and a host of fragmentary sources, cultural historians think through patterns of representation and experience that shape the conditions in which histories of all kinds—economic, political, social—happen. They investigate often overlooked subjects and offer new angles of vision on familiar topics through a cultural lens. The ambition of *A Cultural History of Western Empires* is to advance conversations about the work of culture in shaping how empire took root, took shape, was maintained, and faced challenges whether its regimes were of long or short durée. Indeed, no thoroughgoing histories of the subject can afford to ignore the influence that culture has had on the shape of empires in local, regional, and global contexts.

The geographical remit of *A Cultural History of Western Empires* is indicated in its title. As compelling a topic as the wide variety of imperial formations is, and as interconnected as west and non-west have been along the axis of empire from Greece to Beijing and back again, the authors in this volume explore empire's cultural histories in a broadly western European setting. And while the differences between French and German and English imperial experiences are often notable, what is equally striking are the features that cultures of labor, trade, sexuality, race, war, mobility, natural worlds, and resistance share across imperial locales. Even allowing for specificities of time and place, there is a value to taking a very long view of the concept and practice of *imperium*—not simply to note commonalities or differences but to be able to discern through lines across such widely distinctive terrains as the Frankish kingdoms and the world of the post-Versailles settlement. In no small respect, attention to cultural forces, identities, rhetorics, tropes, relationships, and imaginaries make this kind of discernment possible. Reading for culture—which is to say, developing the capacity to plumb a variety of sources and archives for evidence of how meanings and forms were constantly made and struggled over across a range of domains—reveals the work of historical forces that have undergirded and, at times, have redirected or undone imperial power. Empire simply cannot be understood in all its limits and possibilities without an analysis of its cultural histories.

This is a work of scholarly synthesis rooted in the original scholarship and intellectual vision of the volume editors and their contributors. Its audience is students seeking a comparative, interdisciplinary, and evidence-based account of how empires worked at multiple scales. Readers will get a sense, then, of the cultural impact of large-scale territorial expansion and hegemony *and* of the meaning and experience of conquest and colonization in more intimate environments. Contributors have written their essays to make available a broad overview of their theme or topic. Each one draws on a range of materials and case studies to make a larger argument about the history of cultural formations and influences that pertain to their subject. The series is structured around six time periods: Antiquity, The Medieval Age, The Renaissance, The Enlightenment, The Age of Empire, and the Modern Age. These are conceptual and pedagogical, signaling a periodization that modern Western imperialism itself has played an important role in shaping and sustaining. Casting Rome as an imperial touchtone and colonized territories as "ancient" or "medieval" in temporal terms remains an important cultural resource for contemporary empire building, and it draws on a long cultural legacy that contributors both address and challenge. Each volume takes up the chronological parameters assigned in critical conversation with the historical evidence, allowing readers to see the pros and cons of thinking about empire itself as a maker—and breaker—of time periods. Of equal significance, each volume is organized with the same chapter titles so that readers can either follow a theme across time frames—mobility in the Enlightenment as compared to the twentieth century, for example—or read through a single period by exploring the range of thematic lenses on offer. This combination of diachronic and synchronic affords us a unique opportunity to cultivate comparisons that are as deep as they are broad, and to appreciate the indispensability of cultural history to practically all aspects of imperial regime making and unmaking across this particular swath of the global past.

Such a purposeful focus on culture at this juncture in the history of the historiography of empire is worth remarking on. As an object of historical inquiry, culture is arguably the carrier of a number of historical forces that attention to politics or economics alone cannot capture. Though embedded in and constitutive of every aspect of imperial geopolitics, race, gender and sexuality were long invisible to the historians' eye because they were considered trivial, or at best inconsequential to, the workings of real power. Cultural history practices, which bring new forms of seeing and reading as well as new subjects to our sightline, open up the imperial archive to aspects of the past which, in turn, shed new light on old paradigms. Thinking with and through culture also reorients our gaze, pulling us toward sources—diaries, images, discursive motifs—in a diverse array of formations and spaces that illuminate dimensions of hegemony and power otherwise invisible: dismiss-able, even, as immaterial because they are ostensibly "only cultural." What the collective example of this series accomplishes is to suggest how, why, and under what conditions culture has been a maker of imperial history—indeed, that empires have been done and undone by the cultural forces they sought to control but which were not always completely in their grasp. As twenty-first-century forms of imperial power emerge, claiming historical newness and relying on past models of conquest and occupation all at once, we need narratives that insist on the power of histories attuned to the ideological and material work of culture more than ever.

Culture is at the dynamic heart of all imperial histories. It operates in spaces of high command and conjugal intimacy; in ceremony and in ordinary life; in military documents and botanists' texts; at court and on the plantation; through trade routes and refugee settlements; in the pronouncements of empresses and the movements of the lowly beetle; in the signing of treaties and the violence of the battlefield and the inner workings of the household. Thinking through cultures of empire, in turn, throws us back on the protocols and presumptions of the discipline by encouraging us to be ever vigilant about where—in what spaces and through what repertoires—history happens. Empire is not, perhaps, unique in this regard. The irony is that while imperial ambition and self-regard have often been steeped in convictions about the power of culture to conquer and colonize, imperial narratives on a grand scale are often the most impervious to the argument that culture matters. What follows is a wide-ranging and lively set of arguments about how and why that has been incontrovertibly so from antiquity to modern times.

Introduction

Culture in an Age of Empire

KIRSTEN MCKENZIE

A British officer reads aloud to his female companion, the figures affectionately entwined against a peaceful domestic backdrop. The setting is likely Lahore, northern India (now Pakistan), around the middle of the nineteenth century, a time and place of recent and violent colonial conquest.[1] The Indian artist and European sitters who created this graceful scene were brought together by the turmoil of Western imperial expansion.

The image on the cover of this book has much to say about the way we understand the cultural history of Western empires. The soldier at the center reminds us both of the ubiquity of the military in European states across the nineteenth century and that colonization was invariably a process involving violence at some level. It was also, and often no less traumatically, a process of cultural exchange and negotiated identities in which both colonized and colonizer were repeatedly made and remade. Such identities were always unstable: if imperialism was about creating new ways of seeing, it was no less about creating new ways of being. This is a portrait of a European couple in their distinctive dress and material culture, accoutrements both closely observed and occasionally mistranslated.[2] Yet the unknown painter has represented them in an artistic idiom largely located within the Indian subcontinent (Archer 1992). The Mughal-style archway, itself encased within a frame of distinctively stylized flowers and vines, was routinely used as a proscenium to emphasize the importance of the sitters. And if the exaggerated size of the reading officer appeared quaint to eyes tutored in nineteenth-century western notions of perspective, it made perfect sense to an artist likely following particular conventions of signifying relative status in Indian art. To our eyes it is a reminder of the important focus on gender, in concert with other social and identity differentials, as a category of analysis in the most recent developments of imperial historiography. As this painting itself suggests, cultural historians have located the power struggles of empire as much in ways of seeing as in materiality, as much in the intimacies of the domestic sphere as in the movement of armies or the signing of treaties.

If the long nineteenth century covered by this volume was the "Age of Empire," what makes it so in a series devoted to the cultural history of Western empires across a far longer period? Most obviously, its distinctiveness lies in the way in which both the territory and the influence claimed by Western empires between 1800 and 1920 came to cover a greater geographic proportion of the globe than at any time before or since. Empire might be defined as a system of geographically dispersed and expansionist power, one which routinely "reproduces difference and inequality amongst people it incorporates" (Cooper 2005: 27). Not only is the manner in which that power is exercised and felt highly varied, but approaches to empire by historians have also broadened well beyond a focus on formal sovereign power. Environmental and technological factors, resistance on the part of the colonized, shifts in costs and incentives on the part of the colonizers, all of these variables and more influenced the degree to which European metropolitan power was exerted in colonial situations. Furthermore, if colonies were fundamental to European power and prestige, imperial systems could function without them. What historians have termed "informal empire" (a term popularized in Gallagher and Robinson 1953), one that exerts its power through inequitable trade and commerce, does not require establishing territorial sovereign power over colonies. Colonialism itself is also a varied system, particularly in relation to the degree of settler migration, though it invariably involves some degree of dispossession and (depending on labor needs) intentions of population replacement (Hall and Rose 2006). Such is the internal diversity of European imperial power that John Darwin, writing of one example at the height of its global influence, rejects the term "British Empire" in favor of "British world system" (Darwin 2009). Even in the myriad and very different ways in which it touched their lives, however, some iteration of Western imperialism became an increasingly common experience to an ever-larger proportion of the world's population across the Age of Empire.

While this introductory essay cannot hope to offer a systematic overview of world events between 1800 and 1920, I begin with a brief account of how European imperial dominance became increasingly pervasive across the globe in the long nineteenth century. I then move toward considering how historians have approached the question of culture in empire, in particular the relationship between imperial power and identity. Imperial systems became both geographically larger and structurally more complex as the nineteenth century progressed. In the last part of this essay, I consider some of the ways in which historians have sought to grapple with new methods for understanding how these systems were interconnected.

* * *

If the nineteenth century ended as an Age of Empire, it did not begin so, nor would this outcome have seemed inevitable to observers in 1800. The period covered by this volume is bookended by global wars that had their origin in conflicts that convulsed Europe itself. Both the revolutionary (and subsequently Napoleonic) wars, and the Great War of 1914–18 radically redrew the world's geopolitical maps. Europe emerged from the Napoleonic conflagration in 1815 with all but one of the great maritime empires of the last two centuries, that of Great Britain, either eliminated or much reduced. With the exception of Canada, and toeholds in coastal South America, the formal decolonization of the continental Western Hemisphere was largely complete by the 1820s. In 1783 the United States won independence from Britain following a war so ruinously expensive that it hastened the demise of colonial America's ally, *ancien régime* France. This French Revolution in turn set off a train of events that would bring almost a quarter of a century of near-continuous war to Europe and its colonies. After the Battle of Trafalgar (1805) British sea power was undisputed, though war continued almost unabated for another decade. Many French colonies, along with those of their European allies, were taken into (and remained in) British hands. The French Revolution had spiraled into a global turmoil that, in the wake of Napoleon's invasion of the Iberian Peninsula, also lost the once-dominant Spanish and Portuguese empires their possessions in Latin America.

Without the support of Britain, the newly-restored monarchs of Spain and Portugal could not regain their colonial possessions after Napoleon's defeat (Wesseling 2004). In 1823 President Monroe's Doctrine declared the United States' opposition to European colonialism in the Western Hemisphere. As Jennifer Sessions explains in this volume, the revolts of the late eighteenth and early nineteenth centuries, conflicts that initially sought to recast the terrain of empire from within, ended with the "liberation" of the continental Americas and of Haiti in the Caribbean. Yet ironically, as she argues, this decolonization of the Age of Revolutions held within it the seeds of a renewed imperial era. In the wake of these upheavals in the Atlantic world, with only Britain left standing as a European world power, the center of gravity of Western imperialism shifted.[3] While historians have rightly critiqued assumptions about a rigid separation between the so-called first and second British empires, what is not in doubt is that the predominant focus of British attention moved away from the Atlantic world and toward the Indian and Pacific Oceans. While the majority of the Caribbean remained as European colonial possessions, its once-prized sugar economies gradually collapsed under pressure from slave emancipation and European sugar beet (an industry developed to circumvent Britain's blockade of the continent during the Napoleonic wars). European power (once confined largely to maritime entrepôts in Africa and Asia, particularly of the Portuguese, Spanish, and Dutch) began to increase in the eastern hemisphere. Voyages of exploration and scientific inquiry into these regions from the late eighteenth century placed Oceanic peoples and environments at the center of evolving European ideas on nature, culture, and race, ideas that would have profound consequences for both the theory and practice of Western empires. As Ruth Morgan's chapter outlines, imperial expansion saw encounters with unfamiliar environments and cultures that molded the production of knowledge in metropolitan and colonial contexts. Colonies would become laboratories where particular metropolitan ideas about the relationship between the body and the natural world were developed and tested. The expansion of British East India Company possessions on the Indian subcontinent, Britain's conquest of African and Asian colonies held by European rivals in the Napoleonic conflict, and the establishment of a convict colony in Australia, would turn the Indian Ocean into a British lake. Meanwhile, the United States and Russia engaged in conquest and settlement across their respective continental landmasses in circumstances of both indigenous dispossession and violence. Broader (and specifically maritime) expansion by Western empires, however, remained largely muted until the period of so-called "New Imperialism" from around the 1870s.

Lasting until the outbreak of the First World War, New Imperialism was different to previous western iterations of the form in a variety of ways. It saw new European imperial powers (Italy, Germany, and Belgium) as well as resurgent ones such as France, the Netherlands, and Portugal, emerge as eager competitors to British global dominance. German and Italian unification, and intra-European rivalry (encapsulated by pre-unification Germany's humiliation of France in the Franco-Prussian War of 1870) linked imperial expansion to heightened European nationalism. By the end of the nineteenth century, a modernized Japan and an increasingly bellicose America were taking their place as avowedly "western" empires in competition with those in Europe. The late nineteenth and early twentieth centuries marked a high point in western dominance over the rest of the globe.

New imperialism saw the formal colonization of a greater proportion of the world's surface, and at a greater pace, than at any previous time in history. Even uninhabited islands, polar regions, and barren deserts became subject to it. As imperialist muscles were flexed in this scramble for both resources and status, almost the entire African continent and much of Asia and Oceania fell under formal European sovereign rule (if not entirely control) across a thirty-year period. The Great War of 1914–18 readjusted imperial dominance but did not end the global ubiquity of Western empires. The defeated powers, Austria-Hungary, Turkey, and Germany, saw their empires collapse, but only a proportion of formerly subordinate territories secured national independence. Those deemed unfit for immediate self-determination, predominantly Asian and African colonies, were effectively redistributed among the victors under the League of Nations mandate system.[4]

* * *

What enabled this Age of Empire to come into being? If it is the late nineteenth-century period that saw it in full flower, the roots can be traced back to much earlier transformations. Key among these was the development of industrial capitalism, beginning with Britain in the eighteenth century and a crucial factor in ensuring that country's global dominance for much of the nineteenth. As Utathya Chattopadhyaya's analysis of labor in this volume attests, industrialization's transformation of European economic structures, social organization, and ideology would have profound consequences for the Age of Empire.

The impact of changes in transportation and communication technology cannot be exaggerated. At the start of our period the fastest ships could make it from London to Calcutta, India, in two months. By the first decades of the twentieth century, steam power and the construction of the Suez Canal in 1869 (see Robert Aldrich in this volume) reduced travel time on the same route to around two weeks (Wesseling 2004). Undersea telegraph cables, increasing in reach from the 1860s, meant that information connections were even faster. Even at its most advanced (the tea clippers of the middle decades of the nineteenth century) ocean travel in the age of sail was both slow and unreliable, dependent upon an unpredictable energy source. It took the advances of coal-fueled, propeller-driven steam technology to bind far-flung imperial possessions tightly together. Regular shipping timetables were now possible. The rate by which surplus could be transferred from colonized to colonizer was drastically increased. As the price of freight dropped, extracting raw materials through plantation economies (expanding into new crops like rubber that were required for other forms of mechanized transport) became ever-more economical. Yet, as Aldrich reminds us, the economic relations of empire were never uni-directional or purely extractive. Colonized peoples were not just producers of goods. As consumers with purchasing power, they exercised discernment and choice that had economic clout.

These new transport technologies accelerated the demographic consequences of imperialism. Emigrants of all kinds, both voluntary and coerced, could be rapidly and cheaply moved around the globe. As Jennifer Sessions describes, around sixty million Europeans left the continent across roughly the period covered by this volume, half to the United States and half to the expanding settler colonies of the Age of Empire. They were driven by push factors such as famine, persecution, and political unrest, as well as pull factors such as increased opportunities and access to land. The demographic and other consequences for indigenous peoples in these new settler colonies were profound, though policies of displacement (or "genocide" in the view of some historians) were not always implementable in practice.[5] The flow from Asia and Africa was much smaller though arguably more disruptive as it involved various levels of coercion. If the slave trade was formally abolished by Britain in 1807 this did not end either legal slavery (which lasted until as late as 1888 in Brazil and 1896 in Madagascar, for example) or other forms of bonded labor, as Utathya Chattopadhyaya explains in this volume. Systems of indenture took off in the wake of slave abolition, moving large population groups from Africa and Asia and creating distinct communities and cultures around the world as a result. Convict labor—shipped both outward from metropole to colonies and multi-directionally between colonies themselves—remained integral to Western empires, as it would across five centuries. A convenient method of transporting labor to where it was required, regardless of the wishes of those forced to work, convict transportation was perceived as cheaper than slavery. As abolition sentiment mounted across the nineteenth century, it was also considered more morally justifiable. Criminals, after all, could be presented as the agents of their own suffering (Anderson and Maxwell-Stewart 2014).

As Miranda Spieler emphasizes in her chapter, these mass population and trade movements saw the development of new commercial and state surveillance techniques, designed to track goods and people, along with the bureaucracies necessary to sustain them. It was part of the general nineteenth-century explosion in statistical recording and record keeping, the inadvertent result of which was to lay down a vast data set for future historians and (as Ruth Morgan explains) practitioners of other disciplines such as climate scientists. The forced migration of around 165,000 convicts to Australia between 1788 and 1868, to give one example, was enabled and sustained by an increasingly detailed system of record keeping. In its attempt to track and utilize criminal labor, the resultant paperwork preserved a matchless record of nineteenth-century working lives. (It was inscribed in the UNESCO Memory of the World Register in 2007.) These changes in technology and practice did not "annihilate" distances like the vast Pacific Ocean, despite the common parlance of the time. Rather they transformed the ways in which such spaces were known, traversed, and imagined (Steel 2014: 317) and, as Spieler demonstrates, became prominent in the art and literature of the Age of Empire. By the end of our period, routine imperial travelers were not confined to emigrants (whether voluntary or coerced), the military, or administrators. Increasingly they included tourists, traveling for pleasure and recreation. When Sir Joseph Banks joined James Cook's first scientific and exploratory voyage to the South Seas (1768–71) rather than embark upon the traditional Grand Tour of Europe, the decision was deemed highly eccentric. Yet by the late nineteenth and into the early twentieth centuries, the economic model of companies like Burns Philp in the Pacific were based as much around tourism as they were around transporting goods such as copra. Their advertising material drew on exotic images of paradise and savagery that might have been familiar to men like Cook and Banks, even if the comfort in which the Burns Philp passengers traveled would not.

Steam-powered shipping bound empires together, but the development of inexpensive, high-quality steel through the Bessemer process (first developed in Britain in the middle of the century) had even more immediate implications for Western imperial expansion (Choate 2014). In a context of heightened European nationalism and Great Power competition it fueled an accelerating arms race. It was one that tipped the military balance of power in East Asia decisively in Europe's favor for the first time and most of East and South Asia fell under formal European colonial conquest. The notable exceptions were China and Japan, though with very different outcomes. With a stronger central government emerging out of a decentralized Shōgunate, Japan modernized and industrialized, becoming an imperial player in its own right by the early twentieth century and defeating a European Great Power in the Russo-Japanese War of 1904–5. When the Japanese fleet commanded by Admiral Tōgō Heihachirō annihilated two-thirds of the Russian navy in 1905, expanding Japanese control over Korea and Manchuria and humiliating one of the Great Powers of Europe, the German Kaiser described it as the most important naval battle since Trafalgar. It was a harbinger of things to come and a major source of inspiration to anti-imperial nationalists from Turkey to Vietnam (Mishra 2012). By contrast, the Anglo-Chinese Opium Wars (1839–42, 1857–60) were followed by repeated military incursions by both western powers and Japan. Chinese territory was seized, unequal treaties and trading relations were enforced, and the erosion of internal power structures in China witnessed increasing European interference through "informal empire" (Bickers 2011). As Aldrich's chapter underscores, "free" trade was never as beneficent as European ideology would have it.

Industrial production and new metal technologies allowed precision small arms and artillery to be mass produced. Breech-loading weapons and later machine guns enabled reliable and rapid rates of fire. Steamboats and railways (especially important to continental empires) meant that troops carrying such weaponry could be moved rapidly around the globe, including up the navigable rivers of Africa and Asia. Nevertheless, improved military technology was not always decisive and should not be reified in explaining European global expansion. Gunships provided only maritime advantage, for example, and tropical diseases were as least as significant as local resistance in stopping colonial incursions. As Morgan points out, the effect of foreign climates on white bodies became almost an obsession among medical experts and social commentators across the nineteenth century, creating a series of disaster tropes in western thinking that reach into our own time. Improvements in western medicine were decisive factors in imperial conquest and the economic exploitation of new territories in the late nineteenth and early twentieth century. Until that time, European activity in Africa was restricted to the temperate areas of the continent, or to working through African mediators on pre-existing trade routes. With the exception of settler colonies located outside the tropics, such as French Algeria or British Australasia and Southern Africa, the numbers of Europeans on the ground were small. As Susan Kingsley Kent's chapter explains, imperialism relied heavily on the participation of non-Europeans—participation that was both coerced and opportunistic as colonized peoples negotiated the possibilities open to them. It is impossible, as Sessions reminds us, to draw a clear line between resistance and acceptance. Rather, subject peoples made a continual and varied series of choices (however constrained) in how they responded to imperial incursions and rule. For Europeans to pursue their interests, local collaborators were vital, as were the use of indigenous troops. The ideological work done by concepts such as "martial races," as Kent explores, enabled the incorporation of mercenary and conscripted foreign populations into the European war machine. Colonial warfare was not always formalized or even declared, with enemy combatants not a hostile army or government but rather the population itself. Colonized people were highly adept at fighting back on their own turf. Advances in weaponry could prove a double-edged sword, and not only when it was employed by the enemy (as in Afghanistan or New Zealand, for example) against Europeans. When the Zulu army annihilated British forces at Isandlwana in 1879, the victory was as much the result of British over-confidence in their recently-improved military technology (breech-loading Martini Henry rifles) as it was the consequence of superior Zulu battle tactics.

    The global impact of New Imperialism was rooted as much in cultural as in geo-strategic transformations. As Esme Cleall and Susan Kingsley Kent explain, the intensive rivalries of the New Imperial era were shot through with concerns about racial degeneracy arising out of ideas of the struggle between evolving species. Mid- and late nineteenth-century scientific theorizing about race was premised upon a quite different set of ideas about race, culture, and power to the concepts underpinning imperial expansion earlier in the century. While Matt Fitzpatrick's chapter rightly insists upon the disparities and irregularities of imperial racial hierarchies, the late nineteenth century nevertheless stands in contrast to the theories (if not always the practice) of imperial expansion that held sway between the 1820s and 1850s. Cleall's chapter in this volume explains the significant impact of missionary endeavors, notions of moral upliftment, and the civilizing mission on patterns of behavior in a range of European empires across this period. The influence of such endeavors on imperial policy, however, varied over time. To take Britain as an example, what historians have identified as the "humanitarian" influence of evangelical Christianity was on the wane by the middle of the nineteenth century. It was a profound force in both domestic and imperial British politics for the first decades of the nineteenth century, peaking with the abolition of slavery and investigations into the treatment of indigenous subjects in settler colonies in the 1830s. The resultant protectionist policies toward indigenous populations were frequently exerted against settler self-interest, though seldom with any lasting benefit to those colonized (Lester and Dussart 2015). By the 1860s, however, Britain had suffered a series of severe checks both to its power and to its confidence in this particular model of empire. These included widespread uprisings against the British East India Company in India in 1857 (known as the Indian Mutiny to outraged Britons), the protracted New Zealand Wars across the middle decades of the century (in which the Māori proved themselves highly adept with European military technology, including artillery) and the Morant Bay rebellion of 1865 in Jamaica which saw the aspirations of former slaves suppressed with extreme violence by Governor Edward Eyre. There was widespread disillusionment in the ranks of evangelical humanitarians at the desire for both emancipated slaves and colonized peoples to go their own way rather than conform to the dictates of colonialism and the "civilizing process," a desire clearly strong enough to inspire armed revolt. In the wake of these mid-nineteenth century developments, a "less benign view of empire" emerged, with humanitarianism losing the political clout it had wielded earlier in the century (Hall 2004: 47). Instead a more innate, biologically-defined and immutable sense of racial difference increasingly held sway, one coupled with assumptions about the inevitability of a struggle between those deemed fit and those races fated to extinction.

Rising levels of literacy and a growing mass media made these new ideas of imperialism more visible and more widely held among Europeans than ever before. Technological innovations such as engraving, and later photography and film, made empire and its multiple locations increasingly visible to the general population. A new term, "jingoism" entered the English language. Denoting aggressive, expansionist patriotism, it was drawn from the lyrics of a popular music hall song. The modern definition of the word "imperialism" was itself popularized during this period by the English economist and vehement critic of British imperial policy John A. Hobson. His 1902 publication *Imperialism: A Study* appeared three months after the conclusion of the bitter and bloody South African (Anglo-Boer) War, arguably the last conflict of the so-called "Scramble for Africa" (Hobson 1902). Hobson saw the leading cause of the South African War in a pressure group of investors and financiers who would profit from this expansion. He argued that imperialism, not only in Britain but also as enacted by other leading players such as Germany and the United States, involved the aggressive search for, and international conflict over, territory or spheres of influence providing markets and outlets for investment. While it is generally Hobson who is remembered in accounts of imperial historiography for first emphasizing trade as the "economic taproots" (as he phrased it) of empire, he was not alone in criticizing the foundational structures of empire at this moment of High Imperialism. Dadabhai Naoroji, Parsi merchant, British member of parliament, and former mathematics professor in Bombay, published *Poverty and un-British Rule in India* in 1901. His "drain theory" was a comprehensive economic critique of empire that predated Hobson's by a year and went even further in his critique of capitalist expansion and its impact on colonized peoples (Visana 2016).

* * *

New ways of thinking and being, therefore, were as important to the history of imperialism as the conquest of new territories. If improved technology, in the literal sense, was essential to enabling the expansion of western power across the globe in the nineteenth century, then "technologies of power" were fundamental in other ways too. The phrase has come to take on a distinct meaning in the cultural history of Western empire, one quite different from (though related to) the factors outlined earlier, and no less important in explaining how empire works. I now turn to this historiography to investigate the ways in which scholars have approached questions of culture in understanding imperial power and in determining the consequences of Western imperialism for colonized and colonizer alike.

"Technologies of power" (of which more later) was a phrase coined by the French philosopher and historian Michel Foucault to explain the interface between language, knowledge, and the disciplinary structures of the state. Foucault elaborated these ideas in a series of studies published in the 1960s and 1970s that explored the relationship between the individual self and mechanisms of social control through topics such as madness, punishment, and sexuality. (Among a large body of work see Foucault 1977 and Foucault 1990.) The impact of industrial capitalism, the associated rise of the middle class and the elaboration of the bourgeois self were important frameworks connecting his analysis across these works, though colonialism itself was a notable absence from his published work (Stoler 1995). Foucault's scholarship first appeared during a period in which imperial history writing was in a moribund state, viewed by many historians as both irrelevant and (especially by those on the left) apologist. In the immediate aftermath of rapid and widespread decolonization in the 1960s, the focus for scholars working in and on former colonies was toward writing nationalist histories, or pursuing interconnections through area studies. For historians working on European countries, there was little sense that their histories had to be integrated into a wider global perspective. Surveying imperial history writing in the 1980s, David Fieldhouse wondered whether it would be "condemned to share the midden of discredited academic subjects with, say, astrology and phrenology?" (Fieldhouse 1984: 10). Several congruent scholarly developments, however, were about to revitalize imperial history in ways that would have seemed inconceivable in the preceding decade. While the historiographies that brought about this transformation had diverse strands, what united many of them was an emphasis on placing culture at the heart of studies of imperialism.

The transformation was so profound that it became known as the "new" imperial history, though by no means all revisionist imperial scholarship aligned itself with a label that had rather distinct theoretical roots.[6] While a highly diverse group, new imperial historians (and scholars in the fields they were associated with, such as postcolonial studies) frequently were, and remain, characterized by their overt political engagement in feminism, anti-racism, and minority rights. They articulated a close connection between their scholarly work and their activism—urging the need to mount criticism of Western empire and its continued legacies in postcolonial and metropolitan societies alike. In contrast to their highly empirical, even positivist predecessors, these new iterations of imperial history were overtly theoretical and interdisciplinary. They turned away from the field's traditional focus on high politics and economics to highlight the explanatory force of culture and identity in the power structures of empire.[7]

New imperial history came out of a series of broader shifts in scholarship in the late 1970s and early 1980s, variously called the cultural and linguistic turns. It traced even deeper historical roots back to social history. Although European social history was resolutely domestic in its focus, histories from below sought to recover the stories of marginalized individuals and peoples in ways that would prove influential to new forms of imperial history writing. History writing in these decades became increasingly influenced and energized by theoretical formulations in linguistics, philosophy, literary criticism, and anthropology, to name but four of the dominant influences at that time. As these influences were gaining strength, Edward Said, a Palestinian exile working in the United States, published a short and highly polemical book called *Orientalism* (Said 1978). It became, in the minds of many scholars, "the iconic text which linked culture with colonialism" (Hall 2000: 14). At its most basic level, Said's argument was that in western literature, art, and scholarship "The Orient" was produced as a discursive formulation by the West. These forms of cultural power, argued Said in *Orientalism* and his follow-up volume *Culture and Imperialism* (Said 1993), were as significant as the political, economic, and military matters which had thus-far dominated studies of empire. The greatest importance of Said's work, since then much criticized and much extended by scholars both sympathetic and vehemently opposed, can perhaps be found in the way it acted as a catalyst for a new field of study. Said's argument traced roots to the work in the 1950s and

1960s of Martinique-born scholar, psychiatrist, and activist Frantz Fanon who, studying identity in the midst of his own anti-colonial struggles, insisted that colonialism made both colonizers and colonized (Fanon 1952, 1961). In elaborating Fanon's ideas on representation and identity, Said drew on concepts articulated by Foucault whose work was becoming increasingly influential in many branches of English-language scholarship at this time. For Foucault, culture is the discursive construction of meaning, and thus of knowledge, through language. In his formulation, discourse is a process of producing knowledge that is inextricably tied to the power relations within which it is articulated, creating what he called "a regime of truth." Foucault's "technologies of power," therefore, centered on the operation of discourse, especially in relation to the disciplinary structures of the state.

The insights of Foucault- and Saidian-influenced postcolonial studies were only one of the ways in which imperial history writing was revitalized in the 1980s and into the 1990s. Subaltern studies was an associated, and powerful, influence exerted at the same time, with the work of Gayatri Chakravorty Spivak having an especially significant impact on the work of feminist historians (Spivak 1988). Identity politics and activism such as second-wave feminism, gay liberation, and environmentalism were all important contemporary developments. The resultant scholarship insisted on the importance of identities (such as gender) as categories of historical analysis, while emphasizing that they were never *a priori* but always contingent and bound up in power relations. If the influences were many and varied, it was particularly the linguistic and cultural turns that were lambasted by their critics as the "killing of history" (Windschuttle 1994). While this hostility can in part be attributed to the reservations about theory and interdisciplinarity felt by many more traditional imperial historians, some iterations of postcolonial studies can be criticized not only for an overindulgence in jargon, but also (and more seriously) for making totalizing claims based on isolated and decontextualized readings of particular texts. Properly employed, however, discursive theories are eminently suitable for use by historians. Whatever the shortcomings of Foucault's original investigations as works of historical scholarship, his concepts of language and power are bound up in the historical specificity of a particular system of meaning, and thus properly require precise contextualization. Matt Fitzpatrick outlines some of the methodological challenges involved in so doing in a later chapter of this volume. Despite the criticism voiced by historians skeptical of linguistic influences on the cultural turn (for example Darwin 2009) the best work in this tradition has not precluded an analysis of material realities or economic and political contexts. It has proceeded through deep archival engagement, even as it has highlighted innovative critical readings that demonstrate how archives (and the historian working within them) constitute a knowledge-producing discourse in themselves (Burton 2006).

While the "postcolonial condition was global" (Chakrabarty 2009a, 58), much of the academic literature in these new iterations of imperial history initially focused on the British Empire, particularly on the moment of High Imperialism in the late nineteenth century. While this genealogy has not attracted significant scholarly debate, there were likely several convergent reasons for this. The Subaltern Studies group had political imperatives to write back against the heritage of British imperialism in their own region of South Asia, with the high point of the British Raj looming particularly large in their consciousness. Many prominent postcolonial theorists, Said and Spivak among them, found academic positions at elite institutions in the United States, where pioneering work was also being done in fields such as gender and cultural history. All these factors influenced the choice of Britain's empire as the research terrain, and cemented the Anglophone emphasis of these initial methodological interventions. Circumstances in Britain itself in the 1980s and 1990s also lent themselves to a focus on both jingoistic empire and its cultural heritage, as I outline later.

If technological change had profound implications for nineteenth-century Western empires in the most material and literal sense, then Foucauldian "technologies of power" were equally significant in relation to identity, the body, and notions of the self. Perhaps even more remarkable than the transport technologies that bound imperial possessions together across the globe, were the vast range of human behaviors nineteenth-century imperial states increasingly sought to control (Lehning 2013). Esme Cleall's chapter charts the immense effort—discursive, judicial, and reformist—that was put into policing the boundaries between acceptable and unacceptable sexuality, a function of the ways in which this effort was always and everywhere disrupted. The essays of this volume repeatedly touch on this important theme: the biopolitics of colonial rule reached into the most intimate aspects of human existence with an ambition that faced continual resistance and renegotiation on the part of colonized and colonizer alike. Drawing on the theoretical insights about power, culture, and identity I have outlined earlier, the work of Ann Laura Stoler on nineteenth-century Dutch Asia[8] insisted that colonialism played a central role in the creation of bourgeois identity for Europeans both at home and abroad: "Colonialism was not a secure bourgeois project. It was not only about the importation of middle-class sensibilities to the colonies, but about the *making* of them" (Stoler 1995: 99). Taking her cue from Foucault's *History of Sexuality*, Stoler argued that Europe's discourses on sexuality could not be understood outside of empire and that the affirmation of a bourgeois self could not be separated from a racialized context. Her analysis was based on detailed attention to quotidian practices by which European dominance was generated, asserted, and resisted—to childrearing, to control of sexual behavior, and anxiety over bodily functions in the tropics, and to community and state responses to *métis* communities (Stoler, 1995b, 2002).[9]

The "civilizing mission" (upon which Cleall's chapter elaborates) was not a stable, uni-directional projection from the center to the periphery. It was fractured, disrupted, and directed as much at colonizers as at the colonized, implicated with power struggles at home and abroad. Catherine Hall's entwined study of nineteenth-century Birmingham and Jamaica was suggestively titled *Civilizing Subjects*. This was a history of "the making of selves through the making of others" (Hall 2002: 20). In tracking the patterns of identity, representation, and social formation that unfolded in the tumultuous debates over slavery and its aftermath, it demonstrated the impossibility of separating Britain and the Caribbean from one another. Hall's and Stoler's work on British and Dutch empires respectively, and increasing numbers of complementary studies as the field exploded across the 1990s, cut across the boundaries between metropole and colony. They were insistent on the need for connecting places and developments which had previously been dealt with separately in *either* imperial *or* European historiography.

New imperial histories became increasingly caught up in the difficulty of achieving this multi-centered vision, particularly given the increasingly global reach of empire across the nineteenth century. Until the 1990s, most works on empire were conventionally arranged around a divide between a metropolitan core and a colonial periphery, even if they differed in the degree to which local crises and frontier situations were given causative power to shift the core's direction. Fieldhouse's assessment of imperial historiography in the 1980s argued that one of the symptoms of its current weaknesses was a failure to bridge this divide (Fieldhouse 1984). In the decades that followed historians found new and increasingly diverse ways of doing so.

Calls for rethinking the research agenda insisted on the importance of placing "metropole and colony in a single analytic field" (Cooper and Stoler 1997) and on the need to move away from a spatial division that replicated the hierarchical view of the world subscribed to by imperialists themselves. In arguments that have now become axiomatic in imperial history writing, Cooper and Stoler urged that "social transformations are a product of both global patterns and local struggles" (4) and that "colonial historiography has been so nationally bound that it has blinded us to those circuits of knowledge and communication that took other routes than those shaped by the metropole-colony axis alone" (28). As this quotation suggests, these new approaches to imperial history were closely aligned with frameworks that questioned rather than assumed the centrality of the nation-state (Burton 1997). In the decades since the late 1990s, therefore, locating studies of Western empire in place has become at least as important as locating them in time. As Alan Lester, historical geographer and influential proponent of this approach, argues "concepts of place, space and scale now seem just as integral . . . as do those of chronology and periodization, and spatial claims of causation just as relevant as temporal ones" (Lester 2013).

Many historians turned to networks to recast their spatial orientation of nineteenth-century empire and to bypass the rigidity of particular frameworks, such as the nation, in favor of the nodes, both big and small, thrown up by tracking the flows and connections of particular people, goods, ideas, or influences. Tony Ballantyne's conceptualization of imperial connections through the metaphor of the web (a shape that acknowledged a degree of metropolitan centrality as well as recognizing the importance of transverse connections, such as cross-colonial ones) has been particularly influential (Ballantyne 2002). Others used a focus on the links that bound oceans together as distinctive spaces in order to reframe imperial relations, as did Clare Anderson and Sujit Sivasundaram in their respective work on Indian Ocean networks and connections (Anderson 2012; Sivasundaram 2013). Approaches such as these have recently seen histories of imperialism and globalization come closer together than ever before. Historians have abandoned formal political divisions as their *a priori* category of analysis in favor of seeking connections that break out from both the national and the imperial. Western empires intersected and competed with much older sets of networks, both maritime and littoral, such as the trade and migration routes that had long crossed the African continent and linked it to Asia. They also fed into much newer conceptualizations of unity and division based, for example, on race and culture, as Marilyn Lake and Henry Reynolds have explored in their analysis of "White Man's Countries" (Lake and Reynolds 2008).

An important strand in this work on networks was a revival in methods of biography, often tracing the lives of peripatetic individuals and interconnected families. European empires may have been geographically vast, but they were held together by individuals, and even the most marginal historical actors and localized events could have real (and unexpected) impacts on imperial policy and governance (McKenzie 2016). If the structure of state archival collections inevitably privileges national frameworks, individual lives have a way of ignoring such boundaries, breaking free from the grip of the national. The technological innovations I have outlined earlier, as well as the bureaucratic, military, and labor needs of ever-expanding imperial systems, all fostered movement. Tracking mobile lives across space has allowed us to come to new interpretations of these interconnections. Nationally-focused histories tended to treat an individual who left the nation-state (or its colonial precursor) as if they had disappeared into utter irrelevance. A network-based analysis focuses instead on how such men and women bound multiple nodal points together in a widening mesh of ideas, contacts, and experiences, and were themselves transformed in the process. What is frequently referred to as "transnational biography" (though the places connected are not always nation-states) presents the opportunity of showing how place, space, and identity all interconnect in forging both individual fates and transforming imperial social structures

(Ballantyne and Burton 2009; Deacon *et al.* 2010). Where once histories of colonial officials and bureaucrats were ignored as the driest of traditional topics in imperial history writing, such "imperial careering" has enjoyed a resurgence of interest from new historiographical perspectives (Lambert and Lester 2006). Transnational biography is vulnerable to criticism for a focus on elites. Tracking their lives (particularly those of white men) is often easiest within the constraints of the surviving archival record. Recent work by Clare Anderson, however, has demonstrated the impact of subaltern lives on colonial structures as she traces the individual networks crossing and connecting the Indian Ocean world across the long nineteenth century. Anderson's recovery of the lives of convicts from South Asia was made possible by the records generated from growing state surveillance techniques outlined previously. Her careful reading of this archive allowed her to place men and women from the very margins of society front and center in her analysis of the biggest picture issues of imperial history (Anderson 2012).

A significant strand of the new cultural historiography of empire set out to explore its place "at home," another means of breaking down a rigid divide between metropolitan "core" and colonial "periphery." In a period that Antoinette Burton calls "after the imperial turn," we have seen "an accelerated attention to the impact of histories of imperialism on metropolitan societies" (Burton 2011: 2; Burton 2003). If this attention marked a major shift in academic historiography, it is not new in public debate. The impact of empire on European societies were topics of intermittent and heated debate in the Age of Empire itself, often associated with military or political crises or the identification of new social trends. New wealth derived from empire and from industrial manufacturing were considered equally disruptive to the social structures of England, for example, as both took off in the late eighteenth and nineteenth centuries (Raven 1992). The wealthy "nabob" (whose fortune derived from India) and the West Indian planter became figures of public debate and popular satire. Yet much of this history of self-reflection had since become erased from national narratives. Empire had largely disappeared from European national historiography around the time of decolonization and immediately after. Two important early works to buck this trend were John MacKenzie's *Propaganda and Empire* (1984) and his edited collection *Imperialism and Popular Culture* (1986), studies of imperial culture in nineteenth-century Britain. These books would become foundational works in a highly-influential "Studies in Imperialism" series published by Manchester University Press, a series premised on the conviction that "imperialism as a cultural phenomenon had as significant an effect on the dominant as on the subordinate societies." These were claims reminiscent of the arguments of Frantz Fanon I have outlined earlier, despite the different historiographical path followed in MacKenzie's own work (though not always in his series) from that of postcolonial studies.[10]

When MacKenzie's series began in the mid-1980s, imperial history was at a low (perhaps its lowest) ebb (Thompson 2013). The consensus of historical scholarship considered it utterly marginal to internal British society, politics, and culture. Yet this was belied by its renewed and overt presence in wider British society outside the academy. The Brixton riots (1981) focused attention on race as a pressing social division in Britain and the "neo-jingoism" of the Falklands War (1982) was a recent memory. A seductively nostalgic "Raj revival" was becoming ubiquitous in British popular culture, with France experiencing its equivalence in "Indo-chic" (Norindr 1996). "These are dark days" complained British Indian novelist and essayist Salmon Rushdie in 1984, referencing Said's *Orientalism* in his critique of feature films like Richard Attenborough's *Gandhi* and television melodramas such as *The Far Pavilions* and *The Jewel in the Crown*. This "zombie-like revival of the defunct Empire," in Rushdie's view, had produced work as inaccurate as it was dangerous (Rushdie 1992: 87, 101; Hill 1999). There was, as Stuart Ward has reminded us, "much to be said for [MacKenzie] pursuing the idea of a deep-rooted British popular preoccupation with the culture of empire" at this time, even if it swam against the prevailing historiographical tide (Ward 2013: 31). Other scholars espoused related arguments about the centrality of empire at home from very different theoretical and political perspectives. Coming from post-structuralist, feminist, and postcolonial orientations, they were determined to critique the insularity of national history making. Such assertions were given political urgency in reaction to public discourse claiming that ethnic multiculturalism was a recent (and problematic) phenomenon in Europe. Exclusionary and homogenizing narratives, such scholars claimed, shut out the legacy of empire in European dominance. As Fanon had claimed in *The Wretched of the Earth*, "Europe is literally the creation of the Third World" (Fanon 1961: 58). They also ignored the place of "internal 'others'" in European national stories (Tabili 2006; Hall *et al.* 2014). Since the first studies appeared in the 1980s there has been a flowering of scholarly work on imperial high and popular culture in Europe, from music hall ditties to architectural style, as well as major exhibitions on European empire and the visual arts (Benjamin *et al.* 1997; Smith 2016). Scholarship on the iconography of empire, partly inspired by Said's initial work, has become one of the richest seams of imperial cultural history.

Skepticism about the strength of empire at home has been articulated by Bernard Porter (2004) who engaged in a robust debate about the British case (Porter 2008; MacKenzie 2008). Historians have increasingly moved away from a maximalist versus minimalist position, or (as Andrew Thompson puts it) "an imperial Richter scale for measuring the magnitude of empire in national culture" (Thompson 2013: 15; also Thompson 2005) in order to pay as much attention to the diversity of *how* imperial influences were manifested in the metropole, and how they connected with domestic concerns. When antislavery rhetoric, for example, was harnessed in early nineteenth-century Yorkshire politics against a candidate whose wealth derived from plantations in the West Indies, it need not be read as a barometer of the informed knowledge of voters about the plight of black slaves. Rather it was an imperial concern that could be harnessed to very specific local conditions—the industrialization of the wool industry—that touched voters directly. Thus regional, national, and imperial identities overlapped to construct and contest European identities at the most local level (McKenzie 2007). As Robert Aldrich's chapter in this volume makes clear, empire increasingly suffused the quotidian details of everyday domestic life in nineteenth-century Europe. Imperialism did not need to be overtly discussed in order to be ubiquitous. It was frequently assumed rather than articulated (Hall and Rose 2006).

* * *

In charting approaches to writing the cultural history of the Age of Empire developed over the last four decades, I have sought to track at least some of the influences manifested in the contributions that follow. While studies of British imperialism dominated the first cultural histories of empire (much as Britain came to dominate overseas expansion in the Age of Empire itself) the diversity of examples raised in this volume demonstrate both these early influences and our distance from that moment. Historians of empire can only benefit from this wider lens and from more consideration of the history and historiography of diverse imperial circumstances. As these chapters insist, representation and identity cannot be separated from the material power relations of empire, for each is intimately bound up in the other. Cultural history is not a distraction from or distortion of the hard realities of imperial expansion. Taking such an approach is to demonstrate that even phenomena such as climate or time, encompassing measurements that might seem entirely rooted in the physical world, do not stand outside culture. Rather, they are inextricably part of the cultures of empire: manifestations of the struggles, large and small, that bound together the intricacies of colonial relations.

CHAPTER ONE

War

The Racial and Gendered Contours of Conflict, 1800–1920

SUSAN KINGSLEY KENT

Between 1800 and 1920, the Western empires engaged in nearly constant warfare in pursuit, defense, and control of their imperial holdings. Even as they fought one another, as in the Napoleonic Wars of the late eighteenth and early nineteenth centuries and the Great War of the twentieth, their conflicts extended beyond the European continent to encompass imperial lands and peoples. But for most of the period under review, the Western powers waged war not against one another but against local inhabitants who resisted their efforts to establish, maintain, and expand their colonies. From India to Indochina, from the antipodes to British North America, from North and West Africa to South and East Africa, displaced peoples within the Western empires fought hard against their overlords. In virtually every instance, the imperial powers depended on local indigenous peoples to provide the military forces with which to put down rebellions, "pacify" their subjects, and enlarge their territories. In 1914, the inter-European rivalries and tensions that had been displaced onto the colonies after 1880 exploded in the outbreak of the Great War, a conflagration that engulfed millions of colonized peoples, as the Western empires mobilized their subjects to help them preserve their power.

Wars have profound and dramatic impacts on the societies and cultures that engage in them. In addition to provoking demographic, technological, political, social, and/or economic transformations, warfare frequently introduces significant cultural alterations as well. It both sharpens and challenges the identities of those who fight them and, just as powerfully, those who do not. As the nature of warfare changed over the course of the period under consideration, ideas about warriors—their gender, race, and the characteristics of the ideal fighter—underwent important modification as well. The qualities, attributes, and valuation attached to peoples involved in military conflict took on a centrality to the identities of the Western imperial powers, their military collaborators, and their adversaries, informing how they understood their societies and cultures for decades to come.

Almost every society we know of has organized itself according to gender, assigning certain responsibilities, obligations, and privileges to some people—and forbidding them to others—on the basis of the different attributes those people were purported to possess as gendered individuals. We conventionally think of gender as the cultural or social qualities attached to a sexed body. What societies assume about differences between male and female and beliefs about the ways men and women do or are supposed to act informs virtually every aspect of life, but nowhere more prominently than in ideas about wars and those who fight them. Importantly, these ideas of gender were—always—inflected by other status categories such as race and class.

Gender is almost always embedded in some kind of power relationship. Ideas about sexual difference are used to create, justify, uphold, challenge, or resist some kind of power differential in any given society or era. But gender is an amazingly protean entity, amenable to all kinds of interpretations and claims: societies and cultures use it in often contradictory and inconsistent ways to describe themselves and others. As the nature of warfare changed over the period of 1800–1920, the gender and racial identities of those who fought them and those who did not altered, too.

THE NAPOLEONIC WARS AND THE ERA OF CITIZEN ARMIES, 1800–15

Revolutionary wars in America and France ushered in a new kind of citizen-soldier in those lands. Until the late eighteenth century, warfare occupied people of a particular status in society and was fought by mercenaries and/or those unfortunate enough to fall prey to press gangs. Now, however, in America and France, war became an affair of citizens fighting on behalf of one another in the interests of the people and the nation. The ideals of the warrior mirrored those of the citizen: the virtuous citizen was also a manly fighter for the nation. Honor, previously bestowed on men of a certain high status, now attached to men of a much lower rank as well. Manliness became identified with service to the nation and the soldier the model for all men in French and American societies. But even in a republic, empire loomed large, and the manly citizen-soldier played a significant role in the dynamics of getting and keeping it. Napoleon's battle to take Egypt in 1798–1800, for instance, had both a strategic and a symbolic intent. On the one hand, control of the country would hamper Britain's access to India; on the other, defeat of the country that Alexander the Great and Julius Caesar had conquered would position Napoleon and his armies as the inheritors of their glorious legacies. The successful campaign against the Egyptian Mamluks, descended from the warrior caste that had rid the East of the Crusaders in the thirteenth century, gave the French armies a heroic stature that outlasted their eventual defeat at the hands of the British.

In Britain, defeat at the hands of the American colonists in 1783 and the threat of French invasion during the Napoleonic Wars compelled contradictory responses. The wars with France provided the patrician class that ruled Britain and commanded its armies with an opportunity to redeem themselves. Humiliated by upstart citizen militias in America, the men who led the British army found themselves cast as effeminate poseurs who had nothing to contribute to the nation but only vitiated its strength. War with France gave them a second chance to present themselves as manly and heroic leaders, and they took it up with a vengeance, contributing to a cult of heroism that surpassed virtually all previous instances in intensity and display. Men like Lord Nelson, the hero of Trafalgar, set themselves apart from others of their own status, and certainly those of a meaner station, by touting their patriotism, their courage, and their honor—their manliness. At a time when the "other ranks," the enlisted and conscripted men described by the Duke of Wellington as "the very scum of the earth," were regarded as unreliable, uncivilized, and even dangerous, the elite military class presented themselves as the protectors of the nation and the progenitors of imperial expansion. Men only slightly lower down on the social scale joined in the celebration of heroics as well, taking up positions in the army and navy in a burst of patriotism and pride. The officers in the Royal Navy grew from 2,000 in 1792 to 10,000 in 1806; those in the army increased even more. The local volunteer and militia units exploded in size as middle-class men of every age sought to be seen doing their duty for nation and empire. The home guard and volunteer militias possessed some 500,000 members by 1804 (Colley 1992: 183–5. See also Hagemann *et al.* 2010.). Manliness and military service had become intricately connected with one another.

The demonstration of military masculinity led officers to sport uniforms of the most elaborate type and tailoring. Closely-fitted coats and breeches, colorful epaulets, shiny medals, and spectacular plumed helmets set off patrician elites from the popular classes at just the moment when plebeians had become instrumental to the war effort. Uniformed officers might be the quintessential manly figures in early nineteenth-century British society, but the ideal had a distinct class bias. The Napoleonic Wars had become total in nature, requiring the input of everyone. When in 1798 and 1803 the government put out an appeal for recruits, Britons of all ethnicities responded in great numbers. The army grew to 250,000 men in 1814, up from 40,000 in 1789. The navy saw an even greater expansion, growing from 16,000 sailors in 1789 to 140,000 in 1812. Unlike in America or France, however, enlistees volunteered not because citizenship demanded it of them—they were not, in any meaningful way, citizens at all. Fear of invasion by French forces, rather, seems to have driven them to answer their country's call (Colley 1992: 183–5). Nevertheless, the very act of appealing to working men to act as patriots in defense of their nation set up the prospect for citizenship in the future, a gamble the government had no choice but to accept if the country were to be saved from invasion. Fabulous uniforms helped to demonstrate that class distinctions would continue to characterize British society, as did the policy of refusing awards and distinctions to soldiers and sailors of the "other ranks." Only in 1856 did Britain's queen challenge this kind of thinking about the plebeian men who fought for their country with courage, valor, and heroism: she insisted that the newly-created Victoria Cross be conferred on junior officers and common soldiers as well as the elite officer class (Braudy 2005: 297).

MARTIAL RACES, 1815–1914

In the years following the Napoleonic Wars, Britain established control over huge areas in South Africa, Asia, the West Indies, and Canada. In the decades between 1840 and 1870, it expanded its holdings by adding new colonies in Australia, New Zealand, British Columbia, Hong Kong, Lower Burma, Natal, the Transvaal, parts of what would become Nigeria and Sierra Leone, the Gold Coast, and the Punjab, Sind, Berar, and Oudh in India. In the course of building its empire, Britons promulgated a body of systematized racial thought portraying Asians, Africans, Native Americans, Australian Aborigines, and Maori as childlike, feminine, or savage peoples in need of guidance, discipline, and control (see Fitzpatrick in this volume). The presence of a virtuous, manly British imperial master, under whose firm tutelage these benighted people might learn the attributes of civilization, justified their incursions into foreign lands and cultures. While it granted various measures of representative government to the white settlement colonies in Canada, South Africa, Australia, and New Zealand by 1860, it progressively tightened its control over millions of peoples of color. Having essentially lost its first empire with the defeat of Napoleon in 1815, France began to acquire the lands that would make up its second empire in 1830. That year it claimed territory in Algeria; during the reign of Napoleon III (1852–70), it established colonies in Senegal in West Africa and Vietnam, Cambodia, and Thailand in Indochina.

In the last quarter of the nineteenth century, many of the European powers, the United States, and Japan embarked upon a path of what is called "new imperialism." Believing that Britain's great economic prosperity derived from its holding of colonies, politicians and business interests in France, the US, Italy,

Belgium, Germany, and Japan resolved to gain their own. In the early 1880s what has come to be called the "scramble for Africa" took place, whereby the various European powers carved out large areas of the continent they deemed to be their "spheres of influence." France took the lion's share, expanding its claims in North Africa with the creation of a protectorate in Tunisia; in West Africa, it extended control over Senegal and claimed Mauritania, Guinea, Mali, Ivory Coast, Benin, Niger, and Chad. Expansion into the center of the continent brought it the Republic of the Congo, the Central African Republic, and Gabon, while it claimed parts of Somaliland and the island of Madagascar in the east. In Asia, France enlarged its territories in Indochina to include Tonkin and Annam in northern and central Vietnam, respectively, establishing the colony of French Indochina by 1887. Faced with competition for imperial power they had not seen since the end of the eighteenth century, British statesmen and politicians responded in kind, formally annexing vast territories in Asia and Africa—Egypt, the Sudan, Afghanistan, southern Africa, Uganda, Rhodesia, Kenya, and Nigeria—and placing them under the administrative control of the crown in order to protect British "interests" there from encroachment on the part of other European countries.

The ability of Europeans to seize control of and rule over the lands of Asia, Africa, South America, and Oceania stemmed in large part from the new technologies in transportation, communications, medicine, and armaments thrown up by rapid industrialization (see Aldrich in this volume). For the first time, Europeans had the means of administering millions of people with a relatively small number of officials and soldiers. Railroads and steamships enabled explorers, entrepreneurs, and settlers to open up country that had barred their passage in earlier years. The telegraph kept colonial officials in contact with their subordinates in the "bush" and outlying regions and with their superiors in the metropolitan capitals. New medicines like quinine enabled Europeans to cope with diseases like malaria that had decimated their ranks. But above all, it was the invention of new modes of firepower that made it possible for small numbers of Europeans to impose their will over indigenous peoples armed mostly with ancient muskets, spears, and bows and arrows. The breech-loading rifle, the "repeating" machine gun, the gunboat—these weapons gave the Europeans the power to destroy those who resisted their onslaught. This kind of technological might in many ways rendered European warriors less relevant to military success— overwhelming firepower rather than individual prowess and courage determined the outcome of battles now. In this kind of environment—a modern, mechanized society incessantly seeking out material wealth, one in which working-class men and women of all ranks sought participation in the political structures of the nation—how was the manly warrior ideal to be sustained?

In at least two ways. Increasingly, European societies looked to the past for models. Tales of King Arthur's exploits in pursuit of a spiritual end gained purchase, and an emphasis on honor and glory harkening back to the cavalry units of eighteenth-century warfare re-surfaced. Secondly, and relatedly, fighting off the savage barbarians of the uncivilized of Asia and Africa offered a means of regenerating a warrior identity. Ironically, however, it would not be the manly citizen-soldier under the command of valiant commanders who enabled the Europeans to acquire empire. Following the end of the Napoleonic Wars, Britain and France had demobilized their mass armies, and reintroducing mass conscription in pursuit and defense of empire was deemed politically untenable. Their imperial adventuring, which involved enormous levels of deadly violence against a multitude of groups resisting them, required them to turn instead to local indigenous troops to establish and maintain order.

Europeans chose peoples they believed to be especially "martial" to carry out the functions of conquest and policing. An elaborate theory of martial races, historians note, emerged in the second half of the nineteenth century in conjunction with the development of social Darwinism (Streets 2004; Walker 2012). But notions that certain "racial" and "ethnic" groups possessed particular martial talents, energies, capacities, and outlooks had a long history (Rand and Wagner 2012). The belief that Highland Scots, for example, were especially warlike went back centuries. It derived from clans that fought endless pitched battles over cattle, the sign and source of wealth in the Highlands. Clan chiefs enjoyed a system of land tenure that provided them with soldiers: tenancy carried with it the obligation to perform military service. Following the defeat of the Jacobites at the battle of Culloden in 1746, parliament outlawed this system, and made it illegal for any Highlander to possess arms, to wear the traditional Highland plaid and tartan, or play the bagpipes. During the Seven Years War, however, William Pitt recruited into the army many of the Highland clansmen who had been languishing since Culloden. Turning disaffected Scots into soldiers of empire turned out to be a brilliant stroke: these battle-hardened men and their former chiefs proved to be excellent fighters for the crown, and their loyalties to their local clans were transferred to Great Britain and the empire.

Participation in the Atlantic slave trade had convinced Europeans that Africa was a place of "continual," "interminable," and "ceaseless" warfare: the French singled out the Toucouleurs and the Mandinka of West Africa as possessing superior martial abilities. Believing that Africans could better withstand the climate and diseases of the regions they colonized, and convinced that some Africans were simply too fierce to be defeated by European arms, the French in 1857 organized the tirailleurs sénégalais, a military battalion made up of men from "races" they believed to be quintessentially warlike in nature. They used the battalion in numerous instances to police other African peoples as they claimed and conquered more land and people during the scramble for Africa. In 1909, General Hippolyte Langlois voiced the opinion of many of his fellow soldiers and citizens when he asserted that "those who belong to the black race take their qualities as warriors from their heredity, because, as far back as we can go in history, the state of war has been normal in Africa—their social situation that teaches them discipline; the harsh conditions of their existence which render them persistent; their carelessness, which makes them tenacious in the long struggles that characterize the modern battles; their bloody and fatalist temperament, which renders them terrible and shocking" (Ginio 2010, 63) (Figure 1.1).

FIGURE 1.1: Poster celebrating French African and Colonial forces fighting on the Western Front. Lucien Jones, 1917.

In New Zealand, the Maori people had long celebrated their military exploits and victories in *haka*, dances punctuated with shouted words. In defeat, they named their children after failed battles in hopes that their offspring would avenge themselves on their enemies in the future. In 1770, James Cook identified war as Maori's "principle profession"; sixty-five years later, Charles Darwin allowed as how "a more warlike race of inhabitants could not be found in any part of the world than the New Zealanders" (Thompson 1997: 112, 110) (Figure 1.2).

In India, so-called warrior races had arisen in the course of the decline of the Mughal empire. Rajputs and Bhumihars in eastern Uttar Pradesh and Bihar, respectively, fashioned themselves as high-caste warriors in service to local rulers. In Punjab, Sikhs did the same in the early eighteenth century; by the early nineteenth century, they parlayed their military prowess into the creation of their own state. In the second half of the eighteenth century, as the East India Company increasingly took on the functions of ruling India, it turned to those groups that had established themselves as warriors with a long-standing military tradition and incorporated them into the sepoy armies of Bengal, Madras, and Bombay. During the Indian rebellion of 1857, sepoys of the Bengal army rose up against their British officers and marched to Delhi, where they proclaimed the descendant of the last Mughal ruler, Bahadur Shah, "emperor of Hindustan"

FIGURE 1.2: *Danse de Guerre des Maoris*, Émile-Antoine Bayard, 1860, after Arthur Saunders Thompson. Credit: Photo12/UIG via Getty Images.

(Figure 1.3). From Delhi the rebellion spread across much of northern India, attracting alienated groups from all parts of society. For more than a year, Hindus and Muslims, merchants and landowners, princes and peasants fought against and in many cases ousted local British authorities, till it seemed that the British might be ousted altogether. They were not, but it took at least fourteen months before the army that had remained loyal to Britain, made up predominately of the "manly" warrior "races" of Sikhs, Punjabis, and Nepalese Gurkhas, was able to re-establish control in large parts of Oudh and the Punjab, and reassert their authority and rule over the subcontinent as a whole.

Europeans admired those they considered especially martial; they attributed to them a manliness that other Africans and Asians lacked. But the gendered and racialized ideology was not consistent and the French and British sometimes held ambivalent views. They often distinguished between what they saw as the "civilized" warfare conducted by Europeans and the "savage" warfare carried out by certain warrior "races." Colonel Charles Callwell, for instance, who wrote one of the most influential works on imperial conflict, *Small Wars* (1896), cautioned that while superior weaponry alone might not be sufficient to

FIGURE 1.3: Bengal sepoys. *Magasin Pittoresque*, 1857.

overcome the ferocity of "savage" warriors, determined and bold action would "cow" them into submission. "The lower races are impressionable," he argued. "They are greatly influenced by a resolute bearing and by a determined course of action. . . . The records of small wars show unmistakably how great is the impression made upon semi-civilized races and upon savages by a bold and resolute procedure." (Reid 2007, 15). Savagery had for centuries connoted a disordered gender system and a promiscuous sexuality that reduced indigenous peoples to the level of the primitive; these sexualized and gendered images served to justify European intervention in order to tame and discipline the unruly impulses of these subhuman creatures.

It wasn't only men who displayed martial prowess, a fact that introduced complexity and contradiction into the notion of manly, martial races. Since the late seventeenth century, armed, uniformed, disciplined women had served as palace guards to the king of Dahomey in West Africa. By the time Europeans arrived in the early eighteenth century, they had taken on the functions of warriors. Their size, strength, and demeanor led Europeans to dub them "Amazons," after the ancient Greek stories of savage women warriors. Europeans regarded Amazons as superior to male soldiers in discipline, skill, loyalty, effectiveness, and ruthlessness. They trained hard and often; in 1861 a French missionary watched one of their training exercises. "At a given signal," he wrote, "they throw themselves with indescribable fury upon the bank of thorns, cross it, leap upon the thorny house, retire from it as if driven back, and return three times to the charge—all this with such rapidity that the eye can scarcely follow them. They clamber over the thorny obstacles as lightly as a dancer vaults upon a floor, and that though their naked feet are pierced in all directions with the sharp thorns of the cactus." Their training stood them in good stead on the actual battlefield. British Commander Frederick Forbes, who was in West Africa as part of an anti-slavery squadron, watched an attack by Dahomean forces on the city of Atakpame in 1840. Most of the inhabitants fled, but some 400 defenders of the city fought back tenaciously, "kept the Dahomeans in check, killed many, [and] put the males to the rout." It was the Dahomean women who determined the outcome, Forbes noted. "Had it not been for a rally of the amazons, [the defenders] would have discomfited the Dahomean army" (Bay 1998: 228, 231).

The Dahomean women warriors confounded conventional European notions of a proper gender order and marked Dahomean society as, therefore, especially savage. By the middle of the nineteenth century, stories circulated widely in Britain and France of Amazons who engaged in horrific hand-to-hand combat using sharpened fingernails and razors to kill, mutilate, and then eat their foes; of women who brought back the scalps, genitals, and internal organs of their fallen enemies to display as trophies. As explorer Richard Burton's widow claimed, Amazons were "crueler and fiercer than men," creatures who tortured their prisoners and cut open the bellies of pregnant women (Matera, Bastian, and Kent 2012: 52). During the French war against Dahomey in 1892, the women warriors, who made up about one-third of the army, fought courageously and tenaciously, harassing French troops as they made their way into the hinterland (Figure 1.4). The French reported the women's exploits in fulsomely positive terms, impressed by their willingness to attack and attack again the dug-in French forces. Ultimately, the Europeans prevailed, deeply cutting into the women's numbers, eventually compelling them to retreat, and establishing French rule in the colony.

FIGURE 1.4: Female Warriors of King Gezu of Dohomey, 1870. Credit: Lanmas/Alamy Stock Photo.

In many ways, martial race theory highlighted anxieties about its absence at home at the turn of the century. Defeat at the hands of Germany in 1870 had introduced all kinds of questions about the fighting qualities, the very manliness, of the French people. Moreover, dramatic depopulation instilled fears that the country would not be able to defend itself against an increasingly bellicose Germany. In 1910, Lieutenant-Colonel Charles Mangin published *La Force Noire*, calling upon authorities to recruit Africans for the defense of the nation. He was joined by colleagues such as General Henri Bonnal, who argued that in the "coming war . . . the 'black' troops will have no rivals when it is a matter of delivering the final shock . . . their savage impetuosity in attacks with the bayonet" would terrify the German soldiers, a prospect reinforced by the German press in its outrage that France would consider the idea of using barbaric and uncivilized Africans against a European neighbor (Ginio 2010: 64). For many French civilians, the German response was reason enough to go along with the proposal.

Anxieties about a society gone soft plagued Britain as well. Although its population had grown dramatically in the late nineteenth century, it was dwarfed by those of the United States and Germany, and its birth rate had slowed considerably. Fears of population decline joined concerns about the quality of the British population, especially in light of a growing awareness of the depth and degree of poverty and of the high levels of infant mortality that existed throughout the country. The conditions of city life, many believed, enervated formerly healthy specimens, demoralizing them and causing physical deterioration. The solution lay in gathering up the remaining "unoccupied" territories of the world and peopling them with Britons. It was through acquisition, possession, and rule of colonies overseas that Britain's health was to be maintained. "New imperialism" gained momentum from the social Darwinist theories that saw in competition with the other European powers, the United States, and Japan the means by which to create a robust society of virile men and proper, moral women (see Cleall in this volume). As Lord Rosebery put it in a letter to *The Times* in 1900, "an empire such as ours requires as its first condition an Imperial Race—a race vigorous and industrious and intrepid. Health of mind and body exalt a nation in the competition of the universe. The survival of the fittest is an absolute truth in the conditions of the modern world." (Soloway 1990: 39; Porter 1975: 130).

For others, conflict offered the most effective means of strengthening the citizens of a nation. In the eyes of many who embraced Darwin's notions of the survival of the fittest and applied them to the species of human beings as well, war constituted a positive good, an arena in which men could be hardened and those who were unfit could be selected out and prevented from procreating, and thus passing on inferior or degenerate traits to a subsequent generation. Through war, the "effeminate" could be weeded out, the manly preserved. "The stimulus of a great patriotic excitement," wrote one apologist for war and empire, "the determination to endure burdens and make sacrifices, the self-abnegation which will face loss, and suffering, and even death, for the commonweal, are bracing tonics to national health, and they counteract the enervating effects of 'too much love of living,' too much ease, and luxury, and material prosperity. . . . Strength is not maintained without exercise." (Porter 1975: 129).

The fears of deterioration that informed the writings of imperialists and social Darwinists were confirmed and exacerbated in the very last years of the nineteenth century, when Britain provoked a war against a small but determined group of Dutch Afrikaner farmers—called, derisively, Boers—in the Transvaal in South Africa in 1899 in order to secure its hold on the gold mines of the Rand. Confident of their success and determined to teach the Boers a lesson about the power and glory of the British empire, politicians and the public were stunned when their armies suffered a series of humiliating and embarrassing defeats in the first months of the war. Despite being heavily outnumbered, Afrikaners inflicted a series of losses on British forces. The British performance in the first months of the war proved so inept that calls for an inquiry soon arose. By late 1900, those losses had been reversed, but the defeat of the 45,000 Afrikaner guerrilla soldiers required an additional eighteen months and 450,000 British soldiers (Meredith 2008; Nasson 2011).

The Afrikaners constituted not an army per se as much as an irregular commando force made up of virtually all Afrikaner men, showing up when they felt it necessary—and departing when they had more pressing issues elsewhere—on the backs of their own horses in homespun clothing that barely resembled anything like a uniform. Their discipline was lax, and they elected their own officers (Figure 1.5). But in addition to the modern weapons they brought to the battlefield, they possessed extraordinary skills of horsemanship and knew the terrain like the backs of their hands. Consummate hunters, they responded to the needs of the moment, flexible in their tactics and responsive to whatever the situation they faced might demand. They knew what they were doing in defense of their land and their way of life.

The terrible failures started to turn around in February 1900 with the relief of two towns, Kimberley and Ladysmith, which had been under siege. The war continued, the fighting bitter and ugly and seemingly endless. Britain carried out a scorched earth policy, firing farmhouses and fields. Both sides executed prisoners in the field, ignoring international rules governing warfare. The British threw women and children into concentration camps, among the first the world had seen, whose terrible conditions left their inmates diseased and malnourished. Twenty-two thousand Britons died, two-thirds of them from disease. Twenty-four thousand Afrikaners died, 20,000 of them women and children who had suffered in the camps. The remaining Afrikaners found themselves destitute and nearly starved when the fighting stopped in May 1902.

FIGURE 1.5: General Piet Cronje and Boer Combatants, Mafeking, Second Anglo-Boer War. Credit: Popperfoto/Getty Images.

The concentration camps brought women into the narrative of the South African War, and called British manliness into question. General H.H. Kitchener, who became commander-in-chief of the armed forces in 1900, established the camps as part of his military strategy. Because "every farm is to [the Afrikaners] an intelligence agency and a supply depot so that it is almost impossible to surround or catch them," he declared, he ordered the inhabitants of the farms—almost exclusively women and children—into camps where he could keep them from spying and otherwise aiding the Afrikaner cause. In other words, he imprisoned women because they were acting as combatants. When the existence of the camps became known in Britain, an uproar ensued. "What civilized Government ever deported women?" demanded Irish MP John Dillon in the House of Commons. "Had it come to this, that this Empire was afraid of women?" he scoffed. The secretary for war replied that "women and children who have been deported are those who have either been found giving information to the enemy or are suspected of giving information to the enemy." This had the effect of spurring Dillon onto even greater rhetorical outrage. "I ask the honourable gentlemen," he sneered, "if any civilized nation in Europe ever declared war against women. ... A pretty pass has the British Empire come to now!" In more ways than one, the South African War was certainly the "last of the gentleman's wars" (Krebs 2004: 60, 55). Britain won, but its grubby victory left Britons with a very bad taste in their mouths.

In the process of recruiting for the South African War, British officials discovered that fully one-third of those who sought to enlist did not meet military standards of physical health. They were too short, suffered from heart trouble or rheumatism, had weak lungs or flat feet or bad teeth. The small-chested "New Town Type" could not stand up to the rigors of physical training and war, and even many of those who passed through the initial screening had to leave the army later when their health failed. Major General Frederick Maurice reckoned in 1903 that when both the first rejections and the subsequent drop-outs were counted, only two of every five volunteers had proved to be competent soldiers. These figures promised disaster, he warned, for "no nation was ever yet for any long time great and free when the army it put into the field no longer represented its own virility and manhood" (Davin 1997: 93–4). When compared to the Germans—indeed even to the Boers and the Japanese—the British "race" of men paled. Near panic about "race degeneration," "physical degeneration," and "deterioration" ensued.

The embarrassments of the British army during the Boer War and the hysteria over "race deterioration" in the following years helped to give rise to an organization designed to prepare boys for the rigors of life in a world fraught with imperial and international competition, to prepare them, even, for war. In 1908, R. Baden-Powell published *Scouting for Boys*, a handbook that described the process of training boys in the attributes and characteristics necessary to create a race of men capable of upholding Britain's place in the world. Boys, if they were to grow into the right kind of men, would have to accept and obey the orders given them by their elders or superiors; they would have to accept that violence was a part of the natural order of things and be prepared to act violently themselves, which would require them to learn to handle firearms capably; and they would have to recognize and reinforce clear rules of separate spheres for men and women. Baden-Powell's Boy Scouts were "*real* men in every sense of the word, and thoroughly up on scout craft, i.e., they understand living out in jungles, and they can find their way anywhere, are able to read meaning from the smallest signs and foot-tracks; they know how to look after their health when far away from any doctors, are strong and plucky, and ready to face any danger, and always keen to help each other. They are accustomed to take their lives in their hands, and to fling them down without hesitation if they can help their country by doing so." (MacKenzie 1987, 177.). The imperial frontier, and one of its most cherished activities, hunting, provided the best means, short of actual war itself, for developing an imperial race. On the frontier, a man learned how to train for war. A man of action rather than reflection, he relied on his senses and his wits, lived off the land, endured nature's dangers, and ultimately triumphed. Free of women and of the society they inhabited, he displayed a virility that "town types" could not possibly possess, a manliness upon which the survival of Britain and the empire depended.

THE GREAT WAR, 1914–18

The test of the Western empires' survival arrived in 1914. Europe went off to war on a gorgeous summer day in August 1914. Everyone believed that the war would be over "by the time the leaves fall," a sentiment that helped governments recruit the soldiers they initially put into the field. European men went off to a war they were sure would be won by Christmas, a war they were certain would be fought gloriously and valorously. They were badly mistaken.

The 100,000 men who made up the British Expeditionary Force (BEF) had only just ensconced themselves along the western front by the third week in August 1914 when they and the French armies were forced by German advances toward Paris to beat a hasty retreat. At the Battle of the Marne, the French forces held firm, blocking the German path and causing its planners, in frustration, to turn toward the Channel. In October 1914, as the exhausted BEF—what was left of it—clung desperately to its position in the Ypres Salient in Belgium, German troops with far superior numbers, weaponry, and equipment threatened to break through the line that separated them from the Channel ports and possible victory. On October 22, sepoys of the Indian Corps arrived a mile or so from the front and made their way to the makeshift trenches occupied by the BEF. Thus relieved, the British soldiers withdrew to the rear to replenish themselves and gain much needed rest. Over the next week, the Indian troops came under sporadic but deadly assault from rifle fire and shelling, suffering serious losses, especially among its British officer corps. On October 31, nine German battalions attacked the Indian Corps at Messines. Fierce fighting over the next several hours left heavy casualties on both sides, but the Indian Corps held the line, thwarting the German offensive designed to drive the British from the continent. As one military historian has noted, their stand, undertaken in circumstances in which they had lost most of their officers, could not speak the language of those around them, and ended up in motley units made up of soldiers from any number of companies, was truly remarkable. They might not have saved the empire, as some have claimed, but, asserts this historian, "it was certainly true that they had saved the BEF." (Corrigan n.d.: loc 1739).

This account of the Indian Corps impresses upon us the global and imperial nature of the Great War. This was a war of empires as well as, ultimately, a war for empire. Having mobilized its colonial subjects to preserve the power of their imperial overlords, the British and French empires emerged from the conflict with their territory expanded dramatically and their control—at least for the time being—extended to unprecedented reaches. Britain mobilized not just its own citizenry, but called up virtually all of its colonial subjects as well. From the dominions, 630,000 Canadian enlistees and conscripts joined them, as did 417,000 Australians, 103,000 New Zealanders, and 146,000 white South

Africans. Indigenous peoples from South Africa serving in the effort amounted to some 85,000; 4,000 Canadian Indians, 2,700 Maori, and at least 580 Australian Aborigines joined up as well. India sent a million and a half soldiers to support the British war effort, while the West Indies contributed 15,000, 10,000 of whom hailed from Jamaica alone. The French military effort was joined by 200,000 tirailleurs sénégalais and at least as many African laborers.

We tend to focus our lenses on the war in Europe, but the Great War involved fighting on other continents as well. In fact, the first shots fired by the British in the war occurred in German Togoland—where the British were concerned to defend their shipping from German attacks originating from its colonial ports—by a sergeant-major in the West African Frontier Force by the name of Alhaji Grunshi. When the German commander Paul von Lettow-Vorbeck embarked on his dash around southern and eastern Africa, British troops were forced to follow. Not all Britons shared the view that fighting the Germans in Africa was a priority. In Kenya, white settlers protested that the most important task for Europeans was not to fight one another but to secure control of Africans. Vastly outnumbered by blacks and insecure in their hold on the territory, whites feared that fighting among themselves would diminish their prestige in the eyes of Africans; moreover, enlisting Africans in the fight among Europeans would result in blacks killing whites and therefore threatening the fragile white supremacy on which their position was based. In fact, these fears did not materialize; while Europeans certainly took part in the African campaigns of the Great War, their numbers were small. By far the majority of participants in the fighting were Africans. More than two million saw action in the Great War. More than ten percent of them—over 200,000—lost their lives, either killed in action or dying from disease or malnutrition in the horrific conditions under which they worked. Some 25,000 Africans from West Africa; 30,000 from Uganda, Nyasaland, and Kenya; and 2,400 from Rhodesia served as actual soldiers under British (and occasionally French) command, but by far the majority of them worked as carriers. Carriers—or porters—were required in such large numbers because the fighting in Africa took place in areas where roads, railways, and motorized vehicles were scarce, and where the presence of tsetse fly and other biting insects made it impossible for draught animals to survive. The heavy and unrelenting work of supply fell to human beings over the four-year period of the conflict.

The contributions of colonial troops made the difference between defeat and continued stalemate. Until Britain's new army could be recruited and trained, Indian and Australian and New Zealand troops filled the breach following the collapse of the BEF in the winter of 1914–15. The first German gas attack at Ypres in April 1915 did not result in a German breakthrough on the western front only because Canadian troops stood their ground and prevented it. The French and Algerian troops had fled, as had the British artillery gunners, as the gas wafted over them, leaving four miles of Allied line undefended. The Canadians stepped up to man the defenses, and fought for the ground for five days against their persistent foe, gasping for air, eyes streaming, and throats burning as additional gas attacks came their way. Improbably, they held, giving up two miles of ground and losing 208 officers and 5,828 men. But they prevented the Germans from breaking through.

The disasters of the war on the western front decimated French forces. By 1916, huge losses of soldiers and threats of mutiny compelled French authorities to turn to their colonies for help in the fighting. The so-called *force noir*, made up of some 140,000 North and West Africans, entered the European theater in support of its French overlords. The tirailleurs sénégalais proved their mettle immediately, leading the October 24, 1916, attack on Fort Douaumont at Verdun and ousting the Germans from their entrenched position. The battle of Verdun has gone down in French mythology as the moment when the French army displayed its determination to counter German aggression and stand steadfast in defense of its homeland. French commanders believed that African soldiers' "savagery" and "bloodlust" rendered them effective against the enemy, a prejudice that prompted them to send Africans on missions deemed too dangerous for French *poilus* and that resulted in a disproportionately high death rate among the tirailleurs. Germans were said by French officers to be possessed of "an almost irrational fear" when faced with the "aboriginal ferocity" of Senegalese troops, savages, it was rumored, who returned from battle with a "pocketful of white men's ears" (Ginio 2010, 65; Nelson 1970, 608). As early as 1915 the Germans began to compile accounts of atrocities alleged to have been committed by "black" troops against their soldiers. For their part, African soldiers described the war as brutal beyond anything they had ever seen, and they suffered intensely from its effects. Men like Kande Kamara from Guinea, who joined the French Army "out of a sense of masculine pride and martial sense of duty," often returned home grievously wounded and "shell shocked" by the experiences they encountered (Lunn 2009: 136–9).

The Great War had powerful effects on the identities of those who participated in it. The courage and perseverance of the Canadian stand at Ypres, for example, instilled in people at home a fierce pride in their men, even amidst the grief of having lost so many in the assault. Canadians had not regarded themselves as a particularly effective, let alone martial group of British subjects, and had entered the war cognizant of their lack of fighting history. Almost overnight, however, the battle at Ypres changed all that. Suddenly the respect and credence earned by the men under the prolonged gas attack gave Canadians as a people a new standing in the world. In the longer term, the actions of the Canadian troops, their "sad but sublime blood sacrifice," as one historian described it, would serve as a catalyst of the development of a Canadian nationalism (Sheftall 2009: 54).

A similar process occurred among Australians and New Zealanders, only in this instance it was the tragedies of Gallipoli that sparked a new pride and sense of national worth. The bravery and determination of the ANZACs, as the Australian and New Zealand troops were known, had made possible the establishment of the first beachhead on the peninsula, and although the entire campaign—the "splendid failure"—turned into a debacle, Australians and New Zealanders at home gained from the stories of the resolution, spirit, and valor of their fighting men an appreciation of themselves as a distinct people with singular characteristics. The British effort had been ill-planned and badly-executed; their Tommies had not acquitted themselves particularly well; so it was easy to contrast ANZAC resilience, independence, and insouciance to the lack of those qualities among Britons. These attributes became mythologized to all Australians and New Zealanders—the white and male ANZACs at any rate—and formed the core of a manly national identity—mateship—that would take root over the next few decades.

Among Europeans, the outbreak of this war of and for empire in August 1914 was experienced by millions of men as an ecstatic, liberating moment, a release from the stifling domesticity and conflicts of industrial bourgeois society. The war offered an opportunity to escape from a society in which wealth, class status, and domestic ideology limited one's range of activities and experiences, one in which the conflicts of gender, class, and ethnicity could be left behind. Escape from it meant escape to the world of men, to the domain of the masculine, the army or navy, to the world of discipline, obedience, action; an effacing of the partisan conflicts, of the feminine. Politicians, writers, and critics viewed the war as an antidote to the diseased and decadent state of Edwardian society, characterized, in part, by a militant feminist movement that challenged and contested traditional roles and behaviors for men and women. "We have awakened from an opium-dream of comfort, of ease, of that miserable poltroonery of 'the sheltered life,'" wrote English writer Edmund Gosse, in terms usually applied to the lives of privileged women. "Our wish for indulgence of every sort, our laxity of manners, our wretched sensitiveness to personal inconvenience, these are suddenly lifted before us in their true guise as the spectres of national decay; and we have risen from the lethargy of our dilettantism to lay them, before it is too late, by the flashing of the unsheathed sword." (Kent 1993: 13–14). The sudden and dramatic prospect of a newly masculinized English manhood had its counterpart in the reassertion of women's traditional roles.

By 1915, the need of the nation for more soldiers required women to take up the positions they vacated. As men went off to war, women joined the workforce in unprecedented numbers, taking jobs as munitions workers, agricultural laborers, tram conductors, ambulance drivers, frontline nurses, and, finally, after the disasters of 1916, auxiliary soldiers. The exigencies of the war after mid-1915 dramatically upset the perceived gender system of the Victorian and Edwardian periods. Mary Somerville exclaimed in the *Women's Liberal Review*, "Oh! This War! How it is tearing down walls and barriers, and battering in fast shut doors." (Kent 1993: 35). The dismantling of barriers between men's and women's work fostered a blurring of distinctions that had helped to form traditional versions of gender identity. Mrs. Alec-Tweedie rejoiced in the fact that by the events of the war, "women have become soldiers." Moreover, she predicted, it might not be long before "we may have to have women fighters too. . . . For . . . the war has literally metamorphosed everything and everybody. To-day every man is a soldier, and every woman is a man." She argued for the formation of a woman's battalion, foreseeing the day when "rather than let the Old Country go under, the women of the Empire would be willing, aye more than willing, to take a place in the firing line. . . . Give them the chance of the trenches . . . and they would step in right royally and loyally again. . . . Women have done more for their country than handle a rifle, and thousands of us are ready to do that, too." Winifred Holtby realized that "so far as modern war is concerned, the old division of interest between combatant and non-combatant decreases, and the qualifications of the combatant lose their dominatingly masculine traits. . . . War ceases to be a masculine occupation" (Kent 1993: 36) (Figure 1.6).

A perception of blurred gender identities appeared at the front as well as at home. Non-commissioned officers in charge of supplying or transporting

FIGURE 1.6: Salvation Army making Doughnuts under bombardment of German Guns. Front Line—France. Postcard, *c*. 1914–18.

troops, for instance, might regard their work in maternal terms, as in the case of the sergeant-major in Ford Madox Ford's *Parade's End*, whose "motherly heart ... yearned ... over his two thousand nine hundred and thirty-four nurslings," and who wished even "to extend the motherliness of his functions" to officers. Collecting the wounded, battle-hardened men carried them "tenderly, soothing [them] with the gentleness of women." The altered lyrics of a sentimental song about Old England gave explicit recognition that traditional gender identity had broken down under the extremes of war: "Oh, they've called them up from Weschurch, /And they've called them up from Wen, /And they'll call up all the women, /When they've fucked up all the men." (Kent 1993: 38).

The war made many men anxious about their masculinity: Captain McKechnie, in *Parade's End*, agonized, "Why isn't one a beastly girl and privileged to shriek?" (Kent 1993: 39). The unprecedented opportunities made available to women by the Great War—their increased visibility in public life, their release from the private world of domesticity, their greater mobility—contrasted sharply with the conditions imposed on men at the front, where they were immobilized and rendered passive in a subterranean world of trenches. Instead of becoming heroes as they had hoped as they marched gaily off to war, they felt emasculated by the horrors they faced and their incapacity to do anything to alter their situation. The terrors of the war and the expectations of manliness on the part of the frontsoldier combined to produce in large numbers of men a condition that came to be known as "shell shock." These cases of shell shock were in fact cases of male hysteria, in which, given the prescriptions of masculinity that saw in fear a sign of unmanliness, men could articulate their terrors only through a language of the body, as women had done for decades. The masculine imperial British soldier had become feminized.

THE BLACK HORROR ON THE RHINE

At the end of the Great War, some 25,000 to 40,000 Allied forces occupied the German territories of the Rhineland. Starting in October 1919, France sent colonial troops from North and West Africa, a decision driven both by concern about the presence of large numbers of "black" troops in France and by a desire to capitalize on depictions of Africans as especially savage fighters to cow the German people and their leaders. The French especially wished to impress upon Germany that they were a force to be reckoned with, even after the devastation of its fighting men over the past four years. "France does not stop at the Mediterranean, nor at the Sahara," asserted General Mangin; "she extends to the Congo; ... she constitutes an empire vaster than Europe, and which in half a century will number 100 million inhabitants." (Nelson 1970: 612–13). German leaders felt the humiliation keenly, seeing in the presence of African troops an affront to civilization itself. In April 1920, Chancellor Hermann Mueller despaired that "Senegalese negroes occupy the University of Frankfurt and guard the Goethe House!" (Nelson 1970: 616).

Earlier French assertions and wider European beliefs about the intrinsic brutality and violence of Africans, useful perhaps as a means of intimidating enemies, now served to excite condemnation of France's actions. Professions of African ferocity shaded readily into claims that Africans displayed a primitive, savage sexuality. Almost immediately, reports of German women engaging in sexual relationships with Africans gave rise to rumors that tirailleurs sénégalais had embarked on a campaign of rape and assault wherever they were stationed. German authorities played upon these prejudices, instigating a campaign to remove "blacks" from their lands by decrying what they called the "Black Scourge," the "Black Shame," and the "Black Peril" imposed by the French upon their people (Wigger 2009: 557, 558). Racist imagery and diatribes filled the newspapers and all kinds of media: novels and short stories, postcards and posters, plays and movies, depicted wild-eyed, drooling African soldiers preying upon innocent German women and children.

The resulting furor took on international dimensions. In Britain, it was fomented by the publication in the *Daily Herald* of E.D. Morel's "Black Horror on the Rhine." The language employed by all of those publicizing the use of black troops by the French burst with imagery of excesses of every kind. "Frankfurt Runs with Blood," screamed the *Daily Herald* on April 9, 1920. The next day the paper declaimed the "Sexual Horror Let Loose by France on the Rhine. Disappearance of Young German Girls." In the accompanying article, authored by Morel, readers heard in frankly sexual imagery that "France is thrusting her black savages still further into the heart of Germany. . . . There they have become a terror and a horror unimaginable to the countryside, raping women and girls," which, "for well-known physiological reasons," Morel explained, recalling centuries of lore regaling the sexual capacity of African men, "is nearly always accompanied by serious injury and not infrequently has fatal results." Day after day for over two weeks, the *Herald* rehearsed the charges against the black troops, which it described as "an invading horde of savages." "Brutes in French Uniform," ran one headline, followed by "Danger to German Women from 30,000 Blacks." The author despaired that "it is impossible to control the black levies." In a subsequent pamphlet, Morel told his readers that mobilizing African troops to occupy the Rhineland, given their "sexual requirements," necessitated that "in the absence of their own womenfolk *they must be satisfied upon the bodies of white women.*" In the most scurrilous language, he warned that "in ones and twos, sometimes in parties, big, stalwart men from warmer climes, armed with sword-bayonets or knives, sometimes with revolvers, living unnatural lives of restraint, their fierce passions hot within them, roam the countryside. Woe to the girl returning to her home village, or on the way to town with market produce, or at work alone hoeing the fields." (Kent 2009, 55–6).

These stories inflamed public opinion in all the Western empires, prompting outraged calls for the French to withdraw their colonial troops from the Rhineland. They did not, but they did feel compelled to answer the charges leveled against the tirailleurs sénégalais. They had difficulty deciding upon their response, given their desire to keep Germans in a state of fear and, thus, obedient to French authority; they faced the problem, as one historian has pointed out, of having "to refute the image they themselves had helped to create" in presenting Africans as a martial and manly race. (Ginio 2010: 67). Ultimately they settled upon a strategy of both denying the charges made against black soldiers and moderating the picture of Africans, rendering them more childlike than manly, more brave than ferocious, more loyal than warlike. In one effort to counter the charges of sexual assault, for example, French authorities cited the testimony of a purportedly high-class German woman engaged to a Senegalese soldier. She argued that German women favored relationships with Africans owing to the fact that they were more polite and civilized, gentler and kinder than white French troops. (Ginio 2010: 68). This paternal image of an innocent, generous, faithful, and trustworthy defender of the French nation, the virtual opposite of the martial masculinity of the prewar and war years, found purchase among the French during the interwar period as they sought to reconcile their gratitude for the contributions made by their colonial forces with the deep-seated fears created by the presence of Africans in their country. Neither stereotype reflected the realities Africans themselves experienced during the Great War (Lunn 2009).

* * *

The Great War underscores the intrinsic relationship of empire to war we have seen throughout the entire period under review. The interactions of war and empire play out on every level of state and society, from the highest political and economic institutions to the most intimate details of individual daily life. The consequences of wars of and for empire, moreover, result not only in broad global transformations but also in dramatic alterations of self and society. Historians and critics have argued that war provides an arena in which masculinity—and therefore femininity—is starkly and definitively defined. But as the events and developments within the Western empires during the period 1800–1920 demonstrate, definitions of gender proved to be eminently malleable, subject to ruptures caused by class and race that had the possibility of rendering them utterly unrecognizable. The pressures of war deeply informed and challenged the gender and racial orders of the Western imperial powers and their subjects.

CHAPTER TWO

Trade

Trade, Colonialism and Culture, 1780–1920

ROBERT ALDRICH

Picture a middle-class home in late Victorian Britain. Rising in the morning, the family would have washed with soap made from copra, the dried meat of coconuts, likely harvested in the South Pacific, and the lady of the house might have dabbed on scent distilled from the essence of patchouli from India, sandalwood from Oceania, tropical ylang-ylang, or frangipani flowers. The family would dress in wool from Australia, cotton from India—"madras" and "calico" cloth taking their names from Indian cities—with perhaps a scarf of cashmere (named for another Indian region) or pashmina from the Himalayan foothills. The wife would certainly squeeze into a corset whose uncomfortable stays came from the baleen of whales killed in the Pacific or Arctic Oceans, and she might slip on a ring made from South African gold and diamonds, or earrings with rubies from Burma or sapphires from Sri Lanka.

The Victorian family's breakfast would be served on porcelain from China, placed atop tables carved from Asian teak or African mahogany; central to the meal would be Ceylon tea, or perhaps a brew from Assam or Darjeeling, sweetened with sugar from Jamaica or Mauritius, Natal, or Queensland. (Walvin 1997) The husband might then leave for work at an import-export firm such as the Royal Niger Company; a shipping company that transported goods and passengers around the world like P&O; one which insured the ships and cargo such as Lloyds of London; or Barclays Bank, which provided the capital to underwrite the commerce. His spouse—whom bourgeois ideals held should not work outside the home—might write letters to a sister or cousin settled in

Canada or Rhodesia, attend a meeting of a missionary group gathering donations for evangelization of "heathen," or enjoy an exhibition of colonial arts and crafts, and purchase a "curio." The family's sons would learn to identify the pink British outposts on the map, read novels by John Buchan and poems by Rudyard Kipling, and play the imperial game of cricket. The family's evening meal could include lamb from New Zealand (now that meat could be shipped in refrigerated cargos), or mulligatawny soup, or a curry inspired by Indian cuisine, finished off with chocolate and coffee from Africa, and for the gentleman a cigar made from colonial tobacco. If the man were very louche, he could venture into the seedier quarters of the city to smoke opium from Asia or hashish from North Africa, or even indulge in the services of a prostitute trafficked from one of Britain's colonies or another distant place.

By the end of the nineteenth century, if not earlier, many Britons were surrounded by the products of empire and used them daily (Berg 2015). The larder, closets and sitting room of a prosperous family constituted a virtual display of products from the monarch's "domains beyond the seas." The *fin-de-siècle* home was a small domestic version of the panoply of domestic and foreign commodities put on show at the 1851 Crystal Palace exhibition. Many of these goods, notably the all-important tea, were no longer luxuries for the happy few, but were appreciated by a broad range of people, though the beverage drunk by the working-class was not of the same quality or served in such fine chinaware as in more favored families. The story was similar in other European countries, as households compiled shopping lists of requisites from distant countries where their traders operated and, often, their national flags flew. The French drank rough red wine from Algeria and smooth rum from Martinique, and flavored their sweets with vanilla from Tahiti or Madagascar; one Dutch treat was a "rijstafel," an assortment of spicy dishes cooked in the style of the East Indies. In the Germanic countries, consumers bought specialized provisions at shops selling "Kolonialwaren," a catch-all appellation for exotic imported goods (Figure 2.1). Soon if not already, Europeans would ride bicycles, take trams, and drive the new-fangled automobiles equipped with tires made of rubber from "the Far East," buy foodstuffs from gardens fertilized with phosphate from North Africa or the islands of the Southern Ocean, and work with tools manufactured with copper from Zambia and nickel from Canada. They would consume the thousand-and-one other goods offloaded at the docks of Liverpool, Rotterdam, Marseille, and Hamburg.

In his magisterial study of consumption since the fifteenth century, Frank Trentmann argues that "empire changed the terms of consumption," and that "in the age of empire, [trade goods] were associated with superior European technology, science and gunboats." Trade and empire led to the commercialization of new products, and it was "in the liberal atmosphere of the nineteenth century that Europeans truly took command of global consumption." With imperialism,

FIGURE 2.1: Colonialwaren in Germany. Postcard, Private Collection. "Colonialwaren" (sometimes spelled "Kolonialwaren") was used in German-speaking countries as a generic name for exotic and specialty items and smallgoods, especially those imported from outside Europe, such as the "cacao" advertised on the sign of this shop in an unidentified Germany city, a business that is evidently a family affair of several generations of women.

Europeans established themselves as colonial masters and also as "master consumers, relegating the rest to the role of coolies or peasants" (Trentmann 2016: 120, 121, 273, 129). Yet Trentmann also offers a reminder that as well as being producers, the colonized were also consumers, and exercised discernment in preferring one or another type of European cloth or metal goods over others. Trade occurred not along a one-way street but at multiple crossroads: the meeting points of producers and consumers, indigenous and foreign people, old and new consumer desires, militant colonialism and proto-nationalist resistance.

Trade is about economic cycles, commercial balance sheets, the buying and selling of shares on stock exchanges, and the business strategies of entrepreneurs, but it is also profoundly about culture. It involves identifiable cultural perspectives and emotional turns: a lust for profit and a desire for goods beyond basic necessities procured locally. It draws on existing and created consumer needs, from luxury goods to quotidian articles manufactured from imported raw materials. It encompasses aesthetic appreciation of new objects, textures, and tastes, a marveling at the wonders of the wider world, and a yearning for products not traditionally available. It points to fads for the foreign: Orientalism (in the sense of fascination for the Muslim, Arabic, Persian, and Turkish cultures), *Chinoiserie*, and *Japonisme*. Trade takes in the allure of colonial exhibitions and world fairs, broadening travel, innovative strategies of merchandising, and the spread of scholarly and vernacular knowledge about overseas practices and commodities. These aspects of cultural life found greatly increased geographical scope and commercial manifestations in the late 1700s and 1800s.

It is hard to overestimate the effects on international trade, and on colonialism, of two phenomena of the nineteenth century. One is the development of industrial production, which created demands for specific resources—coal to fire furnaces, raw materials for transformation into finished goods—and also produced, in larger volumes, and at lower costs, items for trade by Europeans. The products of the European factories posed severe and sometimes fatal challenges to manufacturers using artisanal technologies outside Europe. Though the stereotype is somewhat exaggerated, the result was a global economy increasingly based on the exchange of primary products from Asia and Africa in return for factory-made goods, industrial technology, and capital investment from Europe and America. The second major change concerned transport, the appearance of railway lines (including those built in the colonies) and deep-water ports, the opening of canals (across the isthmus of Suez in 1869 and Panama in 1914), and the replacement of sailing ships by much larger and faster steamships (Spieler in this volume). The train and the steamship stood as monuments to progress and technological prowess, and they created new cultures of mobility for commodities, as well as for the people of empire, the settlers, slaves, indentured laborers, soldiers and, increasingly, tourists who moved about the world (see Burgess 2016; Tindley and Wodehouse 2016).

Changing technology and transport created remarkable demand for novel products over the long period from 1780–1920, not just an expansion in markets for known commodities, such as coffee, tea, and chocolate, or cotton and wool. Emblematic of the new products is rubber, first obtained from South America and, by the late 1800s, cultivated on plantations in British Malaya and Ceylon, the Belgian Congo, Dutch Sumatra and, somewhat later, French

Vietnam. Rubber, initially used for insulation, came into its own with the invention of bicycles and automobiles, making it one of the most profitably traded commodities by the early twentieth century. A company such as Michelin sourced rubber from plantations in Indochina, manufactured tires in central France, and promoted tourism through its guidebooks. The recreational journeys encouraged by Michelin, with advertising for travel around France, to Indochina and other destinations, provide a particularly evident link between trade and culture, extending to hotels, restaurants, and souvenir shops. Travel on steamships also depended on the new sorts of commodity trade, for instance the mining of nickel that provided an essential alloy for steel hulls (and the soldiers' weaponry that made new conquests easier if bloodier). Growing travel also gave birth to travel agencies, most famously the company formally established by Thomas Cook in 1872.

Given the significance of trade and its wholehearted promotion by colonialists, it is not surprising that historians have devoted much attention to commerce. Indeed, trade has long provided a key theme in analyses of colonial expansion. It has suggested competing theories: what John Hobson called the "economic taproots" of expansion (1902), imperialism as the "highest stage of capitalism" (in the words of Vladimir Lenin (1917)), the "imperialism of free trade" in a famous formulation by John Gallagher and Ronald Robinson (1953) and "gentlemanly capitalism" for Peter J. Cain and Anthony G. Hopkins (1986, 1987). Economic historians have chronicled booms and busts, and tried to tally imperial gains and losses; business historians have explored colonial entrepreneurship, the development of colonial companies, capital formation, and capital and technology transfer. Labor historians have investigated the recruitment, employment, and often exploitation of workers under colonial regimes (Chattopadhaya in this volume).

The "cultural turn" rotated historians' gaze in other directions from the economic history of empire, though the economic history of colonialism has recently sparked renewed interest, including volumes that link imperialism and globalization (e.g., Magee and Thompson 2000). There are also studies of consumption and consumer tastes as part of the lived experiences in colonies and metropoles (De Groot 2006; Trentmann 2016). The "geographical turn" in historical studies underlines the commercial, social, and cultural significance of sites of trade, the movement of goods and people, and the networks woven between metropoles and colonies, and between different colonies. Research on gender and colonialism reveals the impact of commerce on domestic as well as public space, the development of colonial domesticity, and the role of women as producers and consumers (e.g., Bishop 2015). Studies of alcohol, narcotics, and prostitution have exposed trade in addictive substances and commercial sex, and attempts to regulate these types of commerce. "Biographies" of trade goods show the place of selected products in markets, homes, and mentalities (e.g., Morton 1999 on nutmeg; Kurlansky 1998 on cod). These new approaches have added flesh to the bones of a more statistical and cost-accounting chronicling of colonial trade.

Having shown at the outset how goods from the colonies entered westerners' day-to-day lives, this chapter will now turn to particular links between colonialism, trade, and culture over the long nineteenth century, with a particular emphasis on the British Empire. It begins with a discussion of the culture of trade, and then looks at two sites of trade: port cities and department stores. Finally, it points to several social and cultural repercussions produced by trade during the triumphalist age of empire. The discussion focuses on material culture, though it should be remembered that other types of trade, including trade in ideas, held enormous importance as well.

THE CULTURE OF TRADE

Trade is itself a type of culture, based on particular needs and desires for goods that are not home-grown or home-made, and the expectation of earning profits by producing and marketing them. The Enlightenment and revolutionary movements of the eighteenth century, by challenging the established order, stimulated individualism and aspirations to social advancement. Political reform ended the monopoly of aristocrats or members of guilds over certain occupations, and also the sumptuary laws that restricted consumption of various articles to limited elites. Optimistic nineteenth-century rhetoric about opportunities awaiting a "self-made man" and the virtue of enterprise bespoke attitudes favorable to commerce. "Having," despite moralists' warnings, became as important as "being," with acquisition and consumption promoted by new forms of marketing. Images of the bounty unloaded on bustling wharves and arrayed in markets in Europe and throughout the empire—stock-in-trade representations in colonialist propaganda—heroically promised progress, prosperity, and modernity.

Meanwhile, "culture contact" and "first encounters" had introduced new commodities to Europeans and "natives." In the newly "discovered" South Pacific, for instance, islanders manifested great interest for fish-hooks, knives, and other items made of iron since metals were little used in their societies; European textiles and beads were also coveted as exotic goods. Europeans mused on the commercial possibilities for tropical agricultural products, including the sandalwood prized on Asian markets, and the riches of the sea, such as the oil and baleen of whales. They filled trunks with the flora and fauna of Oceania, and the weaponry, carvings, and tapa-cloth made by local artists and artisans. By the end of the 1800s, nickel from New Caledonia, phosphate from Nauru and French Polynesia, copra from the New Hebrides, sugar from Fiji, and pineapples from Hawaii circulated around the world. The establishment of new export-oriented economies produced dramatic social and cultural effects, including despoliation of indigenous land, the arrival of indentured laborers and other migrants, and a "scramble" that by 1900 saw all of the islands of Oceania divided among the British, French, Dutch, Germans, and Americans. Islanders, working for European planters or mine owners, or in port entrepôts, or settlers' houses, often now dressed in modest "Mother Hubbard" gowns of European fabric, smoked tobacco, drank alcohol, and used imported utensils; they were as much actors in a global trade and cultural revolution as Europeans. Each new European conquest opened up fresh possibilities for trade.

What was different in the nineteenth century by comparison to earlier periods was the extent of trade created by the "discovery" of the South Pacific, the settlement of Australasia, and the move of European merchants away from coastal ports up rivers and across oceans into the "heart" of Africa and other continents. Europeans appropriated vast tracts of territory in the hinterlands for colonies, and for pastoralism, agriculture, or mining. The volume of trade reached previously unimagined levels; innovative technologies accelerated commerce in unforeseen ways (for instance, communication via the telegraph), as did laws permitting the setting up of joint-stock companies and chartered banks. The twin desires for goods and profits animated much European expansion, just as they inflected reactions from indigenous peoples to European incursions. Such urges were not original to the period covered by this volume, but what was different was the scale on which the quest for goods and profits could be pursued, and the technological, political, and commercial changes that facilitated their satisfaction. Trade became an essential part of the nineteenth-century gospel of expansion, joined inseparably to a "civilising mission" as famously summed up in Dr. Livingstone's injunctions to students at Cambridge to take part in Britain's great crusade for "Christianity and commerce" (Harlow and Carter 1999: 272–7).

Trade was thus integral to the ideology of empire. A harbinger of later views of commerce and imperialism, Adam Smith's *The Wealth of Nations*, published in 1776, enshrined free trade as a central tenet in liberal thought, and identified international commerce as key to Britain's power; Britain was a trading nation (a "nation of shop-keepers," the French remarked) and "workshop of the world." Smith opposed slavery and expressed great reservations about colonialism, but his ideas about the "invisible hand of the market" and the beneficence of trade proved vital to the British architects of empire (Smith 1776). Colonialists elsewhere spread similar ideas. The mid-nineteenth century Saint-Simonians in France spoke idealistically about collaboration between the "industrious" classes of capitalists and workers (a view from which Marx dissented). The Saint-Simonians exercised great influence on Emperor Napoleon III and such men as Ferdinand de Lesseps, engineer of the Suez Canal (Pilbeam 2014). The canal was lauded as a herculean achievement, literally cutting a conduit for trade between the Mediterranean and the Indian Ocean. The canal, as well, was considered a great cultural project, and at its inauguration, the chaplain of the French Empress Eugénie (present there alongside other European royals) intoned: "Today, two worlds are made one. The splendid Orient and the marvelous Occident salute each other.... Today is a great festival for all of humanity." He asked God to "make of this canal not only a passage to universal prosperity, but make it a royal road of peace and of justice; of the light, and of the eternal truth" (Karabell 2003: 254–5). Trade, the canal's *raison d'être* (though its military value was hardly coincidental), was assigned a moral mandate.

The French prime minister Jules Ferry later echoed these sentiments in justifying his expansionist policy in Indochina before a censorious parliament in 1885. Ferry developed a tripartite argument about the intertwined commercial, geopolitical, and civilizational imperatives for empire, and began his oration by declaring that colonial policy was the daughter of industrial policy, and thus linked to business and trade (Aldrich 1996:97–100). Among ardent promoters of French expansion in Asia were the manufacturers of Lyon, who needed access to raw silk to satisfy clients' demands for clothing and furnishings: another link between expansion and consumer goods. Conquests in North Africa and sub-Saharan Africa were similarly promoted by chambers of commerce in Marseille and Bordeaux. Trading companies marketed wine, coffee, chocolate, palm oil, ground-nuts, ivory, minerals, and other goods sought by metropolitan consumers, and sold the products of France to an ever-widening circle of African consumers. In parallel, lobbyists in Hamburg and Genoa used the perceived benefits of trade to convince the German and Italian governments to pursue conquest, while merchants and shippers in Yokohama and Kobe touted the advantages to Japan of a push into Taiwan and Korea. In each case, though economic theories varied—with a move from espousal of free trade to protectionism by the late 1800s in an effort to safeguard privileged colonial resources and markets—the rhetoric combined commerce and civilization, trade and culture.

Arguments about the near-panacea that imperial expansion, commerce, and the export of "civilization" promised did not win unanimous support. Some argued that commercial interests would be better served without colonial conquest and rule, and their human and financial costs. Others pled that the national priorities ought to be economic development and resolution of social problems at home rather than foreign ventures. Yet others damned colonialism for enriching the few at the expense of the many, and for advancing a corrosive culture of greed and corruption, exploitation and violence. Such charges had been leveled at the East India Company, and the profit making of its "nabobs," in the late 1700s. More than a century later, one of the key critical texts concerning colonialism, Hobson's *Imperialism,* indicted capitalists who, despite high-minded language, sought personal profit rather than national wellbeing.

Published following the author's tour of South Africa during the recent Anglo-Boer War, Hobson's richly textured study is most frequently analysed for his proposition about the economic foundations of expansion. However, Hobson's target was, in part, the culture of trade and investment incarnated by the businessmen of London: their unbridled pursuit of gain was sapping the soul of Britain, to the detriment of workers at home and Britain's subjects in the colonies, kept poor and disenfranchised for the profits of plutocrats (Hobson 1902).

Just a few years later, scandals erupted over the Congo Free State, a private colony of King Leopold II of the Belgians. Journalists revealed the forcible recruitment of laborers, miserable wages, and grisly violence that colonial companies committed against Africans. The critics' focus was often not colonialism *per se* but a particular culture of business, largely unregulated and untrammeled, and condoned by the monarch (Hochschild 1999). Leopold's Congo (subsequently ceded to the Belgian state), like other outposts, provided a venue for evangelization, with missionaries working alongside traders and plantation-owners, and questions were raised about the compatibility of their undertakings. In another link between culture and trade, the landscape of the equatorial colony provided inspiration for Belgium's Art Nouveau, the curves and ornamentation visible in design motifs adopted from central African jungles (Silverman 2011).

The culture of trade can also be seen in the way that trade was transacted. Here, too, as with transport, structural transformations occurred between 1780 and 1920. In the late 1700s, much colonial trade still came under the purview of chartered companies with monopoly privileges, the most famous the English East India Company and the Dutch United East India Company (VOC). A century later, most colonial businesses were private enterprises. Some traders were lone adventurers at the edge of empires, the very models of weather-beaten, pith-helmeted men in remote locations buying and shipping tropical hardwoods or gemstones, palm oil or copra, and importing European goods to sell to indigenous people. By the late 1800s, however, an increased number worked for large companies headquartered in the metropole or the major colonial cities. They were cogs in a machinery of "big business," whose strategies involved bank financing, international stock exchanges, managerial organization, and diversified investments and activities. Companies such as the Dutch Shell, Jardine Matheson, Swire's, and Unilever, and the French Bank of Indochina and the French West African Company, exemplified this new business world.

The commercial culture for colonial traders, whether serving big business or operating on their own accounts, still involved mastering the procedures of the home countries and the protocols of doing business with foreigners. They had to learn how negotiations were conducted overseas, what kinds of restrictions and taboos obtained, the often elaborate courtesies expected, and the sorts of emoluments that secured deals. They had to learn languages, or learn how to operate through interpreters and other intermediaries. Good merchants acquired knowledge that surpassed strictly commercial intelligence, or risked failure; if they offended "native" rulers, they incurred exclusion from trade or a worse fate. Slights to traders and other expatriates indeed provided a justification for European governments to send in the gunboats.

Traders continued to brave the dangers of long voyages, tropical diseases, and homesickness, though faster transport, better medicines, and larger settler communities ameliorated conditions. They looked forward to profitable earnings though expectations were sometimes disappointed, and they benefited from the luxury of servants, and the pleasures (especially sexual relationships with indigenous partners) considered "perks" of colonial service. The most successful built mansions overseas or purchased country estates at home, where they decorated their interiors with treasures they brought back, a "conspicuous consumption" (to use Thorstein Veblen's famous phrase) of the goods of empire and the rewards of trade (Barczewski 2014). Successful traders thereby became landed gentlemen.

The culture of trade similarly changed for non-Europeans. Asians and Africans for centuries before the arrival of the imperialists had traded with each other and with Europeans along the great trading networks from the Persian Gulf to the African coast, from India across southeast Asia, along the silk road and on caravan routes from the African interior to the coast. (Indeed, Europeans often inserted themselves into these well-established networks.) Many local producers sold whatever goods they produced to whichever traders came to seek their wares, but they increasingly realized they could gear production to new foreign markets, for example, with the Chinese "export porcelain" for which Europeans proved insatiable consumers. Some indigenous merchants set up their own trading stores or companies, and competed with Europeans. King Ja Ja of Opobo in western Africa, for instance, in the 1830s began to export palm oil directly to European markets rather than through British traders. When they protested, he blockaded African ports the foreigners used; the British responded by overthrowing and exiling the king (Trentmann 2016: 130). Diasporic entrepreneurs were perceived as particularly deft in handling trade: Indians and Middle Easterners in Africa, Chinese in Southeast Asia and the Pacific, and Jews and Armenians around the empire. Trading opportunities and migration changed the very demography of colonized countries (Figure 2.2).

A merchant such as Jamsetjee Jejeebhoy is exemplary of the commercial, social, and cultural fabric of empire. Born in Bombay in 1783 into the Parsi communitary—Zoroastrians who traced their origins to Persia—Jejeebhoy came from a modest background, was orphaned at an early age and had little formal education. He made his first voyage to China, to trade opium and cotton, while still an adolescent; on a later trading voyage during the Napoleonic

FIGURE 2.2: Indian shop in Vietnam. Postcard, Private Collection. Among the goods on offer at a shop run by an Indian in Cap Saint-Jacques (now Vung Tau), in southern Vietnam, are textiles, cosmetics, purses, perfumes, and essences. The image illustrates both the presence of Indian shopkeepers in Indochina and trade between South Asia and Southeast Asia.

Wars, he was captured by the French and taken to South Africa. Back in India, and again engaged in the China trade, he amassed a huge mercantile empire and enormous wealth. He also became a leading philanthropist in Bombay, and was the first Indian to be made a knight and then a baronet (Palsetia 2015). Entrepreneurship and success as merchants were similar achievements of many Parsis, among other indigenous, diasporic, and settler peoples.

Colonial business, in sum, was a key part of the culture of empire in Europe and overseas. From small-scale traders in isolated trading posts to besuited employees of international companies, growing trade provided a way of life as well as an occupation, a mindset in addition to a job. Trade formed part of the cultural history as well as the economic history of empire.

SITES OF TRADE AND CULTURE

Trade is linked to many sites: those of production in farm, fishery, mine, or artisanal workshop; sites for transformation of raw materials into finished products such as factories; the trading floors of stock exchanges, offices where transactions are managed, transport hubs where merchandize is shifted; and shops where vendors purvey their wares. Port cities, where many such institutions clustered, offer the most visible sites of the culture of colonial trade, and an interface between home and abroad.

Marseille, for instance, claimed to be the "gateway to the Levant" and the "capital of the empire," though riverine and ocean ports such as Lyon and Bordeaux vied for their share of colonial trade. With the mooring of ships and off-loading of merchandize at the Vieux Port, the monumental new Bourse standing not far away, and a cosmopolitan population of traders and laborers, Marseille was the model of a colonial port where trade and culture were inextricably linked, not only in the comings-and-goings of merchants, financiers, colonists, and administrators, but also in the rough-and-tumble docklands life of cafés, cabarets, and bordellos. Marseille lived off colonial business. The ships of the Marseille-based Messageries Maritimes provided transport for settlers and cargo. Its industries, including manufacture of soap (a speciality), depended on supplies of tropical raw materials. Members of the city council and powerful Chamber of Commerce promoted trade, organized colonial expositions in 1906 and 1922, and set up a colonial museum and a colonial training academy. They boasted that Algiers, on the opposite shore of the Mediterranean, was a city re-created in the image of their hometown. Moreover, Marseille had the largest proportion of migrants from Africa, Asia, and the Antilles of any French city. Not coincidentally was the city's grand railway station ornamented with allegorical statues of Asia and Africa.

Other European cities, such as Liverpool in England (Haggerty, Webster and White 2008) and Glasgow in Scotland, similarly functioned as nodes of colonial trade and culture. So, too did the overseas metropolises that grew up with trade, none more exemplary than Singapore and Hong Kong, where life for indigenous people, migrants from around Asia (and further afield), and British expatriates revolved around commerce. Wealthy merchants lodged in luxury at Raffles or the Peninsula Hotel; far more of those involved in business toiled at hard labor in the shops and docks. Batavia in the Dutch East Indies, Saigon in Vietnam, Manilla in the Philippines, Bombay in India, and Cape Town in South Africa, among many other cities, were burgeoning colonial capitals that relied on international trade, and that provided the locus for new cultures of work, consumption, and leisure. In a European city such as Glasgow (with a prosperous trade in jute) or a colonial center such as "marvelous Melbourne" (with wealth from the Victorian gold rushes), the erection of grand hotels, majestic city halls and government houses, cathedrals and concert halls, as well as the growth of slums, testified to the power of trade and the diverse cultures colonial commerce engendered.

A second emblematic site of new forms of nineteenth-century trade was the department store (Whitaker 2011). The first department store, Au Bon Marché, was established in Paris in 1838, and still operates from a building designed by

Gustave Eiffel in 1869 (Miller 1981). It resembled both an old-style market with the assortment of goods, and a new-fangled factory, with demarcated sections, a grid-like pattern of long aisles, and adoption of new technologies (such as the mechanical lift). With grand staircases, domes, and balconies, this and other department stores were temples of commerce; an 1883 novel by Emile Zola compared shopping to a new religion (Zola 2008). Department stores also resembled the exhibitions of empire, including the Crystal Palace exhibition in London in 1851, the 1889 fair in Paris for which Eiffel designed his famous tower, and the colonial expositions popular in the early twentieth century (Auerbach 1999; Hoffenberg 2011; Geppert 2013). Goods on show at exhibitions and on sale in department stores advertised the empire, stimulated transcontinental business, and whetted the consumer appetite.

Liberty of London, which opened in 1875, developed a particular line in Asian and colonial goods. The basement of the Regent Street store was the "Eastern Bazaar," and one speciality was Indian textiles, both imported from South Asia and created especially for Liberty in patterns reminiscent of Indian design. (Many were produced in the Scottish mill town of Paisley, and the name "paisley" for a particular motif—in western eyes, a droplet shaped image, but one that Indians associated with the mango—became so popular that the word was adopted in India.) In 1885, Liberty brought to Britain a group of Indian artisans, setting them up inside the store to produce their crafts; though neither a great cultural nor a commercial success, the effort spread an image of timeless villagers making desirable handicrafts for the European public. The wealth and beauty of Indian goods was almost simultaneously on show at the Colonial and Indian Exposition of 1886 (Mathur 2007). London's other department stores and shops, from Harrods, and Fortnum and Mason to the Army and Navy Stores (which opened branches in India) and the aptly named "Home and Colonial Store" retail chain catered to those who needed the requisites for life in the tropics and those seeking to buy colonial imports.

Department stores also appeared in the colonies. Cargill's in Ceylon, which traced its origins to a shop opened in the 1840s, erected a grand emporium in Colombo in 1906. Rowe and Co., housed in a similarly imposing building in Rangoon, was one of the most opulent department stores in Asia, known as the Harrods of the East. Not to be outdone, a French entrepreneur established the Maison Godard (later the Grands Magasins Réunis) in a prime location on a French-style boulevard in Hanoi, its building modeled on Paris department stores (Figure 2.3). In Phnom Penh, the leading department store was the aptly named Au Petit Paris.

Another example of a colonial emporium was David Jones in Australia (O'Neill 2013), founded by a Welsh migrant, the son of a peddler turned shopkeeper and farmer. First apprenticed to a local grocer, the Welsh-speaking Jones then went to London, where he learned English and found a job with a

FIGURE 2.3: Department store in Hanoi. Postcard, Private Collection. The Grands Magasins Réunis was the leading department store in colonial Hanoi, located at a prominent intersection in the French quarter of the city; the building still stands and has been redeveloped as an emporium of international luxuries.

draper. His employer was also developing business in the Australian colonies, and in 1835 sent Jones to Sydney. Three years later, Jones opened a store under his own name, realizing the opportunities presented by a growing and aspirational elite among the city's 20,000 residents. Jones faced challenges, including the one hundred days it took cargo to reach the Antipodes from Europe. One advantage of the delay, however, was that he could acquire the latest European fashions at the end of "the season," when prices were low, and they arrived just as "the season" began in the southern hemisphere. The shelves of David Jones were filled with cloth, ribbons, thread, and scissors for those making their own garments, as well as ready-made fashions, and household furnishing sourced from Europe, America, and Asia. Clients' eyes were always set on trends in London, for instance the "Norwich and Tibet Shawls" popularized by Queen Victoria. Having access to the latest styles proved that the rising bourgeois were respectable, up-to-date and connected with "home." Since many settlers lived in the bush, including pastoralists who made rare trips to the city but whose custom David Jones eagerly sought, the department store developed a "shop by post" option, offering even bespoke clothing by mail and, for those with limited means, with lay-by payment. The store in 1899 set up its own factory, employing 700 workers, and displayed pioneering marketing tactics by having advertising leaflets dropped from an airplane in 1919. Over 175 years after its establishment, David Jones remains Australia's premier department store.

Department stores, in a sense, provided permanent exhibitions of trade goods. Department stores and smaller shops brought the colonies to the metropole, and took the metropole to the colonies (Figure 2.4). They gave Europeans access to exotic and useful items from the wider world, and helped settlers maintain a European style of life. They also made European goods available to indigenous and diasporic populations, at least to the minority who could afford these wares. Laborers on plantations and in mines were often obliged to purchase necessities including foodstuffs, and any luxuries they could afford, from "company stores" owned and operated by plantation and mining firms. Prices were typically high, and clients ran up hefty accounts that drained away meager wages. Salt, tea, and rice provided staples, but sales of

FIGURE 2.4: Colonial produce stand. Postcard, Private Collection. Colonial commodities were essential exports for colonial producers and became necessities for European consumers, with certain shops specializing in these wares—among the products featured in this artful display mounted by a Paris shop for a competition at an agricultural fair are bananas, kola nuts, and vetiver, as well as some examples of "native" artisanship.

tobacco and alcohol boomed, the shopkeepers eager to promote tastes for such products. Opium was also in high demand, especially in Southeast Asia and China; the desire of traders to market opium and of government officials to reap substantial taxes from opium monopolies contributed to the "Opium Wars" fought between western colonial powers and China, and the growth of exports of opium from India to east Asia (Derks 2012; Wright 2013). Opiates for legal medicines and illicit pleasures sold well in the metropole, too, as did the rum made as a by-product of sugar in tropical countries. Dealings in addictive sugar, tobacco, alcohol, and drugs played a vital role in colonial trade and nineteenth-century culture.

Wearing European clothing was important to some of the colonized as a sign or hope of being considered modern and "civilised" (Morton 1995; Hendrickson 1996; Wickramasinghe 2003). Indeed, proof of an undefined European way of living was required in parts of the French empire for an indigenous person to gain citizenship, and possession of European furnishings and fashion characterized those disconcertingly called *évolués* ("evolved ones"). A European coat and tie for a man, or a frock for a woman, constituted visible signs of status, wealth, and outlook for the colonized elite. For the less fortunate, motley apparel mixing European and indigenous items, though ridiculed by colonists, expressed sartorial fancy or creativity. Europeans sometimes forbade the indigenous to wear European clothing, particularly shoes, with sumptuary regulations aiming to maintain distance between settlers and "natives." Whether someone went barefoot, wore sandals, or donned leather shoes was an indication of race, wealth, and legal status. One etching of the drawing room of the Susew de Soyza family in Ceylon shows the wealthy master dressed in Sinhalese-style sarong and jacket, while his young nephew wears a European frock-coat and trousers (Jones 2007:153–7). The adage that "clothes maketh the man" (and perhaps even more the woman) held particular relevance in colonial life.

The sewing machine offers a particularly good example of new technology and a trade good associated with culture and lifestyle in a colony such as Ceylon (Wickramasinghe 2014). The sewing machine was one of the most widely sold new inventions of the nineteenth century, first commercialized to tailors and seamstresses after 1851, when the American Isaac Singer patented his inexpensive and reliable machine. By the end of the century, Singer took ninety percent of the world market, with the spread of the appliance little less than phenomenal; many of those for the colonies were manufactured in Glasgow (Figure 2.5). Singer's first shop in Ceylon opened in 1877, and there were twenty-eight by 1915. One in ten households owned a Singer sewing machine, a comparable level to the market penetration in Turkey and Greece. The Singer became standard equipment for tailor shops, and a valued household asset, often given in a woman's dowry. The machines made easier the sewing of

FIGURE 2.5: Algerian sewing machine. Postcard, Private Collection. By the end of the nineteenth century, Singer sewing machines were sold from Algeria to Ceylon and most other places in the world. They had become essential items in households and tailor shops, and were particularly important in the domestic and professional life of women.

clothing for the family and for sale; whether at home, in a small shop, or a factory, it opened new careers for women as machine-operating seamstresses.

Middle-class houses of indigenous people began to be filled with European objects as symbols of comfort, modernity, and civilization. In Ceylon, for instance, the late nineteenth-century elite like the de Soyzas fancied overstuffed sofas, marble-topped tables, gilded clocks, gas-fired chandeliers, Louis XV and baroque chairs, display cabinets stuffed with bric-a-brac and the other paraphernalia of Victorian drawing-rooms. Chased silver and crystal glassware were sure indicators of wealth and European tastes, though the elephant tusks that graced reception rooms provided a reminder that Colombo was not London. Some of the furnishings were locally produced in western style, other goods imported from India, elsewhere in the empire, and Europe.

Those among the colonized with great means indulged their consumer desires on European tours. The king of Cambodia, visiting France in 1906, so enjoyed his shopping expeditions to the Grandes Galeries du Louvre department store that he presented a royal decoration to its manager; like any tourist, he also picked up souvenirs at the Eiffel Tower shop. Maharajas and other fortunate Indians provided coveted business for European providores (Jackson and Jaffer 2009; Jaffer 2013). In 1865, Sir Jamsetjee Jejeebhoy paid £20,000 for a diamond from Garrard, the royal jewelers in London. In 1875, Maharaja Rajinder Singh of Patiala paid £60,000 for a suite of diamonds, which he wore to a reception for the visiting Prince of Wales. In 1905, the Maharaja of Kapurthala ordered a turban ornament from Boucheron in Paris, an early example of a European jewelry manufacturer working specifically to commissions from Indians. A few decades later, maharajas were buying motorcars, the Nizam of Hyderabad said to own fifty Rolls-Royces; another Indian prince, after being slighted at the Rolls-Royce dealership, bought several of the automobiles that he then pointedly used for rubbish collection. Wealth, style, consumption, and occasional eccentricity intertwined with international trade in the transactions of peasants and princes.

NEW GOODS, NEW HABITS

Such "lifestyle" commodities as western clothing and furnishings counted as important articles of colonial trade, as did other items such as pianos. A piano represented a considerable outlay by a purchaser, whether settler or other, and an investment in culture; a piano was a standard asset of middle-class homes in Europe, and so should it be, residents of colonies reckoned, even in remote corners of the empire. Gramophones as well found eager buyers, providing an entirely new way of listening to European music and of recording local music; in Ceylon, Buddhist monks even recorded the chanting of scriptures, using the new technology to spread a very old religion. Books and newspapers, sources of information and entertainment, assumed enormous importance, local and overseas publications eagerly awaited by readers and providing income for booksellers and newsagents. Photographic studios, camera clubs, and shops selling photographic equipment appeared in the colonies nearly as soon as in Europe (Newton 2008, 2014). As early as the 1840s, for instance, newspapers in Ceylon carried advertisements for producers of daguerreotypes, and a photographic studio opened in Colombo in 1862. The small *carte-de-visite* photographs popular in Europe quickly caught on throughout the colonies, products of technology, marketing, and consumer tastes. Among many other producers, Lehnert and Landrock, a photographic firm in North Africa, produced picturesque postcards of local landscapes and people, and did a thriving under-the-counter trade in soft-core pornography as well. Picture postcards were a new mania, art form, and saleable commodity by the 1890s, testifying to the increasing importance of travel, the efficiency of colonial postal services, and the vogue for "otherness." Each new invention, technology, and commodity thus added to the inventory of trade goods moved about the empires.

Advertising provided an essential connection between producer and consumer, and between trade and culture (Ramamurthy 2003). It was a rapidly developing business in the late 1800s, especially with the growth of the illustrated press and the multiplying of goods on sale. Advertisements in Europe purveyed wares promising comfort in the rigors of tropical heat and arduous expeditions. Solar topees (pith helmets) and "tropical whites," stocks of tonic to mix with gin to stave off malaria (because of the quinine in the tonic water), guns to ward off wild animals and "savage natives," and steamer trunks for packing the supplies, were essentials—the Paris saddler and leather-maker Louis Vuitton sold custom-built steamer trunks to wealthy clients. Products from Europe advertised in the colonial press, and sold at colonial department stores, helped make the foreign feel more homelike, just as colonial wares were promoted in Europe in ways that seduced stay-at-homes. Images of pyramids, camels, and Arabs decorated packets of tobacco, nubile West Indian women appeared on bottles of rum, and fields of happily busy tea-pickers figured on tins of Ceylon tea.

Some images were straightforwardly racist, such as advertisements in Britain for soap said to be so good it could wash even a black baby white. Soap brands such as Lifebuoy, Lux, and Sunlight became symbolic of the missionaries' idea of cleanliness being next to godliness, medical attempts to better hygiene, and the marketing acumen of manufacturers. (McClintock 1995; Burke 1996). Many other advertising images drew on racially- and culturally-inflected stereotypes, such as a smiling African used to sell Banania, a French breakfast food based on bananas. Meanwhile, alluring images of Asian temples, North African casbahs, and inviting tropical beaches featured, as they still do, on advertisements for tourist agencies. Advertising the colonies was not just part of commercial strategy and political propaganda; it created and reinforced impressions about overseas countries, peoples, and products.

A summary example illustrative of trade and culture, which returns to the quotidian nature of consumption of colonial products, is tea (Moxham 2009). One of the very symbols of Britishness, tea supplies depended entirely on production outside Britain, and British colonial tea was exported to populations around the globe. The unquenchable thirst for tea in the 1700s and 1800s also lay behind the opium trade between India and China since the British needed a product that the Chinese wanted to buy in exchange for sales of tea. Moreover, the setting up of tea plantations in Ceylon, India, and such other colonies as Kenya and Mauritius represented "economic development" (in the colonizers' view) with the creation of export-oriented economies. Trade in tea, furthermore, was a significant colonial enterprise, typified by the Twinings Company, established in 1706; other tea merchants boasting a long history include Jacksons of Piccadilly (set up in 1815) and Whittard of Chelsea (founded in 1886). Across the Channel, the aptly named Compagnie Coloniale, dating from 1848, was perhaps the first French firm to sell coffee, chocolate, and tea, followed by Mariage Frères, set up in 1854. These two, like the British firms, still do business today.

Yet another famous British tea firm was established by Thomas Lipton (McCarthy and Devine 2017; Rappaport 2017). The first tea plantations had been set up in Ceylon in 1867, in the wake of failure of production of coffee, heretofore a major export. The former Glasgow grocer and tea importer realized that by growing tea on his own plantations and marketing it directly, he could cut out middlemen, and his tea estates, established in the 1890s, became some of the most extensive in Ceylon. A host of other planters, many Scotsmen like Lipton, set up in the highlands of Ceylon and, with aid from the colonial government, brought in Tamils, mostly women, from southern India to harvest the tea. Tea became colonial Ceylon's major export, and drinking Ceylon tea was a habit for local people, the British, and consumers throughout the empire and beyond (Figure 2.6). The arrival of the Indian and predominantly Hindu Tamils also profoundly changed the social structure of Ceylon, with repercussions far into the future, and foreign ownership of the plantations (until nationalization in the 1970s) rankled with anti-colonialists. The plantations and their bungalows, some now turned into hotels, remain important reminders of the intertwining of agriculture, trade, and cultures of consumption.

The shipment of tea from Ceylon to Britain, and to Canada, Australia, and other colonies, points to an important aspect of colonial trade. It took place between colonies, and between colonies and still independent states, as well as between colonies and imperial metropoles. Products from one colony, like tea, were easily assimilated into the purchasing practices of other societies. One advertisement in the Sydney *Gazette*, advising consumers of the arrival of the ship *Agnes* from China in 1833, listed among the goods on board black and green tea, coffee, chocolate, sugar, rice, tobacco, cigars, "Lisbon wine" and wine from Madeira, candles made from wax and whale oil, Bengal sealing wax and Prussian blue coloring, as well as hats and caps, beds and chair seats, lacquer ware and ivory, silks and nankeens, spices, fireworks, and the curious "japan

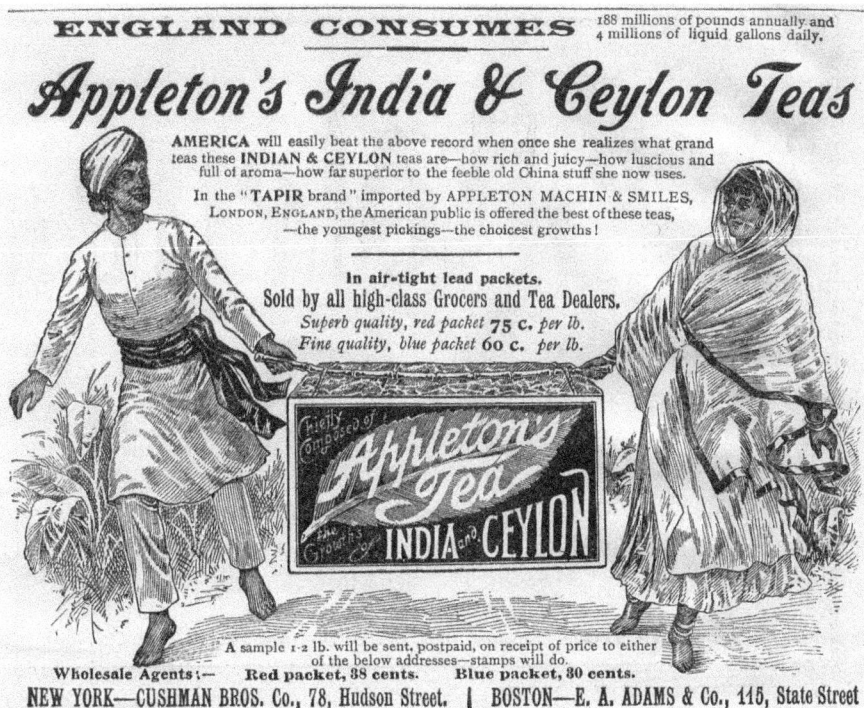

FIGURE 2.6: Ceylon Tea. Printed advertisement, Private Collection. By the start of the twentieth century, Ceylon (Sri Lanka) was one of the world's major producers of tea, and "Ceylon teas" became not only the beverage of the British Empire but also an important and famous trade good in places such as the United States.

footpails": an array of Asian, African and North Atlantic products that no doubt quickened the pace of prospective purchasers to "Edwards & Hunter agents" (Broadbent, Rickard and Steven 2003:58). The list testifies to a global network of trade and also to patterns of consumption that encompassed products from around the world. Early Australian colonial culture, in fact, owed much to imports from India and China as well as from Britain—Indian cottons and furniture, and Chinese ceramics and silks furnished the houses of many Sydney colonists, and in return New South Wales exported, among other goods, "walers," horses in high demand in India.

The story was similar in other empires. For instance, in the late nineteenth century, part of the crop of rice, then Vietnam's major export, was destined for French colonies in Africa and the Indian Ocean. Cod caught around France's tiny Saint-Pierre and Miquelon (off Newfoundland) provided an important foodstuff in the French West Indies, whose sugar and rum were exported to France. A Frenchmen in a colonial outpost as well as in Paris might well have consumed wine from Algeria, coffee from the Ivory Coast, rice from Indochina, and sugar from Martinique or Guadeloupe. In the 1860s, Gaëtan Picon, who had first gone to Algeria as a soldier in the French army, invented a new bittersweet alcoholic beverage, the *sirop de Picon*, or "Amer-Picon," made from oranges and bitters. It won a bronze medal at a London exhibition, and Picon set up factories in Algeria and in Marseille. By the late nineteenth century, Picon's slogan was "There is no longer any part of the globe where Picon has not gone"—an advertising motto that might well have been paraphrased (with perhaps more veracity) by Lipton for his tea, and that would have provided a worthy target for many manufacturers and traders.

TRADE, CULTURE AND SOCIETY: SOME CONCLUSIONS

Colonial trade was about routes along which commodities and their merchants passed, pathways etched across oceans and continents in the process of building commercial and political empires. It was about the cultures of production, commerce, and consumption that created and utilized those conduits. The to-ing and fro-ing of wares encompassed relationships of producers and purchasers, advertisers who touted the products, and shopkeepers who sold the goods, whether in dusty outback trading posts or city-slicker department stores. Also involved were employees of rail lines and shipping firms, banks and stock exchanges, and a host of others. Wealthy colonial and metropolitan manufacturers and merchants reaped the most evident benefits, but small-scale traders, shopkeepers, and grocers were equally agents, beneficiaries, and sometimes victims of trade. Many indigenous and diasporic people owed their wellbeing (or lack of it) to trade in the new colonial and capitalistic systems of production and exchange. Even for those in remote locations and with very limited means, in Europe and the colonies, trade brought in necessities or luxuries otherwise unobtainable, and it thereby brought about changes in cultural life.

The new trade goods were not universally welcomed; Christian, Muslim, and Buddhist temperance groups railed against the evils of alcohol. Gandhi famously told Indians that they must boycott the imported products of British factories, spin their own thread and weave their own cloth. Photographs of the Mahatma sitting at his spinning wheel, wearing a simple *dhoti* rather than a smart British suit, embodied rejection of exploitative British business as part of the campaign for Indian self-sufficiency and independence. Orthodox socialists meanwhile damned the capitalist system that had trade at its heart, and argued that only the overthrow of the system could better the life of workers at home and abroad. Some of the anti-colonialists nonetheless welcomed new consumer goods, such as the sewing machine and the gramophone that made life easier and more agreeable. Many progressive reformers in the colonies avidly pursued a material and cultural modernity they hoped would emancipate fellow men and women from feudalism, anachronistic traditionalism, and the dominance of old elites; it is not surprising that nationalists sometimes adopted European dress and availed themselves of the media of communication, transport, and publication introduced by colonizers. The important point is that the colonized exercised rights—within varying latitudes, depending on country and time—and a considerable degree of choice as to which trade goods to accept or refuse, and how to accommodate them within their inherited cultural beliefs and practices.

Trade was not always beneficent, as colonialists sometimes conceded. It destroyed older types of local artisanal production. It did not necessarily substitute superior products for poorer ones—and Europeans often yearned to purchase the high-quality silks, porcelain, and lacquer that testified to workmanship in Asia while they exported cheap factory-made goods. Trade introduced harmful addictions, and it tempted many to spend beyond their means. Illicit trade in indigenous artworks, taken as booty by conquerors or spirited away by unscrupulous collectors and art dealers, robbed countries of their cultural patrimony. The trade in human flesh—slaves, indentured and coerced laborers, prostitutes—was an even more heinous sort of commerce.

Trade inextricably tied markets and cultures together more tightly in the nineteenth century than ever before, thanks to new forms of transport and technology, the establishment of export-oriented colonial economies and factory-based systems of production in Europe, and new consumer tastes promoted by advertising and innovative types of marketing. Trade brought products, peoples, and cultures together, at colonial expositions and world fairs, on wharves and in warehouses, in open-air markets, boutiques, isolated trading posts, and grand department stores. The labor trade moved slaves, contract laborers, and seamen around the world, just as the promise of trade and fortune-hunting moved about investors, planters, entrepreneurs, administrators, settlers, and job-seekers. Colonial trade was part of the dynamics that created more demographically and culturally diverse societies, especially notable in places such as Singapore with its Chinese, Malays, Indians, and Europeans. Trade also divided people, into those who could afford imported goods and those who could not, those who eagerly adopted new products and those for whom they held limited interest, those whose traditional activities could not compete with European enterprise and those who found opportunities in the new commercial system. With colonial import and export regulations concerning customs and tariffs, new geographical and cartographical barriers appeared and privileged trade routes were created. Under colonial dominion, the hand of the market was not invisible, nor was the market fully free.

Trade created new intersections and hybridities. Picture one of Gauguin's paintings of a Tahitian woman standing in front of a Polynesian statue and wearing a *robe mission* (as the French termed the modest Mother Hubbard frocks) made in a French factory but with raw materials from some cotton plantation overseas; she smokes a cigarette, another trade good and cultural practice. Or think of a photograph of a Ceylonese drinking a cup of tea, listening to Buddhist suttras or European symphonies on a gramophone, perhaps with a sewing machine sitting in the background. Each was living at the crossroads where local and foreign technologies and commodities met, and at the intersection of material life and habits of culture. Trade was a vital form of culture contact and transnational exchange, though it could provoke misunderstanding, conflict, exploitation, and violence, as well as profit and pleasure.

Colonial-era trade brought together multiple practices involved in getting commodities from producer to consumer, and those practices underwent a great metamorphosis in the long nineteenth century with the "new imperialism," the technology of steam and industry, the rail lines and canals, the transformation of business organization. Trade supplied an essential element in the colonial project, and every proponent of overseas expansion identified trade as both imperative and benefit. Some of the lasting legacies of that perspective, and the trade routes pioneered in the colonial age, remain with us in the globalized world of today, in the products we eat, the clothes we wear, the furnishings that fill our houses, the objects we collect, the recreations we pursue. Trade and culture, in fact, are two sides of the same coin.

CHAPTER THREE

Natural Worlds

Cultures of Climate Concern in the Age of Empires

RUTH A. MORGAN

During the long nineteenth century, the spread of European and North American imperialism throughout Asia, Africa, Australasia, and Oceania connected diverse peoples and places on an unprecedented scale, contributing to the globalizing processes that historian Christopher Bayly describes as "the birth of the modern world" (2004). Even in the twilight of the age of sail, however, natural forces continued to guide the extent and form of Western empires—their territories and their trade routes, for example, were at the mercy of the prevailing winds (Griffiths 2005; Bankoff 2006; Bankoff 2017). The ensuing encounters with unfamiliar environments and cultures were shaped by, and produced, particular understandings of the natural world in metropolitan and colonial contexts.

In both cultural and material ways, climate loomed large in these colonial exchanges as imperialists confronted arid, tropical, and variable conditions, which challenged aspirations for empire's enrichment. To make sense of their colonial experiences and observations, Europeans and North Americans applied their own philosophies of climate. During the seventeenth and eighteenth centuries, western climate discourses had begun to bifurcate such that by the nineteenth century, climate was largely understood as both an agent or force and resource, as well as an index, or in statistical terms (Fleming and Jankovic 2011). The roots of the former lay in an historic climate determinism, while the latter had emerged more recently as the product of empirical weather observation and the development of the separate scientific fields of meteorology and climatology (Heymann 2010). Depicted in these diverse ways, "climate" was central to the concerns of empire and provides an ideal entrée into human interactions with, and representations of, the natural world during the Age of Empire. Acknowledging the impact of climate is not to imply determinism. Showing the interactions of climate, human and other non-human factors instead moves the focus of climate studies away from a deterministic tradition to reveal the complexity of climate–human interactions in the past (Carey 2012).

In the colonial context at least, climatology did not supplant or rise at the expense of the agential interpretation, which flourished in the face of new geographies of risk and opportunity. Both approaches thrived where the paucity of instrumental data beckoned measurement, observation, and interpretation, while representations of the colonial climate became instruments of imperial rule and resistance (Endfield and Randalls 2015). The characteristics of a colonial climate tended to form part of a broader environmental imaginary conceived by European and North American imperialists. As Diana Davis (2011) argues, such preconceptions were the lens through which colonized lands and peoples were understood, and their potential for imperial improvement determined, such as whether the conditions were amenable to European habitation or better suited to European management.

Despite the metropolitan potency of such environmental imaginaries, the materiality of colonial climates and peoples often subverted, or at least circumscribed, their imperial logic. The challenges and contradictions that the colonial settings presented all contributed to what Daniel Clayton (2004) describes as the "messy pragmatics of colonial contact" (458). Until the mid-nineteenth century at least, this "messiness" fostered conditions for experimenting with alternative forms of environmental management, as Richard Grove argues in his seminal work *Green Imperialism*. These tended to favor "the long-term economic security of the state, which any ecological crisis threatened to undermine," over "the short-term interests of private capital" (1995: 7). In these colonial laboratories, climate was a subject that engaged a legion of actors in its articulation, measurement, and analysis.

In this chapter I examine key areas of research by historians of climate and environment in the nineteenth century context of empire and colonialism. This research ranges from the reconstruction of past climates, the study of medical climatology, and the social and political consequences of climate events, to understandings of climate change and climate modification, the practice of colonial climatology, and the emergence of a "global" climate. For European and North American empires, colonial climates inspired particular environmental imaginaries that sustained imperial visions and policies of settlement, development, and trade, while the reach of empire facilitated the measurement of colonial climes and the development of trans-imperial networks of science and observation during the long nineteenth century. These imperial understandings and representations of colonial climates demonstrate the extent to which the seemingly "natural" world is, in fact, enmeshed in human power dynamics and therefore implicitly cultural.

RECORDING COLONIAL CLIMATES

The expansion of European and North American empires during the eighteenth and nineteenth centuries helped to facilitate the rise of western science, the growth of which in turn reinforced the imperial enterprise (Palladino and Worboys 1993). Among the sciences aligned with empire, such as botany, geography, and geology, was the emerging science of meteorology. Jan Golinski (2007) and Vladimir Jankovic (2000) have shown how an increasingly quantitative approach to weather observation surpassed locally-focused folk traditions in Britain by the early nineteenth century. In the colonies, meanwhile, both practices thrived, encouraging the recording of colonial climates in qualitative and empirical terms. The former required observers to describe the quotidian and the extraordinary, while the latter noted variables such as temperature, pressure, rainfall, and wind. Such a quantitative approach to weather recording fostered imperial understandings of climate in statistical terms, as an index by which to assist the achievement of imperial objectives.

European and North American empires established observatories to foster the systematic collection of meteorological statistics in their colonial territories. The English East India Company, for example, established observatories in Madras (Figure 3.1), Calcutta, St Helena, Bombay, and Singapore during the early to mid-nineteenth century (Sen 2011; Williamson 2015). Later, such observatories became hubs for the collection of climate data recorded around the colonies (often by volunteers and native peoples) and from other colonial outposts. Stocked with European instruments and staffed by military, if not scientific, observers, these observatories were to be sites of colonial science and imperial authority. These were also sites of adaptation to colonial climes—Jesuit scientists at the Manila Observatory, for instance, developed instruments better suited to tropical conditions (Bankoff 2011). Katharine Anderson (2005) has shown, however, that the lack of a uniform pattern of observation, the absence of the standardization of instruments, and the poor training of observers severely undermined the usefulness of colonial climate data until the latter third of the nineteenth century.

Despite such challenges, these networks of climate knowledge became increasingly important to scientific communities and cultures in both the colonies and the metropole. In the colonies, the collection of meteorological data over time and space allowed for colonial meteorologists to attempt to interpret local climate patterns. Facilitated by the advent of the telegraph

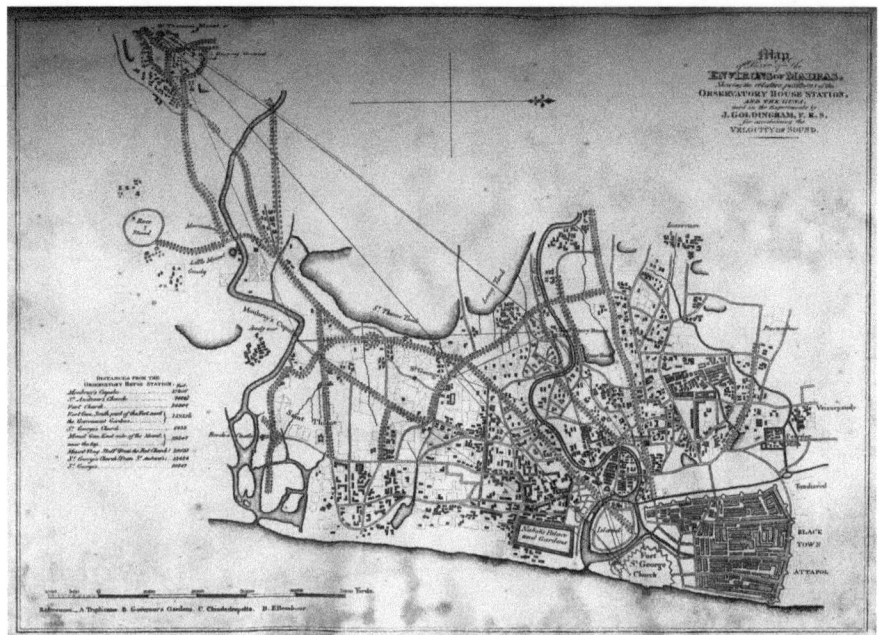

FIGURE 3.1: Map of part of the environs of Madras, showing the relative positions of the Observatory House Station, and the guns, used in the experiments by John Goldingham, FRS, for ascertaining the velocity of sound. John Goldingham, *Madras Observatory Papers* (Madras: College Press, 1826), Courtesy: University of Cambridge, Institute of Astronomy Library.

(1830s), their interpretations were critical to the development of weather forecasting, a predictive science vital to the agricultural and maritime endeavors of empire (Anderson 2005). In the wake of the Madras famine of 1876–7, the meteorological reporter to the Government of India observed similar conditions elsewhere and speculated on the presence of a "barometric see-saw" that influenced rainfall between what he described as the Indo-Malayan region and the Russian plains (Blanford 1880; Davis 2001: 217–18). The associated exchange of meteorological data subsequently allowed Australian meteorologists to speculate that there was a "teleconnection" between the failure of the Indian monsoons and Australian droughts (Grove 1997; Grove 1998). Meteorologist Jacob Bjerknes would later describe these patterns as a consequence of an atmospheric-oceanic phenomenon, the El Niño Southern Oscillation (ENSO).

The imperial collection of meteorological data provided the statistics necessary to contribute to the emerging field of climatology. Alexander von Humboldt's definition of climate was "crucial" to the field's development, as Matthias Heymann observes (2010: 587). In *Kosmos* (1845), Humboldt suggested that "climate ... indicates every change in the atmosphere which sensibly affects our organs," from temperature and humidity to "electrical tension" and "gaseous exhalations" (von Humboldt 1845: 96). Humboldt's approach to climate as both the atmospheric phenomena specific to a particular location and the atmospheric phenomena across different locations was especially suited to the wide networks of meteorological observation that European and North American empires were developing in the nineteenth century (Figure 3.2) (Heymann 2010: 587). Humboldt himself recognized this wider scientific potential, urging the British Royal Society in 1836 to establish geomagnetic observatories in British colonies to aid the study of the Earth's magnetic variation (Ratcliff 2016).

By the late nineteenth century, the emergence of climatology as a quantitative and systematic science was slowly supplanting Humboldt's more cultural approach. Aspiring for climatology to depict "the interaction of all atmospheric phenomena over a patch of the earth's surface," Austrian Julius Hann sought to average long-term time series of meteorological data for a particular location (cited in Coen 2010: 846). His vision for climatology, Deborah Coen (2011)

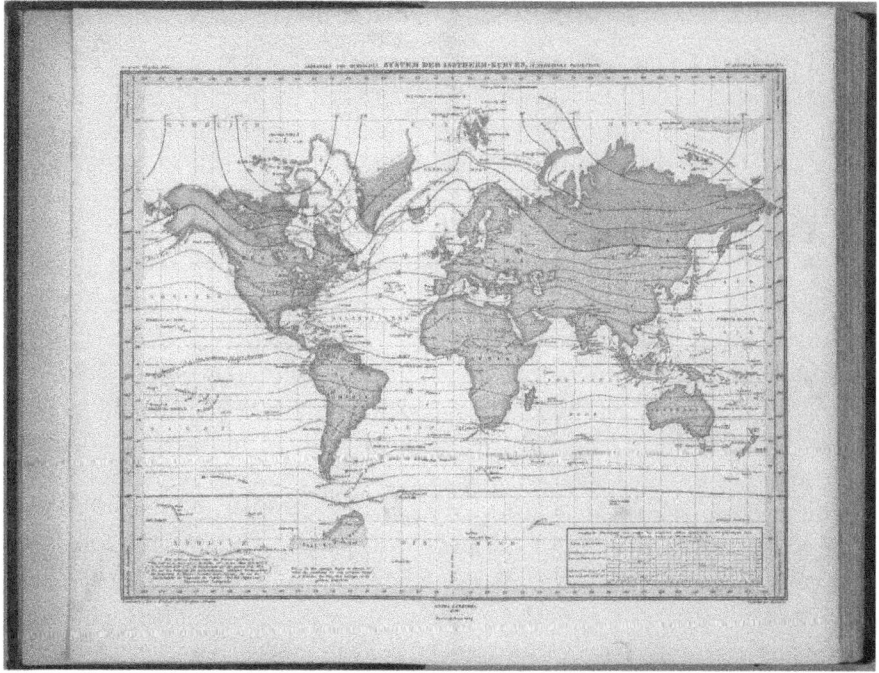

FIGURE 3.2: An 1838 map based on Alexander von Humboldt's concept of isotherms. Heinrich Berghaus (1849), *Alexander von Humboldt's System Der Isotherm-Kurven*, 2nd edn, Gotha: Justus Perthes. Courtesy of the David Rumsey Map Collection.

argues, implicated the developing field in a project peculiar to the Austro-Hungarian empire, that of "imperial climatography." Through the study of the physically and ethnically diverse Habsburg territories, imperial climatographies reinforced the "naturalness" of the empire, united by climatic continuity. Although the International Meteorological Organisation was established in 1873 as a means to advance global, cooperative climate research, the politics of empire continued to shape climatological and meteorological research well into the twentieth century (Mahony 2016).

More recently, the documentary archive of empire has proven a valuable source of climate information for historians and others seeking to reconstruct and recover past climates over wide spatial and temporal scales. Researchers can trace the climate monitoring of European and North American empires and their agents through a range of documentary sources, such as government records and gazettes, the accounts and diaries of missionaries and early settlers, newspaper articles, ships' logs, military records, physicians' journals, and weather records from colonial observatories and observers. This quantitative and qualitative information has been vital to international and regional endeavors to extend the global climate record; reconstruct past climates for former colonies; and to understand cultural concerns about climate in colonial contexts.

In addition to instrumental observations, other documentary sources of climatic data have offered climate historians insight into the colonial past. Although the use of such documentary sources has been commonplace in analyses of European and North American climates, historians and geographers are increasingly turning these techniques to the study of the climates in southern Africa, South and Southeast Asia, the Caribbean and Mexico (Nash and Adamson 2014). English-, French-, and Sesotho-language missionary accounts have revealed precipitation and temperature variability in Lesotho, the Kalahari, and Natal and Zululand (Endfield and Nash 2002a; Kelso and Vogel 2007; Nash and Endfield 2002; Nash and Grab 2010; Nash *et al.* 2016), while private diaries have allowed a climate reconstruction of early nineteenth century Bombay (Adamson and Nash 2014; Adamson 2015). Similarly, ships' logs as well as missionary and plantation papers provided the basis for the reconstruction of rainfall variability and hurricane activity in the southern Caribbean (Chenoweth and Divine 2008; Berland, Metcalfe and Endfield 2013). Such work has also shed light on the nature of extreme weather events. For example, Jesuit records from the Spanish Philippines provided insight into typhoons in the archipelago (Warren 2015); French, English, and Norwegian missionary accounts revealed the tracks of the tropical cyclones that made landfall on Madagascar (Nash *et al.* 2015); and the colonial archives disclose the nature and extent of drought and flood events in Mexico since the sixteenth century (Endfield 2008).

DIAGNOSING COLONIAL CLIMATES

In addition to the collection of meteorological records, the human body was also an important instrument by which to measure colonial climates. Imperial discourse on the merits of exploration, colonization, and emigration was rooted in Hippocratic thought, which emphasized the dependence of human health on local geographical conditions. By the nineteenth century, the question of how white bodies would fare in foreign climes, particularly the tropics, was becoming a source of considerable consternation. Once an Edenic vision of plenty, the tropical environmental imaginary had darkened: rather than the veneration of the tropics that Humboldt and Darwin espoused, the region between the Tropics of Cancer and Capricorn was increasingly conceptualized as a threat to the health of colonizing peoples (Arnold 1996: 141–68). These fears were deployed to justify European and North American imperial ambitions; to support arguments for slavery; and to account for the challenges that imperial powers encountered in colonial contexts.

The climate of prospective territories provided the basis on which European and North American powers could rationalize their imperial ambitions. If climate determined racial character and capacity, as contemporaries believed, then the civilized, white peoples of temperate nations were entirely fit to subjugate those of the uncivilized tropics. Following from this cultural alignment of climate with civilizational progress was the view that the heat of the tropics limited industriousness, encouraged laziness, and fostered despotism. As the Presidency Surgeon of Bengal observed in 1839, for instance, "When we reflect upon the habits and customs of the Natives; their long misgovernment; their religion, &c; their diet, clothing, and withal, their *climate*, the problem of their moral and physical depravation is solved" (Martin 1839: 79, emphasis in original). Such moral discourse, most commonly associated with eighteenth-century thinkers such as Abbé Jean-Baptiste Du Bos and Montesquieu, had significant implications for questions of emigration and the mobility of imperial agents throughout the Age of Empire (Fleming 1998).

During the eighteenth century, western medical thought had reassured colonial ambitions that whites could adapt or acclimatize to colonial climes. Dress, housing, behavior, and creolization were each important elements to the successful management of European health in the colonies (Harrison 1996). A spell of seasoning was another approach to condition bodies to their new environs. For both the free and unfree, physicians recommended seasoning to allow their bodies to adjust to the foreign conditions and reduce their susceptibility to the climate and diseases (Smith 2015). As the Scottish physician James Lind observed in a 1768 essay, "By length of time, the constitution of Europeans becomes seasoned to the East and West Indian climates, if it is not injured by repeated attacks of sickness, upon their first arrival. Europeans, when thus habituated, are generally subject to as few diseases abroad, as those who reside at home" (Lind 1768: 146). These notions of acclimatization were predicated on a climate determinism that a human body was best suited to its (evolutionary) "home" or birth climate. Leaving there could risk that body's degeneration, which could in turn imperil the racial purity of future generations (Valenčius 2001).

By the early nineteenth century, however, human acclimatization was coming under question. Western medical geography increasingly attributed high rates of disease and morbidity among Europeans in the tropics to the heat and humidity of these climes, especially when these conditions were made worse by the excesses of the colonists (Livingstone 2002). Under this schema, tropical climes posed the greatest threats to European constitutions and therefore, to European rule (Arnold 1996). Experience only heightened these fears. For Spain, the climate of its Caribbean territories was thought to be a safeguard against military incursion. A proposed British military intervention in Caracas in 1808, for instance, was met with concern from one colonel, who argued, "My fears on that subject are the climate, the climate, the climate" (cited in McNeill 2010: 277). In Sierra Leone, nearly 500 per thousand of the British troops garrisoned there between 1819 and 1838 died each year (Curtin 1998). Meanwhile, in India, although the British had triumphed in the First Burma War (1824–6), climate and disease exacted a heavy toll on both sides of the campaign (Harrison 1999). These experiences confirmed shifting perceptions of tropical climes, their implications for the defense of European empires, and their prospects for colonial settlement. The emerging field of medical topography identified the environment, particularly the climate, as the most important determinant of both physical and moral health, and its practitioners sought to identify the healthiest areas for Europeans abroad (Harrison 2000).

In the Dutch East Indies, however, a more optimistic view of European acclimatization prevailed. There, the prospects for the acclimatization of Dutch colonists became significant to wider debates about the future of the Indies as a colony of extraction, which had flared in response to the introduction of the (forced) cultivation system (*cultuurstelsel*) in 1830 in Java (Pols 2012). Designed to boost Dutch state revenue, the cultivation system attracted criticism for its exploitation of Javanese peasants and contribution to the occurrence of famine (Protschky 2011). In addition to these concerns, European residents had their own interests to consider—the colonial government limited European settlement to reduce competition with its own commercial interests, and offered few opportunities for educational and career advancement for colonists in the Indies.

By the mid-nineteenth century, these grievances gained a voice in the metropole, where the 1848 "Springtime of the People" had encouraged the formation of a parliamentary democracy in the Netherlands. Such a program of political reform would not be extended to the Indies, nor would emigration restrictions be relaxed on the grounds that the tropical climate was ill-suited to European colonization (Pols 2012). Colonial reformers, however, mobilized medical evidence that suggested otherwise. A cultural and scientific renaissance in Batavia since the 1820s showed, argued advocates such as the physician Willem Bosch, that Europeans could thrive in the Indies with careful attention to their behavior and morality (De Knecht-Van Eekelen 2001). As Ann Laura Stoler (1989) notes, the responsibility for these matters fell to European wives and mothers who were the colonial bastions of Calvinist morality in the Indies. The reformers eventually prevailed and in the 1870s, the opening of the Indies economy, the introduction of agrarian reforms, and the loosening of immigration restrictions led to an influx of Europeans and Americans to the archipelago (Figure 3.3) (Protschky 2011).

For the British and French empires, meanwhile, segregation became increasingly preferable to acclimatization during the nineteenth century. Physicians now recommended that Europeans would preserve or restore their health by retreating to spaces that were climatically akin to their homeland. As

FIGURE 3.3: Planten van suikerriet bij Tegal, *c.* 1890 (Sugarcane plantation, Tegal, Central Java). Courtesy of the University Library, Leiden, KITLV 10735.

the French physician Alexandre Kermorgant declared in 1899, "Man is like a plant transported to a foreign soil, and the greatest pains must be taken in order to acclimate to that new soil. If hill stations are useful to the weakened in our own climes, how much more useful they are amongst victims of anaemia in our overseas possessions" (cited in Jennings 2006: 27). Consequently, hill stations, spas, and sanitary enclaves became highland refuges in which Europeans could restore or preserve their health away from the ills of the wider tropical landscape, such as malaria and yellow fever (Chakrabarti 2014). In Guadeloupe, Réunion Island, Madagascar, Tunisia, and Indochina, the French empire established climatic resorts or *climatiques* for the moral and physical benefit of Europeans (Edwards 2003; Jennings 2006; Jennings 2011). Local French authorities in Cochinchina even entertained an ambitious 1896 plan to build an enormous "refrigerated sanatorium" in Saigon that would replicate the cooler climes of the metropole (Demay 2014). In South Asia too, hill stations provided cool sanctuaries for Britons to recuperate from the tropical heat of the plains, particularly following the influx of British troops after the revolt of 1857 (Kennedy 1996; Jennings 2014). As European enclaves, these areas became key sites of political and military power that allowed for the maintenance of imperial rule in the second half of the nineteenth century (Kenny 1995).

An alternative approach required Europeans to depart the territory entirely and make for more salubrious climes within the empire, if not the metropole. British soldiers and missionaries—weary from their tropical duties—were despatched to temperate outposts as diverse as British Burma, the Cape Colony, and New Zealand (Curtin 1989; Endfield and Nash 2007; Deacon 2000; Beattie 2015). Commercial and government-sponsored boosters also capitalized on these desires for temperate relief. In the aftermath of the First War of Indian Independence, for instance, the Australasian colonies and the Cape vied for the opportunity to host a sanatorium for European convalescents at the 1859 Royal Commission on the Sanitary State of the Army in India (1863; Morgan 2015). By virtue of their destination's more ideal climate conditions, a visitor would not only improve in health, but also provide much-needed financial and demographic stimulus to the far reaches of the empire.

Although the field of medical topography was primarily concerned with the health of European and North American soldiers stationed in imperial outposts, the fate of colonial women became of considerable interest in the latter half of the nineteenth century. Empire offered women an escape from the crowded cities of Europe, and their emigration was encouraged to further the cause of colonial expansion (Bell 1993). British wives also set sail for the subcontinent in growing numbers to reinforce the imperial presence after the 1857 uprising (Sen 2010). But if men were susceptible to physical and moral degeneration in certain climes, then the weaker constitutions of women and children were especially vulnerable. With the family at the heart of imperial ambitions for the biological reproduction of white society in the colonies, their welfare was particularly important (Stoler 1989; Grosse 2003). Accordingly, colonial medical texts focused on female reproductive health and childrearing, lest—as one obstetrician warned in 1875—"oriental indolence" developed in the "once hardy Englishwoman" (Tilt 1875, cited in Sen 2010: 260).

Concerns that European bodies would not thrive in warmer, tropical climes had grave implications for imperial projects founded on natural resource extraction. This climate determinism had helped to justify arguments for the enslavement of non-Europeans in the era prior to abolition (Arnold 1996; Jennings 2006). If Europeans were weakened by the climate, they would lack the energy to undertake the labors of agricultural production. It was vital then, slaveholders argued, that peoples born in and so accustomed to those climes, should bear those labors instead (Jennings 2006). The German-born explorer Robert Schomburgk summarized this logic in his 1848 *History of Barbados*: "The African, inured to servitude and by constitution adapted to the hottest climate, proved the most effective labourer under the tropical sun" (Schomburgk 1848: 145). Supporting this notion of a climatic aptitude for enslavement was the view that slavery was the "natural" form of the despotic government of tropical places (Arnold 1996).

Such climate concerns continued long after abolition to explain the reliance of European and North American empires on non-white labor in their tropical possessions. Faced with labor shortages arising from the end to African slavery in the British Empire, capitalists turned to skilled and unskilled workers from China and India, many of whom sought respite from famine and poverty (Northup 1995). In a petition to their Governor, planters and merchants in Mauritius claimed in 1839 that "the climate of this island is well known to be very salubrious and congenial to the constitution of the native Indian," that it was "more healthy than their own" (Nicolay 1840: 7–9). A subsequent Calcutta committee into the treatment of Indian laborers dismissed such rhetoric, stating that, "Any benefit derived from the superiority of climate at Mauritius or elsewhere may, we think, very reasonably be put out of the question, as a mere European notion" (Dickens, Charles and Dutt 1841; Hurgobin 2016). Although many labor migrants served in South and Southeast Asia, others moved to the tropical possessions of empire in the Caribbean, Latin America, the Indian Ocean, Africa, and the Pacific. Their work was diverse—from sugar plantations in Cuba and building public works in Malaya to mining guano in Peru and domestic service in Natal (Look Lai 2009).

Despite the enclavism of Europeans in colonial climes, the boundaries between western and indigenous medicine remained fluid into the latter half of the nineteenth century. The philosophies and practices of local physicians had long interested European medics, but the rising faith of imperialists in the apparent superiority of their own medical science tended to elide this earlier exploratory phase of "medical Orientalism." Yet western medical thought did not always have the cure for the unfamiliar diseases of the tropics. In both British India and Saint-Domingue, for example, European physicians turned to local remedies for maladies ranging from cholera to yellow fever (Thoral 2012). If proven curative, imperialists tended to appropriate these insights, rather than entertain a medical pluralism that might undermine the ascendancy of western medical science (Harrison 2001). Most importantly, local practitioners could (reluctantly) reveal the pharmacopeia of medicinal plants and minerals available in the colonies. Their successful exploitation provided a cheaper alternative to the drugs imported from Britain and France, while opening a new source of raw materials for the pharmaceutical industry in the metropole (Harrison 2001; Thoral 2012).

Although plant collection had long inspired imperialists, their fascination with the introduction—the acclimatization—of plants (as well as birds and mammals) gave such ventures another character. These efforts were the latest chapter in the biological expansion of Europe that Crosby described as "the Columbian exchange" (1972) and "ecological imperialism" (Crosby 1986; Rangan, Carney and Denham 2012). Already, trans-imperial networks of botanical exchange had developed as part of a suite of scientific and commercial endeavors with the Dutch establishing a botanic garden at the Cape in 1694 and the French on Mauritius in 1735. Botanic gardens were vital too for the spirit of what Richard Drayton describes as Britain's "imperialism of improvement" (2000: xv). The establishment of gardens at Calcutta, Madras, and Bombay in the 1790s, for instance, would not only encourage the collection of rare specimens, but also provide sites for the cultivation of crops that might withstand drought and prevent the recurrence of devastating famine, such as had occurred in Bengal in 1770 (Arnold 2005; Baber 2016).

For Joseph Banks, these gardens also represented opportunities to facilitate plant exchanges between tropical climates. A Calcutta garden, for instance, would serve "the purpose of conferring on the inhabitants of that circle in the globe who enjoy a climate similar to the climate of Calcutta, what I conceive to be the greatest of all earthly benefits, an increase of their resources of food, in raw material and in luxury by receiving from the West such useful plants as the East did not possess and by sending to the West such as hitherto exclusively belonged to the East" (1794 cited in Arnold 2005). In emphasizing the trade in plants between similar climates, Banks foreshadowed the British school of acclimatization. This approach represented a stark divergence from the French philosophy, which had emerged earlier in the late eighteenth century and focused on the *transformation* of species in foreign climes (Anderson 1992).

Having lost most of their tropical colonies in the Caribbean by the early nineteenth century, the transformative prospects of acclimatization were particularly appealing to French imperialists. Rather than forsake tropical species such as cane sugar and fruits, French students of acclimatization advocated for their cultivation in Algeria (Osborne 2000). Although colonial gardeners had some successes at the *Jardin d'Essai*, their efforts failed to replicate the agricultural riches of their former tropical territories and produced catastrophic results for local peoples. Denied their most productive lands and the mobility required of pastoralism, rural Algerians suffered from a horrific famine in 1867–8 that had not affected the French settler community (Davis 2007). This ordeal hardened Algerian resentment toward the colonial regime, which erupted in the wake of the Franco-Prussian War in 1871.

Although the rise of germ theory in the late nineteenth century encouraged the decline of these forms of climate determinism, the tropics continued to be a source of concern for the expanding European and North American empires (Arnold 2000). As Pratik Chakrabarti (2014) and others argue, the discovery of germs and vaccines had buoyed imperial ambitions for the tropics, but exacerbated the pathological anxieties already associated with those particular places. Tropical medicine emerged in the late nineteenth century to alleviate such climate concerns, but continued to emphasize the role of environmental and social factors in disease transmission. As Warwick Anderson (2006) has shown in the American Philippines, the new science of tropical medicine became a civilizing tool for population management and control that helped to perpetuate the idea of the tropical other in the twentieth century.

CHANGING COLONIAL CLIMATES

Contemporaries also deployed quantitative and qualitative accounts of colonial climates to determine the extent to which the colonial enterprise had affected local climates. In some cases, colonial climate change was a welcome prospect, while in others it was a source of significant environmental anxiety (Beattie 2011). From the tropics to the temperate outposts of empire, the chief method to affect colonial climate change was the planting and removal of trees for medical and agricultural purposes, as well as to enact visions of environmental conservation and restoration.

The association of deforestation with climatic change, principally diminishing rainfall, became increasingly influential in France and England during the late eighteenth century. These desiccation theories grew apace with imperial expansion, as Europeans and North American endeavors transformed colonial environments. Colonial climate change had grave implications for empire's civilizing mission. The imperial anxieties arising from desiccationist discourse encouraged what Richard Grove (1995) views as the "seeds of modern conservationism" (3), whereby colonial expansion led Europeans to re-evaluate the ecological and cultural impact of their activities. In Venezuela, for example,

Humboldt attributed the shrinkage of Lake Valencia, which local inhabitants had observed for several decades, to the clearing of vegetation and diversion of water for plantation irrigation. His critique reflected his wider disdain for European colonialism generally, and its impacts on local peoples and environments (Cushman 2011).

By the mid-nineteenth century, such colonial conservationism had led to the development of forest protection and scientific forestry. According to the logic of desiccationist theory, afforestation was another means to improve colonial climates. The East India Company, for instance, undertook a program of tree planting in St. Helena to counter what it perceived to be a changing climate in the late eighteenth century (Grove 1993). From the 1850s, the Director of the Botanical Gardens in the Australian colony of Victoria, the German-born botanist Baron Ferdinand von Mueller, promoted the planting of particular tree species, such as the Tasmanian blue gum (*Eucalyptus globulus*), to overcome the miasma of swamps. These trees, he argued, had desiccationist qualities that would clean the air, and elsewhere, provide timber for mines and industry (Beattie 2012). Transcending the bounds of empire, their reach was global—from British India to Algeria, from the Cape Colony and the Transvaal to California, and from Tanganyika to Palestine (Bennett 2011; Showers, 2010).

The belief in the capacity of afforestation to improve a local climate was especially evident in the French colonies of the Maghreb. There, as Diana Davis (2007) has argued, a declensionist narrative of environmental decline demanded French colonial authorities restore the region to its "natural" condition of fertility. From the conquest of Algeria (1830), this narrative depicted a region suffering from deforestation, overgrazing, and desertification at the hands of indigenous peoples, which served to rationalize French rule in the region, underwriting colonial laws and policies of dispossession. This declensionist rhetoric was also deployed in Algeria to *conserve* forests as a vital means to prevent the encroachment of the Sahara into the more salubrious areas where European settlers lived (Ford 2016). As a consequence of these environmental imaginaries, colonial forest policies excluded Algerians from forested areas. No longer able to pasture their livestock in the forests or to collect firewood and other food resources, many were left extremely vulnerable to drought, disease, and harvest failures, which contributed to the deaths of some three hundred thousand Algerians in the late 1860s (Davis 2007). Although fears of the climatic consequences of deforestation persisted well into the twentieth century, the associated issues of soil erosion and sand drift came to compete with these anxieties by the interwar era (Beattie 2003; Showers 2005).

An alternative culture of climate modification swept through the semi-arid dryland farming areas of southern Australia between the 1860s and 1890s. Although South Australian Surveyor General George Goyder had demarcated his eponymous "line" of reliable rainfall in 1865, a series of wet years in the subsequent decade emboldened prospective farmers and the colonial government to cultivate the marginal northern fringes of the colony beyond this boundary. They were optimistic that clearing the land for wheat and barley would civilize not only the land, but in a twist on Lockean principles, would do the same for the climate. Certainly, the presence of grassland made their ambitions seem well-founded, and they could take heart from similar efforts underway on the Great Plains of the United States (Douglas 2014). Their faith that "rain follows the plow" was, however, misplaced as drought and rabbits combined to force a retreat by the end of the nineteenth century.

Colonial climate change could also require divine intervention. During the first half of the nineteenth century, European missionaries encountered indigenous peoples in semi-arid southern Africa who believed in the capacity for humans to affect rainfall. Their written accounts provide insight into the geographical imagination of "Africa" in nineteenth-century European science and the power dynamics that mediated their interpretation of local climate knowledge (Barnett 1998). The region's highly variable climate had already been condemned by Biblical standards, and the prevailing local faith in rainmaking only reinforced this othering of the land and its peoples (Duncan 1997). While the missionaries attributed the occurrence of drought to indigenous sinfulness, local rainmakers declared the European presence to be the real cause. Attuned to the authority and influence of the rainmakers, the missionaries adapted their gospel to appeal to this prevailing association among local people of the newcomers with rain (Endfield and Nash 2002b). As Julie Cruikshank suggests in the context of the Yukon and Alaska, the missionaries' claims to the "discovery" of this local climate knowledge elides the very processes of its production through colonial encounters (2005). Decades later in the settler colonies of Australia and New Zealand, frustrated agriculturalists offered special prayers to summon rain and to assure the success of local rainmaking experiments in the late nineteenth and early twentieth centuries (Beattie 2014).

CLIMATES OF DISASTER

Climate reconstructions have allowed historians to better understand how catastrophic weather events affected colonial territories in South Asia, Africa, the Americas, and Australia. Whether drought, flood, famine, or hurricane, the study of climate disasters can reveal the ways in which colonial societies understood and responded to extreme weather events—their cultures of climate concern. Networks of information exchange, as we have seen, enabled colonial observers to show that such seemingly local catastrophes were part of larger climate patterns, which indicated the presence of global phenomena, such as the ENSO (Chappell and Grove 2000). In the Spanish Philippines, meanwhile, the Manila Observatory (est. 1865) provided forecasts of approaching storms and accurately predicted the passage of typhoons over the archipelago. With its connection to the telegraph in 1878, this Jesuit observatory became part of a regional network of meteorological stations, including Macao (1885), Saigon (1887), and Tokyo (1890) that issued weather warnings across the South China Sea (Bankoff 2011).

The Age of Empire provides fertile ground for the study of extreme weather events and their role in the political and social upheavals of the long nineteenth century. Sherry Johnson (2011), for instance, has shown that the far-reaching ecological and socioeconomic effects of El Niño, La Niña, and hurricane activity combined with fomenting unrest to help transform the Atlantic world, culminating in the American War of Independence, the French Revolution, and the Haitian Revolution. Richard Grove (2005) has likewise examined the role that the ENSO events of 1789–93 played in the French Revolution, as well as droughts and famine in India, Africa, and Australia. In Cuba, Louis Pérez (2001) argues, the destruction wrought by a series of hurricanes in the 1840s helped to break down Spanish colonial rule (Figure 3.4). In these cases, climate extremes did not bring about the winds of change; rather they exacerbated grievances that were already festering in these colonial contexts.

Applying concepts from social science research, such as vulnerability, adaptation, and resilience, has offered historians new ways to analyse colonial experiences of climate variability and cultures of climate concern. The lens of vulnerability encourages the study of extreme weather events in terms of social, rather than natural, processes. Differences in vulnerability, which expose some people to more climate risk than others, are the product of complex socioeconomic processes that historians can unravel in order to discern the interactions of human activities and the environment over time (Hilhorst and Bankoff 2004). Georgina Endfield (2008) deploys this approach to her study of droughts and floods in colonial Mexico at the turn of the nineteenth century. There she shows how communities attempted to reduce their vulnerability to the impacts of climate variability through strategies of land and water management. The notion of vulnerability can be extended to animals, as Greg Bankoff has shown in the Philippines, where their domestication suggests "mutual vulnerability, where the nature of the dependent relationship [with humans] compounds the risks to which both are exposed" (2007: 299). Contemporary concerns about anthropogenic climate change have imbued this research with a new sense of urgency to better understand the social and political consequences of short- and long-term changes in climate.

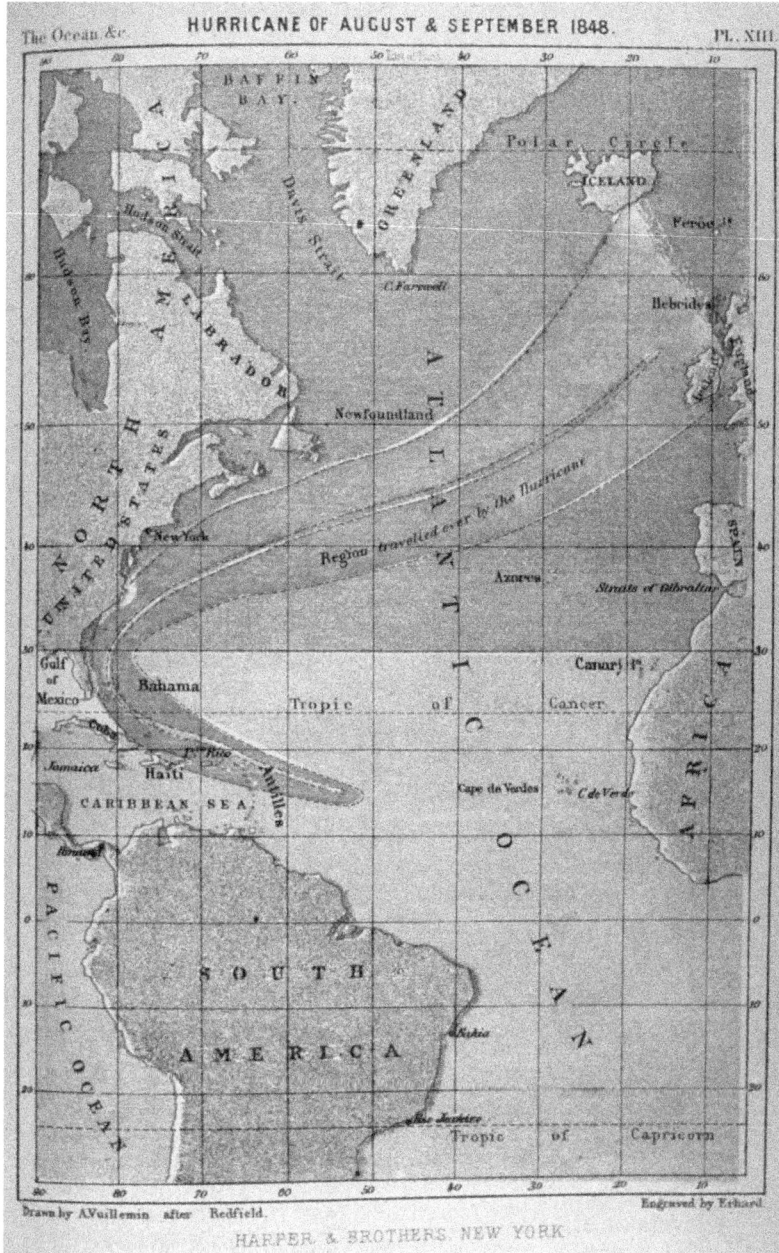

FIGURE 3.4: Storm track of the hurricane of August and September 1848. Elisee Recluse, *The Ocean, Atmosphere and Life* (New York: Harper, 1873). Courtesy of the National Oceanic and Atmospheric Administration and US Department of Commerce.

CLIMATE LEGACIES

Despite the decolonization of the Cold War era, the rise of global climate change discourse has helped to ensure agential understandings of climate continue in the twenty-first century. Mike Hulme (2011) has argued that we face a new form of climate determinism, in which human agency is confined by possible future climates. Within this schema of neo-climate determinism relics of empire persist. The tropics remain pathologized as a space of disaster and disease. This construction of tropical climates serves to portray many former colonies as destined for catastrophe (see Bankoff 2003). Anthropogenic climate change has fueled this image of climate concern, converging with development critiques to conjure a so-called "tropic of chaos": "a belt of economically and politically battered post-colonial states ... [which compose] that violent and impoverished swath of terrain around the mid-latitudes of the planet" (Parenti 2011: 9–11). Such a description suggests that the legacy of European and North American empires continues to manifest in the unequal ways in which anthropogenic climate change is represented and experienced around the globe.

Among the worst-affected by the increased frequency and magnitude of extreme weather events of a warmer planet will be those former colonies that comprise the Global South. There is a dark irony, as Dipesh Chakrabarty (2009b, 2012, 2014) has argued, that these peoples and places are bearing the brunt of a planetary phenomenon to which they have contributed little. For example, excluding low-lying island nations, post-colonial coastal countries such as Vietnam and Bangladesh face the greatest risk from rising sea levels but have received little of the benefit from the economic growth associated with increased carbon dioxide emissions (Hardy and Nuse 2016). This uneven distribution of risk and responsibility lies at the heart of critiques of the Anthropocene concept as well as international climate change governance (Bonneuill 2015; Bulkeley and Newell 2015).

Coined by Nobel Laureate atmospheric chemist Paul Crutzen and ecologist Eugene Stoermer (2000) at the turn of the twenty-first century, the Anthropocene concept proposes that humankind is now a biogeochemical force causing planetary change such that the Earth has entered a new geological age. Although the first exhalation of this "hot breath of civilisation" remains a point of debate, the original proposal dated its onset to the industrialization of the late eighteenth century, or more precisely, James Watt's design of the steam engine in 1784 (McEwan 2010: 109; Lewis and Maslin 2015). Fueling the steam engines of the workshop of the world was coal, the demand for which drove its extraction from South Asia and precipitated the extension of the British Empire's reach to the coal seams of Asia, Australia, Canada, and Africa (Malm 2016). This shared but unequal history of resource extraction highlights the importance of histories that account for the cultures of empire and their lasting impact on colonized peoples and ecologies.

Understanding empire's duress at the planetary scale in the twenty-first century demands the close analysis of the environmental imaginaries that shaped natural worlds during the Age of Empire (Stoler 2016). These imaginaries flowered from particular cultures of climate concern, and informed imperialist ambitions for colonial improvement. The quantitative and qualitative measurement of colonial climates through observation, experience, and theory not only fostered the scientific networks of exchange, but also structured imperial narratives of environmental decline and anxiety that mobilized the unprecedented movement of sojourners and settlers, free and unfree, human and non-human, across the globe for empire's ends.

CHAPTER FOUR

Labor

Identities and Time under Empire

UTATHYA CHATTOPADHYAYA

INTRODUCTION

Histories of Western empires in the Age of Empire have fundamentally pivoted around the narrative of expanding global capitalism and the multiple contradictions immanent in its unfolding. In late nineteenth-century Europe, Eric Hobsbawm (1989: 8–10) found workers at the heart of paradoxes wrought by capitalism—for one, they demanded its undoing while simultaneously pushing the gears that held together imperialism overseas. In the colonies, such contradictions were multiplied manifold as industrial growth was not the only mode of consolidating economic power—empires also relied upon the extractive accumulation of mineral and agrarian resources, the politics of colonial difference in governing labor, imposition of free trade doctrines through multiple strategies in the peripheries, and heterogeneous administrative systems of rule (Robinson and Gallagher 1953; Cain and Hopkins 2001; Bayly 1989; Cooper 2005: 23–5). Colonies were also sites of inter-imperial competition within a political framework already challenged by the dynamic resistance of workers who organized around modes of social belonging other than class, checkering the way capitalism shaped and was shaped by colonial societies. Social and economic histories of labor approached this imperial paradigm by focusing on the formation of social class and the politics of labor in antagonism to and in association with the movement of capital. Social historians explored questions of wage-based exploitation, class consciousness, political militancy, women's work, and techniques of disciplining labor. Despite successfully establishing the disruptive and complicating role of class politics within the larger trajectory of capitalism and colonialism, such histories nonetheless retained a focus on structured social relationships in a framework where class was definitively formed and relatively homogenous, class consciousness arrived at, and capital challenged, or at least troubled, by class organization.

Cultural histories of labor in the Age of Empire emerged from within social history but departed toward analysing cultural objects, identities, and practices that shaped modes of social belonging under imperialism. Following E.P. Thompson's influence, social history had treated class as a historical phenomenon that "happened" relationally across long timespans and tied together the "raw material of experience." (Thompson 1963: 9–10) However, his search for class consciousness had rendered experience an amorphous category that was "embodied in traditions, value-systems, ideas and institutional forms"— consciousness was thus the articulation of experience simply "in cultural terms." Culture, however, was not merely a vehicle for the experiences that shaped class consciousness—newer cultural histories redefined culture through emphasis on the particularity and unevenness in the spread or disruption of capitalism across colonial sites, the experiences of marginal subjects from below as they wrestled with identity, difference, and coloniality, and the nature of power, mobility, and contingency within colonial society. Such histories complicated the presumed fixity of class by focusing on how markers of difference and modes of identification such as race, gender, and religion informed, unsettled, or displaced it. Further, they also delineated how practices of time, performance, dress, and faith were relevant to the historical development of capitalism. The imperial machine was thus rematerialized through an emphasis on the bodies upon the gears that sustained it.

In this essay, I will argue that to think materially about culture and culturally about labor, two themes are fundamentally significant—identities and time. Both indexed empire and labor to reveal the contested and layered composition of colonial working life. Cultural identities were formative modes of articulating the self, social difference, and belonging for the diverse groups that were subjected to Western imperial rule. Colonial institutions enumerated and classified populations by codifying existing dynamic forms of social identification and normativized them through school education, print media, and governmental training. Attempts at reclaiming the reins on multiple identities that existed pre-colonially to navigate the constrained political ambit of the colonial state on their own terms often defined how colonial subjects engaged with governmental knowledges and identity paradigms (Vail 1991; Ranger and Hobsbawm 1983; Glassman 2000). Time was similarly codified by colonial institutions into linear clock time by dominating existing hybridities of seasonal, cyclical, and other modes of biophysical time (Ogle 2015). Assembling imperial authority necessitated that narratives of time among the colonized be brought to heel. How different societies lived *in* their time and imputed coherence and totality to their idea of the present, past, and future, and their experiences of birth, life, and death through diverse interpretive practices of remembrance and expectation were subjugated under European industrial regimes of temporal discipline. However, when seen from below, the conflicts over time divulged not uniformity but the heterogeneity in how colonial subjects inhabited and occupied time, and the contingencies that shaped how they navigated their everyday routines. *With* time, identities also weakened or congealed as expressions of selfhood. The infusion of force and meaning into identities depended upon relations of indebtedness, intimacy, coercion, and violence. Simultaneously, practices and performances of community, individuality, and resistance, also emerged as colonized peoples came to inhabit newer compartmentalizations of time. This essay will dwell on this relationality between identities and time as the signal contribution of cultural approaches to labor.

IDENTITIES

In the Age of Empire, multiple regimes of colonial labor overlapped and co-constituted each other. Slavery continued even after the formal abolition of the slave trade, forced labor was common in African mines, and agricultural labor was conditionally protected, disenfranchised, or used for subsistence livelihood on plantations (van Onselen 1976, 1982; Prakash 1992; Bose 1993; Cooper 1980; Stoler 1995a). Meanwhile, wage labor expanded fitfully, indentured and convict labor was deployed in post-abolition plantations, infrastructure projects and mining centers, and *lascars* emerged as a mobile global maritime workforce. Upon this complex canvas, technologies of colonial power sought to classify cultural practices and social modes of belonging into governable identities, ossifying them even as everyday life tore against the seams of such endeavors (Cohn 1996).

Departing from notions of backwardness or lack on the part of colonized workers and peasants, new cultural histories foregrounded how the political reconfiguration of cultural markers of difference and belonging like ethnicity, caste, religion, gender, race, and sex by colonial governments could better explain how workers made sense of their economic realities. The ensuing emphasis on the production and management of difference under colonial rule incorporated influences from sociology (Calhoun 1994), social and cultural anthropology (Comaroff and Comaroff 1992), cultural studies (Hall 1978, 1996), oral history (Vansina 1985), and postcolonial theory (Gilroy 1993). Critically including diverse sources enhanced both the archive and the practice of history—dance and sport thus became archival complements to strikes and manifestoes to produce rigorous analyses of materiality and culture.

Studying identities channeled labor history toward the materiality of the body under empire. Historicizing the experience of racialized workers, indentured laborers, and convict-coolies, and the legal and governmental endeavors to control miscegenation and inter-racial sexual relationships meant that how labor embodied the discourses that enabled its existence and mobility became a fundamental question for historians (Anderson 2012; Levine 2006b; Tabili 1996; Hall 2000). In the British Empire, discourses constructed by dominant white male culture in the metropole were perpetuated through binaries of colonizer–colonized, self–other, white–black, black–indigenous, respectable–savage, and domesticated–rough (Poovey 1988). Critical theory around race and gender helped historians reveal how coloniality itself undermined the putative stability of these binaries by producing entanglements, not stable oppositions (Ballantyne 2015). The analysis of culture and identities from "above" materialized practices of power that conditioned, ordered, and assembled working colonial bodies for the reproduction of labor whereas the view from "below" refocused historiography toward how laborers made meaning of the profound changes they were enveloped in.

Race was foremost among identities reconfigured under colonialism. However uneven its development, all Western imperial labor regimes were shot through with the discursive and embodied materiality of race. Shaped over centuries by colonial wars, dispossession of indigenous land, and the institution of slavery, race was a political marker of cultural difference and a way of knowing the self and other in colonial and metropolitan societies (Chapman and Frader 2004; Alexander and Halpern 2000). The late eighteenth century witnessed vigorous debates over the abolition of slavery in the British Empire in response to multiple slave rebellions and insurrections across the plantation colonies (Morgan 2007; Gott 2011; see Sessions in this volume). Slaves, maroons, and formerly enslaved men and women militated against imperial armadas and survived diseases like malaria while Quakers, white abolitionists, and dissident religious voices shaped legal and public opinion in the metropole against the institution of slavery (Morgan 2004; Blackburn 1988). But racialized ideas and practices had undergirded the economic enterprise of slavery and the cultural assemblages of Western imperialism since its beginning (Loomba 2007; Said 1994). In each society that came under the shadow of colonialism in the nineteenth century, race was used politically to govern the subjected, making it foundational to the politics of colonial difference. However, far from being a static or stable identity, Laura Tabili (2003: 125–30) argued, pace Stuart Hall (1997), that race was not a thing but an active relationship, a practice of power and a category of codification that made imperial rule possible and was repeatedly reconfigured as raced bodies and ideas collided with each other.

The cultural politics of race fashioned the material lives of people across the color line. The construction of whiteness is instructive of how an invented category based on biological racism meant to segregate plantation laborers in the US South and Ireland came to be accepted and re-articulated by Europeans as a powerful and resilient tool of delineating self from other (Allen 1997; Roediger 1991). Whiteness shaped the identity of the working classes and the immigrant poor in the settler colonies by both deploying blackness as culturally abject and denying indigeneity its history of sovereignty and property (Moreton-Robinson 2015). In Jonathan Hyslop's analysis of how the imperial working class made itself white in the Age of Empire (Hyslop 1999), he argued that white laborism was constituted by multiple cross-imperial vectors enabled by settler migration in an expanding maritime commercial world. In Australia, racist responses to the in-migration of Chinese labor in goldfields since 1850 had led to most Australian colonies penalizing Chinese labor migration or simply seizing, at harbor, gold that belonged to Chinese miners (Loy-Wilson 2017). In 1878, the Sydney Seaman's strike and in 1890, the Sheep Shearers'

FIGURE 4.1: Chinese coolies in Cuba, 1860. Credit: Oldtime/Alamy Stock Photo.

movement both demanded a total ban on Chinese workers. Following the discovery of gold mines in the Transvaal, miners moved away from Australia to South Africa carrying the politics of settler white laborism with them. These migratory vectors were rooted in the dispersed but organized networks of the Cornish mining diaspora which held onto its filial and communal crew culture to find employment and shut out black, Asian, Afrikaner, and Jewish workers in the Rand. As the Second Boer War was fought, white mining capitalists in the Transvaal demanded the introduction of Chinese labor in the mines. This 1904 "Transvaal scheme" had global antecedents in Australia and evidenced how the ideology of settler whiteness was moving away from its ties to Britain and rooting itself more in the settler colonies. However, Chinese workers who were imported, especially into the Witwatersrand's gold mines, resisted white policing tooth and nail, eventuating the failure of the scheme and signaling that indentured exploitation could not continue as it had in the nineteenth century (Ngai 2017; Bright 2013; Park 2009). Transnationally however, pro-worker state welfarism coupled with the protection of racial boundaries in defense of whiteness in Australia, Canada, United States, South Africa, and Britain only further included the white working class within the settler colonial framework. In fact, workers and political elites were complicit in redrawing the color line using developing discourses of white masculinity and white nationalism based on threats of Asian demographic multiplication and the growing influence of Japan, then an emerging Asian empire (Reynolds and Lake 2008a), thus further buttressing a settlerist paradigm built on indigenous dispossession and racial segregation.

Nonetheless, white self-identification, much like imperial power, was prone to coming undone on the ground. The instability of whiteness emerged within the same historical contexts where it was being shaped. In 1893, when 220 Australian workers led by William Lane in search of a utopian "socialist" world of "mateship" and cooperative labor outside of the evils of the industrial class system landed in Paraguay to found "New Australia," they were forced to confront the racism in their notions of miscegenation and "Teutonic" socialism. The attempts to set up the colony failed repeatedly inside a war-ravaged Paraguay that New Australia colonists characterized as a cheap and backward country with lazy natives. More importantly, these racist stereotypes of indigenous Paraguayans in the minds of Lane's followers gradually broke down as they were warmly welcomed by the "natives." Villagers bartered goods with them as hospitable guests and commercial equals. In time, the colonists came to appreciate the diligence of indigenous workers on farms and fields. By 1897, many of them had started living in villages and speaking Spanish and by 1902, started working on sugarcane fields with locals to "produce rum to share" (Mawson 2011). Many thus gave up the movement's founding principles of teetotalism, the color line, and the fear of miscegenation. While Lane continued in his pursuits to colonize other plots of land, he could not avoid the tensions wrought by embodied realities of racial and sexual contact and the gradual undoing of a colonial enterprise on the ground.

Asian workers faced more life-altering decisions—whether to work on other colonial plantations or mines was barely a voluntary choice. The indentured labor system, lasting in the British, French, and American empires between 1826 and 1922, emerged as a response to what Madhavi Kale has called the myth of labor shortage perpetuated by colonial overseers and capitalists in the British Caribbean in the aftermath of abolition. Planters and colonists argued that once slaves were freed they would not want to work for low wages. Cheaper labor was thus essential to keep up competitive production of sugar and other plantation commodities (Kale 1998; Look Lai 2004; Brereton and Yelvington 1999). India and China became the two primary sources of "coolie" labor (see Spieler in this volume). The British administered five-year contracts out of which one or three years would count as an "apprenticeship" period, after which the worker would be able to earn a wage that was previously agreed upon in the contract. Apprenticeship was commonplace during and after slavery—formerly it made slaves more dependent on planters and later denied wages to indentured workers as they were not yet "skilled" for the job (Paton 2004; Tinker 1974). Contracts differed widely depending on the demands of the employer, but in an ideal contract, after the five years, the Indian "coolie" could choose to remain in the host-colony as a wage-earner or avail of the option of repatriation to the homeland.

Besides mirroring features of European slave trading, the "coolie" system was also shaped by the reconfiguration of existing social and economic debt between workers and job recruiters which shaped identities, enabled the limited implementation of contracts and complicated historiographical binaries between "free" and "unfree" labor (Saunders 1984; Northrup 2003, 1995: 10; Mesthrie 2009). Indian workers first arrived in Mauritius in 1834, British Guiana in 1838, Natal in 1860, and Fiji in 1879. They had to spend a minimum of five years away from their farms after a journey in treacherous conditions on boats packed beyond capacity and face severe illnesses and the unfamiliarity of a new land, all based on a contract that was often barely legible to them. Systemic coercion was evident early on—by 1862 in Guiana, the rapid rise in demands by workers for commutation of their contracts despite the loss of wages, led to Immigration Ordnances that removed all termination clauses from contracts and limited worker mobility to two-mile radii outside plantations (Adamson 1984: 45–6).

Indenture also drew upon overlapping networks of enslavement and convict migration in the Indian Ocean (Chatterjee and Eaton 2006). The social dependency and obligation engendered in Indian enslavement, especially of young women, and pre-existing systems of transporting Indian convicts to build

FIGURE 4.2: Coolie Hut, Jamaica, *c.* 1890, by A. Duperly & Sons. Credit: Archive Farms Inc/Alamy Stock Photo.

infrastructure in penal colonies and outposts like Singapore, Penang and, Tenasserim contributed to systematizing Indian indenture (Anderson 2009). Methods of classifying and transporting penal convicts from the mid-nineteenth century were deeply coercive—coolies were thus tattooed, inspected for diseases by medical officials at emigration depots, marched down by watchmen, and organized into work-gangs that resembled penal gangs from the early nineteenth century. Convict passages had been narrated by Indians through stories of the *tapu* (island) and *kala pani* (black waters, to be crossed to reach penal colonies like the Andamans). The experience of indentured labor was articulated by indentured workers being taken to Mauritius or Demerara using the same tropes—cultural categories were thus transposed by subaltern actors to make sense of the global experiment in imperial labor reallocation that they were a part of (Anderson 2009: 93–6; Anderson 2012).

Cultures of trust and community undergirding the sustenance of indenture systems were rooted in debt relations borne out of filial and caste networks connecting the labor recruiter and the workers. The recruiter, often a *sirdar,* was a respected figure responsible for wage-distribution and signing or thumbing *hundis* (promissory notes for remittances). In Fiji, *sirdars* also made workers sign contracts, called "agreements," which Indian workers pronounced "girmit," thus inviting the self-identifying term *"girmitiya"* or *"girmit-wallah"* (Lal 1980; Lal 1983; Carter 1995: 38–42). At any given time, the recruiter could also be the foreman, leader of the work-gang, small-time creditor to needy workers, and scribe for letters. His closeness to the manager centralized his presence further (Roy 2008; Carter 1995). During protests, strikes, or disputes, recruiters were essential to resolving problems. Such clout drew many into the profession of recruitment—competing recruiters then used filial and caste networks to draw more workers into making the journey abroad, often spreading rumors and mischaracterizing the life that they would have on a plantation. Workers were indebted to recruiters from the beginning. Many had to take small debts, often from the recruiter, to arrange the journey from the village to the port town. When boats docked during passage, workers would borrow and spend money on food or medicines to treat ailments contracted during the journey. Such debts fundamentally constituted the identity and position of the worker in relation to the regime of labor and its mechanisms of discipline, and were formalized into institutional practice by British authorities who licensed more recruiters despite the deceit and dependency in recruitment, the disease and death endemic to the system and the inability of most workers to repay debts (Tinker 1974: 133, 159).

The configuration of caste identities within indentured communities was always uneven—its norms disintegrated under severe constraints of plantation life but re-emerged with more immigrant settlement and diasporic politics. As people from different castes were made to travel together and live in close quarters, many barriers shaped by norms of purity and pollution gave way. However, when immigrant workers began transplanting older cultural practices, in Fiji for example, caste identities re-emerged in community relations (Grieco 1998; Lal 2011). In Mauritius, caste as a social basis of discrimination was observably disintegrating until 1910 but between 1910 and 1940, with the rise in political Hindu revivalist movements led by the Arya Samaj, workers tended to take up caste again as a mode of social identification (Hollup 1994: 307).

Initially, Indian coolies in Natal were needed to clear land for plantations, following which they settled outside the estates. After their contracts expired, many stayed on and took to hawking or cane farming and gardening as a peasantry (Freund 1991a; Padayachee and Morrell 1991). Among those who settled in Mauritius, many were re-hired after a period of retrenchment following slumps in profits (Allen 1999). Historians have attempted to capture this structural reality of straddling the labor of farming and industrial or plantation work through categories like "peripheral labor" and "partial proletarianization" (Amin and Van der Linden 1996). Over time, the resulting competition for employment on sugar plantations, public works, and urban businesses in a racially segregated Natal also contributed to the congealing of existing racial divisions between "Black" Africans and "Brown" Indians. Further, the entrepreneurial interests of Natal's Indian mercantilists led them to hire African workers at lower wages than those of settled Indians in the region. Others yet, chose to hire Indians as a policy for safeguarding community interests. Voluntary migration of Indian merchants had increased since 1860 and by 1875, they had established substantial relations of money-lending and trade. Often, they emulated white planters and mining capitalists in order to wield political influence over state policy, albeit in the capacity of junior partners (Harries 1987). As Indian merchants expanded their money-lending practices and liquor sales into communities of African workers, their ability to charge higher interest rates was buttressed further. Violent clashes between African and Indian workers, like in the Natal Government Railways barracks in 1890, exposed the fault lines within the racial and economic system inhabited by different also-colonized peoples which community leaders like M.K. Gandhi were forced to wrestle with (Mahoney 2012; Desai and Vahed 2015; Hyslop 2011). Meanwhile, Indians who became hawkers or flower-sellers in the early part of the twentieth century soon found that Indian mercantilists would hesitate to support their campaigns against racial discrimination in Natal's street-vending policies. Goolam Vahed (2005: 449–79) has shown how Indian mercantile elites who were approached by street vendors to intervene in the racial conflict over street vending negotiated the cultural politics of race by keeping class interests before those of an "Indian" community.

Transformations in religious identities among Indian emigrants, both indentured and passenger, reflected broader cultural politics set forth under colonialism. As the Indian Muslim population in Natal grew, Ismaili leaders from Bombay dispatched trusted followers to establish greater bonds of community. The building of shrines and the discourse of martyrdom helped invent ways of territorializing the lived experience of Muslim workers in a foreign land (Green 2008). In South Africa, *muharram* soon transformed from a Muslim festival into a syncretic celebration with Hindu Indians (Vahed 1999, 2002). In Mauritius, since the high rates of inter-marriage and forced living in close quarters upon plantations had historically created a multi-ethnic social fabric (Christopher 1992), Islam became mostly secular in practice, involving community service, charity, and discourses on morality (Eisenlohr 2006). In Natal, however, differences between Indian and Malay Muslims were prominent and their histories fractious (Vahed 2001). Tensions within Indian Islamic subgroups along lines of caste and language also shaped the life of communal spaces like mosques (Vahed 2006; Vahed and Desai 2010). In Fiji, where the Arya Samaj took up the cause of exploited Hindu workers who were a larger demographic, religious politics deeply divided workers. The development of an identifiable Hindu identity in Fiji occurred through a shift to political devotionalism between 1890 and 1930 and coalesced around the emerging diasporic ambitions of Hindu nationalists (Kelly 1988; Jayawardena 1980). Among voluntary Gujarati migrants in Fiji, notions of virtue and community pride defined their refusal to take up salaried or wage work even in times of economic hardship just as formerly indentured laborers and their descendants rarely ventured into any form of self-employment, indicating how cultural connotations paved the entry into and the distance from wage labor under colonialism (Kelly 1992; Kaplan and Kelly 1994).

The Age of Empire also produced other labor systems that challenged categorizations, such as Indian maritime workers or *lascars*. Their cultural lives were marked by shifting liminal social identities and unstable relations of employment which made them, in G. Balachandran's view, the first modern form of fully globalized labor (Balachandran 2012). This precarious globalization wasn't all fluid—it highlighted an "uneven and uncertain maze" where "globalizing" was about "different and multiple orders and strategies of border-making" and "relentless negotiation and improvisation" (Balachandran 2012: 19–21). These seafarers were, at once, "peasants, coolies, casual laborers, maritime workers, political couriers, militants, sojourners, pedlars, traders,

FIGURE 4.3: December 1928: Lascars at the Opening of the Tower Hill Memorial. Credit: Fox Photos/Getty Images.

workers, farmers and migrants." The *serang*, a labor intermediary for the "Asiatic" maritime world, was a far more agentive, conniving, and complex character when compared to the *sirdar, kangani,* or the *dada*. Coercion was often not the most pressing reason for mobility—his seafarers professed an active and provocative subjectivity in relation to the British Empire and its web of maritime outposts. They crossed boundaries between competing empires, changed their names often, outwitted colonial registrars, bargained for specific benefits aboard ships by capitalizing on the scarcity of rations and mobilized their connections in the service of revolutionary or anti-colonial nationalism. Indian seafarers circulated between crews bound for Australia, the United States, and Canada, creating their own maps of the world. They cultivated relationships with new ship masters, which was essential to long-term survival in a maritime world structured around strict penalties and the undisguised repression of attempts to strike sail. Avoiding working under masters with a reputation for violence was also key. They also avoided working as war labor during the First World War by deserting ships and struck work again just before the war began in 1939 in Durban, Sydney, and Beira.

However, the flux in seafaring lives didn't produce any deracinated subjects. P&O officials used racial arguments about the "inability" of Indian seamen to work in wintry weather to justify containing its Indian maritime labor force within the Indian Ocean arm of its business operations. Using such labor monopolies, P&O could throttle competition and consolidate surveillance. However, Indian seamen routinely jumped ship, crossed over into non-British territory, and refused to serve under *serangs* unfamiliar to them. On the other hand, the British National Union of Seamen became openly racist in the 1880s and after the First World War race riots in England, the National Sailors and Firemen's Union mooted the repatriation of all Black and Asian seamen. On board ships, abuses hurled at Indian workers, such as "bloody niggers," were common and white British sailors resented any equation with Indian workers (Balachandran 2012: 39–40). Generalizing based on the history of Indian seafarers is difficult because few others encountered the world like they did and fewer still had the avenues to switch ships, change names, and bargain using their specialized knowledge of labor markets, multiple languages, and navigational skills but their mobility across Western imperial boundaries reveals the dynamic ways in which coercion and cultural difference were negotiated by those who occupied the interstices of inter-imperial regimes of labor.

Gender identities influenced race and class relationships profoundly as histories of marriage, sexuality, and intimacy transformed how labor was embodied under empire. Among the range of inter-racial relationships that flourished in the nineteenth century, nothing aroused more colonial anxiety than those between white working-class women and non-white sailors (see Cleall in this volume). In the face of metropolitan commentators who blamed inter-racial conflicts on the sexuality of non-white men and ridiculed women for their "unrespectable" choices, the romantic and affective relationships white working-class women in England forged both strengthened and fragmented social solidarities (Tabili 1996; Hall 2000). In British seaport neighborhoods, the proliferation of racially mixed families held together by ties of love, kinship, and personal obligation defied the relentless pathologization and violence that culminated in the 1919 race riots. Since the 1880s, employers, unions, and the British state challenged such affective relationships repeatedly— employers sought race segregation at ports, nationalists represented white women as bearers of racially superior progeny, and unions argued against rights of non-white seamen. After the First World War, many such families moved to colonies like Ghana which had longer histories of inter-racialism that survived despite the late nineteenth century colonial politics of pathologizing mixed-race intimacy (Ray 2015).

In settler colonies, indigenous women were discussed as a moral threat to the virility and racial purity of white male workers. This sexed logic manifested itself in lives of white workers in multiple ways. British Columbia, at the margins of the settler colonial project in Canada, found it difficult to attract white settlers for most of the nineteenth century, making them a demographic minority. The resource-extractive economy driven by gold mining, lumbering, and the fur trade attracted mostly men, both working class and elite. Endeavors to import white women were conceived following white male workers complaining of alienation and developing their own homosocial codes of behavior centered around all-male labor households, dancehalls, and liquor and gambling establishments. Tents and cabins of workers became sites where gender roles were redrawn, household chores were inventively undertaken, and bonds of kinship and same-sex love were formed. Legal and political intolerance toward homosexuality manifested itself in public shaming and violence. Reform efforts undertaken by the YMCA and other upholders of bourgeois white male virtue exposed a desire to protect white labor from the "roughness" introduced by homosociality and inter-racialism (Perry 2001). This inter-racialism was further complicated by Chinese labor in-migration for work in salmon canneries. Racial heterogeneity and colonial proximity between Chinese, First Nations, and white peoples also led to the development of newer colonial knowledges that concretized existing racialism into state racisms. Missionaries and Indian agents considered the culture of Chinese workers and Chinese liquor smugglers to be a potential impediment in their effort to civilize indigenous peoples through social reform and violent regulatory laws like the Indian Acts (Mawani 2009).

Indentured labor regimes reproduced sexual violence and death (Shepherd 2002: 32–8) and justified them through state inaction and pathologizing women's sexuality. Slavery in the New World had been fundamentally shaped by such violence. Under indenture, the social reproduction of labor was deemed less important as more laborers from India and China could be hired for short contracts after which their health and well-being would not be binding upon planters (Daniel *et al.* 1992: 260). Most recruiters preferred male workers. Female workers were recruited in large numbers only toward the 1890s. Family migration depended on workers having marriage registration certificates or witness statements ratified by a magistrate. In Mauritius, only those with access to the Agency *Sirdar* managed to procure such documentation. The cost of registration was an added burden upon the worker, and if the bride was under the age of sixteen, the registration was often rejected (Tinker 1974: 203–5). Many immigrant workers who chose to stay in Natal or Mauritius inter-married with other immigrant communities from a different part of India (Carter 1995: 248–52).

Once the sugar economy stabilized in Natal, women workers were hired for conservancy services on plantations, wives migrated to stay with their husbands,

FIGURE 4.4: Coolie Woman, Martinique. Credit: Archive Farms Inc/Alamy Stock Photo.

and families began to migrate voluntarily from various parts of Western India to avail of increasing employment opportunities. The Hindu joint family was reconfigured among the Natal Indians as a way of expanding the family wage up till almost the 1950s (Freund 1991b). Women plowed and sowed small fields of tobacco and beans whereas men traveled to work in mines or small businesses. They also ran service businesses like laundries and employed other Indians to wash clothes. In Mauritius, many women were brought as servants for planters' estate homes where sexual violence was common. Such histories do not necessarily mean women were silent victims. Women negotiated such inequalities within the domestic while also helping organize and lead plantation workers, besides contributing in other ways such as cooking for those who had struck work (Carter 1994). In Fiji, *girmitiya* women worked harder than their male counterparts, especially in ancillary work on coconut and palm plantations to manufacture coir products. They laid claim to and refigured inherited ideas of honor and dignity to actively counter prevalent threats of sexual violence (Trnka 2008: 103–9).

Both a terrain of political contestation and consolidation, colonial difference manifested itself in everyday cultural practices. Relationships of intimacy and indebtedness, the torsion of violence, and prejudices of otherness contributed to the experience of labor across colonial territories in the Age of Empire. The everydayness of labor, however, was itself the subject of imperial fashioning through the reconstitution of something all human beings experience and inhabit naturally but depict with abundant heterogeneity using cultural categories, idioms, and metaphors—time.

TIME

The experience of time, felt universally by humans through a sense of its passage, is nonetheless rendered culturally particular as societies composed it through narrative and infused it with properties and meaning. Time was fundamentally inhabited—to *be in* the past or present was defined through conflicts over cultural meanings and values. In the Age of Empire, temporality was profoundly constitutive of work and laboring life as European domination imposed linear knowledges of time through clocks and governmental routines. Subaltern actors regularly interrupted and negotiated the European systematization of time calculations even as working hours, postal routines, bureaucratic official schedules, and railway timetables came to share singular timeframes (Prasad 2015: 134–64). Globally, the adoption of time zones across European empire-states in the late nineteenth century carried strong inter-imperial and nationalist motivations just as the contestations between linear and alternative biophysical notions of time shaped anti-colonial arguments over how work could be organized (Ogle 2015).

Within and outside Europe, the working week and the concept of leisure as non-work time were new discursive creations to manage labor, outmode alternative senses of task-time and create governable subjects (Thompson 1967; Le Goff 1980). Constructivist approaches to time saw the colonized inhabiting it coevally with Europeans while also being subjected to discourses that reproduced temporal notions of the backwardness and primitivism of imperial subjects. This contradiction or allochronism was an element of capitalist modernity which pushed historians to denaturalize dominant linear time by showing the alternative ways in which time was inhabited (Fabian 1983). Further, instead of analysing leisure as "non-work" time for proletarianized workers, cultural histories refigured it as a mode of social existence *in* time. Unraveling this fragile but resilient categorical distinction was necessary due to the proportional importance of the Industrial Revolution to histories of modernity and labor—indeed, it was imperative to demonstrate how imperial claims to modernity were legitimated through the discursive and material re-temporalization of the colonized as "archaic" and "traditional" (Cooper 2005: 126).

In western narratives of capitalism, all time had to be spent undertaking "productive" activity. Yet, the ways in which Europeans intended African or Indian subjects to use time were subverted repeatedly. They negotiated the devices of colonial capitalism on their own terms—they imputed their presence and actively transformed the possibilities and limits of such devices (Ferguson 1999). If leisure included practices of sport and music aimed at producing a morally ideal colonized subject, then such subjects engaged with those practices when it suited their own meanings of competition or performativity. Such practices, with their attendant tensions, were not about passing linear time but in effect, inhabiting its compartmentalized logic.

In Britain, between 1830 and 1920, working time was collated into a working week and discursively divided into work and leisure hours. While E.P. Thompson considered it a false distinction, he acknowledged how it objectified the entire social life of the laborer since the late eighteenth century despite how plebeian culture rejected elite paternalism and church morality behind time-discipline (Thompson 1967, 1974). These governmental compartmentalizations of time were inhabited through newer practices of sociality. Drills, brass bands, boy scouting, and competitive sports like football drew dedicated audiences and were promoted by the English middle classes as essential for moral and individual character (Russell 2013; Cunningham 1990). Such activities contained both class struggle and class performance. Greater leisure hours had to be politically wrested from employers to ensure the freedom to decide how one could spend their time. Laundry, church-going, gambling, ale drinking, and communal festivities which resisted industrial time-discipline were examples of how ordinary activities became modes of occupying leisure time (Howkins 1981). On the other hand, leisure brought with it elements of cultural capital and social mobility—those who could afford to travel to a seaside town for a vacation or buy the higher priced ticket at the races or the football match performed their class position a certain way (Cunningham 1982).

Brass bands commonly represented emergent working-class culture in mining districts like the Southern Pennines in England (Etheridge 2012). Industrialists and local working families both contributed to them financially. While industrialists considered it a rational form of recreation, working families saw it as an expression of respectability. Uniforms, clothes, and wages connoted respect and bands created their own trade and festive calendars. In Ireland, arguably England's most intimate colonial space, cycling clubs, football, and cricket kept young men occupied and pubs were sites of dissident republicanism, but brass bands helped form politically affirmative communal identities. In 1840s Cork, against the wishes of important patrons like Father Matthew, brass bands joined the catholic and republican Repeal movement to show how ideas of self-improvement acquired through his temperance rooms made the Irish more responsible nationalists (Borgonovo 2016).

European definitions implicitly held that pre-industrial societies lacked a developed conception of leisure. While social historians read resistance, collaboration, and violence into leisure practices or footnoted them into histories of class, cultural histories of colonial labor situated leisure and fun as practices of making meaning *in* time and a stage for enacting the politics of colonial difference (Ambler and Crush 1992). African practices of leisure never neatly fit into available English conceptions (Zeleza and Veney 2003). Rich indigenous African ideas of leisure or what Africans expected from colonially-imposed recreation have often been obscured in history. Categories like *afuofi* in twentieth-century Asante culture which held meanings of celebrating life as well as wasting time are reminders of such asymmetries (Akyeampong and Ambler 2002: 1–16). Indeed, most European sports took root in African societies for autonomous internal reasons rather than colonial domination—polo, for instance, resonated with equestrian traditions in Northern Nigeria and football was taken up or rejected depending on locally existing beliefs of competitive masculinity and community. In football, the differences in styles of play—whether reliant on teamsmanship or individual showmanship—emerged out of relationships forged by players with spectators. In fact, on the Roan Antelope Mines, the manager found that workers were disinterested in football and expected overtime wages for playing in matches or doing drills because to them it seemed like "work" (Akyeampong and Ambler 2002).

French Brazzaville on the Congo had been an entrepôt for slaves and ivory and witnessed competing colonial endeavors of Belgium and France in the late nineteenth century. The Tio largely avoided French imperial power—they found wage labor to resemble slavery and many families migrated inland or started smuggling absinthe to workers across the river in Leopoldville. Railways brought in migrant labor into a city that was, by the turn of the twentieth century, impoverished by mass hunger and spatially segregated along race and ethnicity. Here, Phyllis Martin found that while the town's French colonists viewed group dancing as frivolous and uncivilized leisure practice, it was their introduction and institutionalization of football that produced social cohesion and tapped into the spirit of communal competition. The rival "villages" of Poto-Poto and Bacongo often took to using magic to change the outcomes of games or used the venues to showcase local dances and brightly colored clothing that missionaries frowned upon (Martin 1995). In fact, Christian missionaries were fundamental in epistemologically refashioning time in Africa and Australia (Nanni 2012). Using rigid disciplinary methods to enforce the observance of Sabbath, the sobriety of dress on Sundays, the ringing of church bells to organize daily rhythms of work, and proselytizing discourses of sobriety, sedentary agrarian life, and Christian civilization, missionaries became vehicles for a European modernist practice of time which undergirded cultures of capitalism. Against such discipline, the active habitations of "leisure time" by Brazzaville workers also produced mass political outcomes—in 1936, they challenged European authorities and their patronage of local clubs when Africans weren't allowed to wear boots in games.

In British East Africa, Terence Ranger found that the *ngoma* (team-dance) called Beni (from the English word "band") that arose in the 1890s incorporated military drills in the performances and indexed how freed slaves and migrant laborers engaged with colonial institutions like the navy, the church, and mission schools (Ranger 1975). Beni groups of freed slaves weren't merely adjusting to the absolute power of colonialism. Despite being unmoored from their communities, they reconfigured their dance and theatrical performance to depict communal prestige, mimic combat, and take out popular processions. In urban working localities on the Swahili coastline which considered themselves urbane and less traditional than the "tribal" interior, the interplay within different Beni groups and between the Beni and other dance teams performing more western-derived dances like the *dansi* popularized by "Bombay Africans" (Africans sent to Indian mission schools for training and relocated to government offices in East Africa) revealed a layered history of hybridity. Coastal dance societies keenly incorporated new elements like fashion, cloth, weapons, and instruments of Arab or Indian origin from Zanzibar alongside "tribal" dancing steps as they competed for popularity among urban localities. Such histories revealed how Africans enjoyed themselves and understood or indulged in fun and challenged straightjacketed top-down colonial impositions of leisure time.

Alternatively, copper miners in Northern Rhodesia developed Beni societies which also worked as self-help and mutual assistance societies for overworked laborers. In Southern Rhodesia, the structure of the Beni societies was also replicated by Burial Societies and dancers who played the roles of king or

FIGURE 4.5: East African Ngoma dancers with painted faces, headgear, and jewelry c. 1910. Credit: ullstein bild via Getty Images.

doctor in Beni, performed similar roles in everyday life as well. For instance, the "doctor" of the Beni society went around the homes of workers checking on their health and well-being and reported cases of medical concern to employers. Suspicion toward Beni was correspondingly widespread among German, Belgian, and British authorities across East Africa. Beni created grounds for workers to actively organize from within the ambit of colonial sanction without necessarily transforming into a vehicle of protest or rebellion but enabling the manifestation of both. Workers did not thus inhabit leisure time through the moral codes brass bands and drills were supposed to inculcate, instead they inhabited it by transforming the very limits and possibilities available through such leisure activities under colonial rule.

The habitation of time on plantations was similarly fractious. On Natal's sugar plantations, six moons in the traditional Zulu calendar meant a work season, which was incorrectly translated by missionaries as a work year. Settler mischaracterization of indigenous time led to confusion and work stoppages by Zulu workers. They resisted the demands of planters by insisting on existing work day rhythms of starting work an hour after sunrise and stopping an hour before sunset. In winter, this meant substantial losses for planters competing with Mauritius or the Caribbean (Atkins 1988). Over prolonged negotiations, the resilient power of "Kaffir time" forced imperial colonists to adapt and navigate Zulu practices. Where contingencies challenged European domination, raced ideas of servility, labor, and efficiency were liberally deployed—many planters thus argued that indentured labor from India would be more productive for sugar plantations in Southern Africa to make them internationally competitive in the late nineteenth century.

In late colonial East Africa, the formerly enslaved took over plantations as squatters. Frederick Cooper recounted how on Malindi's grain estates in 1967, descendants of slaves and slaveowners still disagreed over the time taken to weed an *ngwe* (unit of rope-measure) by formerly enslaved peoples. Meanwhile, in urban Mombasa's docks where seasonal squatters also worked as casual labor in gangs under *serangs* contracted by shipping companies, industrial time-discipline was used to create a new class of African dockers who were more detached or "detribalized" from the surrounding agrarian society. To not fully purchase but materially control the entirety of an African docker's time, employers and administrators successfully segregated the docks spatially and dockers economically through incentivized wage structures unlike the "informal" sector of the economy (Cooper 1992). Although considered irregular and un-European, casual labor was sustained for its cost-effectiveness but once organized mass strikes began in the 1940s, many officials blamed Mombasa's Beni dance societies for fertilizing and structuring rebellion. Again, cultural practices like drills and bands that were introduced under empire to assemble colonized workers into productive subjects during "leisure time" were thus repeatedly turned into articulations of pleasure and politics, effectively undoing or refashioning the imagined horizons of how to inhabit time differently.

CONCLUSION

Under Western empires, the colony was a distant yet intimate site of extraction, transgression, proselytization, and coercion. In the Age of Empire, the imposition of capitalism and free trade within the expanding territories of empire-states and greater mobility of bodies and ideas across the globe welded the colonial governmentality of the state and the logic of capital in newer ways. Cultural histories have excavated how those who labored under empires came to articulate their sense of self and be *at home* with capital—complete with its attendant frictions, heterodoxies, opportunities, and numerous intricately woven entanglements. For them, to be at home with capital implied coming to terms with its power to shape everyday lives and social structures. By centering categories used to make meaning of such forms of power, cultural histories critically expanded historical emphasis from fixity to contingency, the public to the intimate, and from boundedness to mobility (Ballantyne and Burton 2005;

Clancy-Smith and Gouda 1998). As bodies and ideas set forth under Western imperialism collided into dynamic entanglements, the asymmetry of power manifested itself politically through articulations of belonging and difference alongside contestations over habitations of time. These processes checkered the march of capital on the ground, distorted its homogenizing tendencies, and exposed its weaknesses by complicating the paradoxes upon which it was fundamentally constituted. Cultural histories have made such pasts more legible, setting the stage for formidable analyses of imperialism, nationalism, and the contemporary world.

Note of Acknowledgment

I would like to thank Kirsten McKenzie, Antoinette Burton, and David Roediger for their comments on the drafts of this essay. All errors remain my own.

CHAPTER FIVE

Mobility

MIRANDA SPIELER

It seems apt to begin this essay by noting that the movement of people and things has presented both moral and analytical challenges to people who write about culture. Culture in the singular nineteenth-century sense, as a term for sweetness and light, an inward state of becoming, was, for Matthew Arnold, the antithesis of railways, factories, capitalists, and the steam-powered expansion of imperial Britain. Under the reign of the people that Arnold called Philistines, the nation embraced the "worship of machinery" to the point of becoming machines themselves (Arnold 1993).

Arnold was not alone in envisaging the nineteenth century as a mechanized world stripped of culture. Perhaps nowhere is the "particularly stiff-necked and perverse" (Arnold 1993: 105) character of the machine-age Philistine more manifest than in Jules Verne's 1873 novel, *Autour du monde en quatre vingt jours* (*Around the World in Eighty Days*). The tale centers on the unflappable Englishman Phileas Fogg, a man so lacking in wonder and affect that he seems indistinguishable from a waxwork, an automaton, a "chronometer by Leroy or Earnshaw." He travels through the British Empire among routine sorts of conquerors, "diverse functionaries and officers of all rank," yet pursues a different sort of domination, one suited only to a machine. His object—the conquest of time and space—has nothing to do with exotic places, which Fogg ignores throughout the book. Instead he plays endless hands of bridge indoors. As "exactitude personified," Fogg embodies, and achieves, a troubling sort of global mastery: he stands for the disenchantment of the world. There is nothing left to contemplate any longer other than the timetables in *Bradshaw's Continental Railway, Steam Transit, and General Guide*.

The study of cultures, in the plural sense, was also a nineteenth-century development with a highly complex relationship to the imperial movement of people and things. So-called salvage anthropology—ethnography of endangered peoples—was in many respects the outcome of imperial mobility, not least because the objects of study often experienced aggressive and involuntary displacement, sometimes of an exterminatory sort—as with the so-called Bushmen—before becoming ethnographic curiosities (Wolfe 1999; Legassick 2006; Dowie 2009). Moreover, the mobility of ethnographic artifacts from the periphery to the center hinged on the participation of imperial governments and vast caravans of native bearers (Conklin 2013). And yet the method that defined the field of anthropology—structuralism—focused on rootedness, on cultures "localized in time and space" (Augé 1995: 49). There is hence particular irony to the demand by Marc Augé, a self-described theorist of supermodernity, that anthropology reinvent itself as the study of a mobile world.

Whether one looks to *Annales* school studies of mentalités, microhistory, or New Left labor history, the historical study of cultures still hinges on structures specific to time and place. The critic Eric Williams, a founder of New Left cultural studies, describes culture as a "whole way of life" arising from family structure, the organization of production, communication strategies, and common meanings (Williams 2014, 3). Michel Foucault's notion of the episteme—the underlying conceptual framework for all thought across the disciplines—is as rooted in place and time as any other form of structuralism (Foucault 2002a). In short, mobility remains difficult to square with longstanding methods of cultural analysis. And yet, as Stephen Greenblatt insists, "colonization, exile, emigration, wandering, [cultural] contamination" are the very forces that "shape the history and diffusion of identity and language" (Greenblatt 2010: 2).

In view of mobility's central importance to the meaning of culture, this essay seeks to reconcile the analysis of social structure with the study of imperial movement by people and things. It does so by exploring four frameworks that organized imperial mobility during the period from roughly 1780 to 1914. By historical frameworks I have in mind something more robust than mere themes. These frameworks are structuring concepts, which shape both action and thought. The list of frameworks I consider here, which I do not imagine as exhaustive, include: (a) Atlantic slavery during the Revolutionary Era; (b) abolitionism; (c) settler colonialism; and (d) the machine-age conquest of imperial space for extractive and industrial purposes. These four frameworks do not comprise a chronological sequence. Instead, they overlapped, operated alongside one another and became enmeshed in complex site-specific configurations within the same colony.

To take the example of Atlantic slavery in the Revolutionary Era, diverse yet interrelated forms of population movement took shape in relation to Europeans' imperial slave colonies that went well beyond the middle passage and included slave raiding parties and caravans within Africa; the flight of slaves to sites of refuge; the circulation of free and enslaved seamen around the Atlantic; slave ship interception by pirates and privateers; and the deployment of troops summoned in defense of slave colonies during war and insurrection. In turn, slavery, as the organizer of human mobility, caused new things to circulate—from pathogens to books, from fashion to stimulants, from letters, rumors, and folktales, to gold and machinery. With the mobility of people came the mobility of culture: slavery brought forth new systems of belief including Afro-American Maroon Societies and Afro-Catholic slave religion (Price 1983; Mintz and Price 1992; Brown 2003; Harding 2003; Sweet 2003; Parés 2013).

Nineteenth-century imperial history is full of instances in which these structures of mobility crossed one another to then forge distinctive local cultures. In Sierra Leone, for instance, the British government created a settlement colony for former slaves from North America and captive Jamaican Maroons in a region that remained a slave-trading hub; the slave trade continued there, moreover, after the Royal Navy began to police the seas following Britain's abolition of the trade (1807). British captains disembarked most slaves they captured on illegal slave ships in the new colony, which became a place where settler colonialism, slave-related and abolitionist forms of mobility converged. Other examples include Australia, South Africa, and Canada—sites of settler colonialism and steam-powered resource extraction. In the curious case of French Senegal, conquered by General Faidherbe with an army of ex-slaves, government-sponsored abolitionism developed alongside a new peanut industry that hinged on agricultural slave labor and began with the creation of the St. Louis-Dakar railway, built by slaves (Klein 1998).

Although structuralism is ill adapted to the study of people and things on the move, cultural history, a field marked by great diversity of method, supplies ample alternatives. While adapting the study of structure to fit the kinetic reality of imperial societies, this essay also looks to the history of material culture and the history of the body in order to sketch the emergence of a new sort of imperial culture. In light of this approach, I shall venture one broad claim about population movement in relation to Western empires—namely, that mobility *was constitutive of imperial states*. The need to move large numbers of people within and beyond the empire called forth new regulations and institutions and also a need for new personnel (Clancy-Smith 2012). That enterprise also called forth a need for new technologies of movement. In turn, the acceleration of imperial mobility in the machine age would alter the structure of imperial rule. Direct rule over India in the aftermath of the Sepoy Rebellion (1857) would not have been possible without the steamship, the telegraph, and the railway. Through technological change, as George Orwell observed, "by

1920 nearly every inch of the colonial empire was in the grip of Whitehall" (Weiner 2009: 208).

As to the character of imperial states, there were quite a few common traits across empires despite different political traditions in European home societies and divergent institutions for imperial oversight. The imperial apparatus that grew up around the problem of population movement was that of a police state whose material culture, institutions, practices, and notion of science tended to focus on the human body, with the larger aim of converting imperial people into identifiable units tagged for surveillance and use. It is telling that the nineteenth- and twentieth-century French term for colonial workers was never *ouvriers* (workers) but instead *bras* (arms) or else *main d'oeuvre*—a term that, in the eighteenth century, referred to handiwork and literally translates as the "hand of the work." Through these body oriented practices, officials sought to identify, move around, and extract labor from people and also, quite relatedly, to control contagion. Reigning over imperial disease in the age of steam power would involve not only quarantine but also race-specific medical certificates, race-specific travel interdictions, specialized urban sectors, the depopulation of infected regions, and the construction of concentration camps. In view of this later era, streamlined slave ships of the late eighteenth century (Figure 5.1) offer an enduring lesson in the close relationship between moving larger numbers of people and immobilizing them (Rediker 2007).

Within nineteenth-century Europe, regimes of diverse political hue embraced intrusive surveillance methods and also dispatched troops together with paramilitary forces against civilians. For European workers and revolutionists, whiteness proved no bar against state repression. In the case of nineteenth-century France, where martial law and extrajudicial detention became commonplace, state officials oversaw the hygiene of sex workers, made routine use of internal banishment, and devised a rainbow of passports to control the internal movement of suspects, potential or actual, including soldiers, political refugees, workers, vagabonds, and ex-convicts.

The imperial state was not a different state, or an alter ego of the home country (Wilder 2005). The imperial state was, however, an excrescence of Europe with a distinctive legal character that considerably magnified the discretionary power of state officials. In the empire, so-called natives did not enjoy the political rights and legal protections of people at home. In many instances, the very land they occupied lay beyond reach of the domestic constitution. Officials there enjoyed repressive powers as a normal and everyday feature of imperial rule that no one would have countenanced on domestic soil except in times of alarming necessity (Hussain 2003; Spieler 2009). Under these conditions, practices hovering at the edges of European society that targeted vulnerable and marginal groups—formalities for tracking people, modes of extrajudicial search and arrest, techniques of constraint and

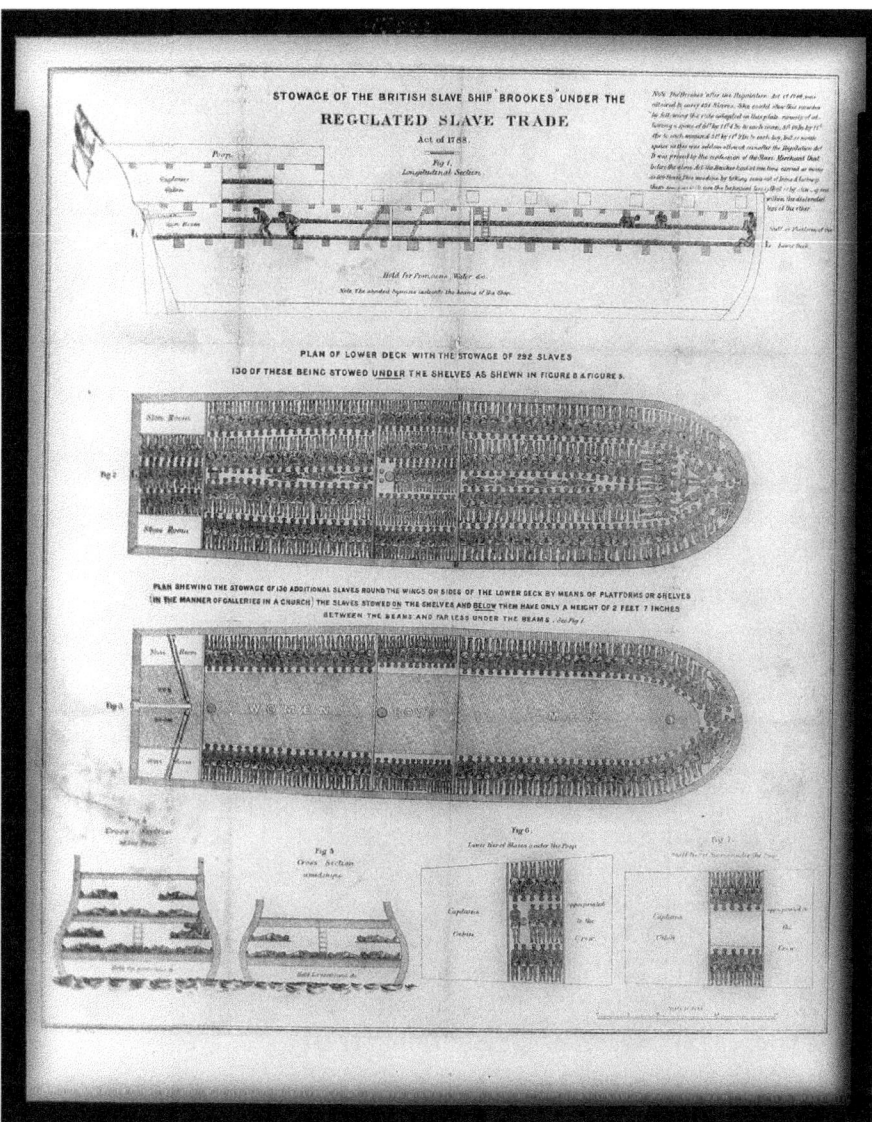

FIGURE 5.1: Cutaway diagram by William Elford of the *Brooks*, a Liverpool slave ship. First published by The Society for Effecting the Abolition of the Slave Trade in November 1788. Public domain.

involuntary movement—applied in the overseas empire to whole populations (Lyons 1992; Levine 2003; Taraud 2003; Howell 2009; Neill 2012; Peckham and Pomfret 2013). The unusual character of imperial legal space and the degraded status of imperial subjects gave a free rein to experiments at managing bodies on the move (Spieler 2012).

SLAVERY AND THE REVOLUTIONARY ERA

The transatlantic slave trade remained the most important form of population movement during the Revolutionary Era and would directly or indirectly structure the movement of people within European empires for years to come. During the period 1780–9, a total of 703,860 African captives embarked for European colonies, of whom 201,169 were bound for the French colony of Saint-Domingue. During this short period, the number of slaves sent to this comparatively small French colony—half the island of Hispaniola, about the size of Virginia—exceeded the number destined for any other colony in the Atlantic world including Brazil. The magnitude of the French slave trade during the final decade of the Old Regime and the antebellum splendor of Saint-Domingue set the stage for regional events during the revolutionary conjuncture, which it seems proper to date from 1776. France's alliance with rebel American colonists against Great Britain (1778) arose, at least in part, from the French Crown's desire to acquire new trading partners for Saint-Domingue. In turn, Saint-Domingue emerged during the American war as the most important site from which France provided aid to the thirteen colonies in the form of troops and warships.

The movement of people between and across empires—smugglers, fugitives, sailors, merchants, soldiers, administrators, jurists, explorers, and deserters—can hardly be described as a specificity of the Revolutionary Era (Clancy-Smith 2012; Armitage 2002; Linebaugh and Rediker 2007; Dubois and Scott 2010; Kwass 2014; Kaps 2017). The novelty of the period from 1776 to 1815 lay simply in the magnitude and political consequences of inter-colonial travel in response to war and rebellion (see Sessions in this volume).

The vast slave insurrection in the French colony of Saint-Domingue, which began in 1791, destroyed the most lucrative European colony in the Caribbean while scattering tens of thousands of its former inhabitants throughout the Atlantic world (Popkin 2011). Planters fled with their slaves and machines to Cuba, Jamaica, and North America; in 1799, the largest and most sophisticated sugar mill in Havana was the fruit of a refugee's technician's ingenuity. The destruction of colonial Saint-Domingue became an opportunity for Cuban planters; by the 1820s the Spanish colony had become the world's largest sugar producer.

The Haitian Revolution assured that news of black liberty would reach slaves throughout the Atlantic world by way of sailors, refugees of all colors, and former slaves who traveled abroad alone or with former masters (Johnson 2012; Scott and Hébrard 2012). In the context of Cuba, this produced an early panic over *negros francese* (French negroes) in Havana, desultory efforts at expulsion, and a rash of insurrections including the remarkable 1812 Aponte rebellion, when a black impostor dressed in the blue and gold braid of a French general circulated about, liberating slaves, with a forged freedom decree (Childs 2006; Ferrer 2014).

Haiti was the most violent instance of anti-imperial war in the Americas during the Revolutionary Era. Other anti-imperial wars unfolded in Latin America in the early nineteenth century under the leadership of Creole elites—Spanish subjects born in the Americas. In common with Latin American wars of independence, the Haitian war against the French had an epidemiological dimension linked, as an irony of history, to earlier imperial mobility in the New World. Malaria and yellow fever became endemic to the Americas due to the deportation of Africans on an immense scale and because of environmental changes—irrigation, deforestation—linked to the exploitation of slave labor. By the late eighteenth century, inhabitants of Caribbean islands and Spanish South America enjoyed what William McNeill calls "differential immunity." Africans, white Creole adults, and their descendants did not succumb to malaria or yellow fever to the same degree as European newcomers for environmental and genetic reasons. During the Age of Revolution, this meant that Spanish, British, and French expeditionary forces, when dispatched to quell anti-imperial revolt, quickly died by the tens of thousands. In South America and in Saint-Domingue, the success of anti-imperial struggles hinged on the rebels' use of delay and an indirect sort of biological warfare. Winning meant enduring military assault until the sickness hit. It meant skirmishing with the enemy until the enemy became extinct (McNeill 2010).

Slave revolt and civil war in Saint-Domingue also transformed European society. Of the planters who scattered throughout the Atlantic world, thousands wound their way back to Europe—often by way of the United States (White 2010). In France they became a bilious victim group who wielded enormous influence upon legislators and imperial bureaucrats (Meadows 2000). Refugee planters clamored for, and received, stipends throughout the 1790s; they demanded, and received, a vast expeditionary force in 1802 aimed at undoing the freedom won by slaves in that colony. Perhaps most importantly, they campaigned for, and received, monumental indemnity checks from the new black state—calculated by head of slave—as the ransom paid by Haiti for recognition by France. The only political failure of the Saint-Domingue diaspora, in 1819, lay in failing to secure a mandate from the Bourbon regime to exterminate the whole Haitian people above the age of six. (Brière 2008) The planter diaspora set the tone of French racial discourse at the turn of the nineteenth century; their clamor for revenge and seething racial hatred altered the political climate, helping to bring about the revival of slavery under Napoleon and the return of Old Regime race law on domestic soil—including a ban on mixed marriage (Heuer 2009). Their presence in France played no small role in provoking a turn toward biological racism among nineteenth-century naturalists and philosophers (see Fitzpatrick in this volume).

MOBILITY IN THE ABOLITIONIST AGE: SLAVES, CONVICTS AND IMMIGRANTS

As an effect of the revolutionary period, both the geography and character of imperial mobility changed, irreversibly. Britain's loss of the thirteen colonies, France's loss of Saint-Domingue (Haiti) and the decolonization of much of Latin America led European empire builders to shift their attentions to Africa, Asia, and the antipodean colonies of Australia and New Zealand. Meanwhile, imperial projects within the Atlantic world assumed a new objective: antislavery (Brown 2005; Drescher 2009). The project of ending the trade, ending slavery, and constructing post-emancipation societies produced new patterns of imperial mobility.

In recent years, historians concerned with the origins of human rights have looked to Britain's naval campaign to end the slave trade as a founding moment. To Fabian Klose, "the practice of humanitarian intervention on the part of the state—that is, state intervention to enforce the implementation of a humanitarian norm—originated in connection with the Congress of Vienna and the campaign against the transatlantic slave trade" (Klose 2016: 119). For Jenny Martinez, "the abolition of the transatlantic slave trade remains the most successful episode ever in the history of human rights" (Martinez 2012: 13). It is nonetheless misleading, for several reasons, to view the abolitionist era (1807–88) as a period marked by the triumph of noble-mindedness and liberty on a global scale.

First, and to a degree that historians of France and Britain have tended to underplay, the transatlantic slave trade was very much a nineteenth-century story. In spite of Britain's naval patrols, 727,280 of the more than one million slaves who disembarked in Cuba during the whole history of the transatlantic trade—spanning four hundred years—arrived there between 1776 and 1866.[1] The Royal Navy only managed to intercept four percent of the 2,484,960 African captives who embarked for Cuba and Brazil after 1807, the year Britain and the United States abolished the trade.[2]

Second, British abolitionism served other purposes in the nineteenth century than the advancement of human rights. Beginning in the new colony of Sierra Leone, the European conquest of Africa took place under the banner of antislavery with territorial expansion assuming the guise of a humanitarian project (Haslam 2012). Moreover, as Lauren Benton and Lisa Ford have shown, Britain did not recognize the slave trade as a crime against humanity or punish non-British traders as criminals. The very courts that judged illegal ships developed earlier, to adjudicate seized property including slaves—maritime prize—during prolonged naval war in the early nineteenth century. At sea, as on the African continent, Britain's campaign against the trade became a mechanism for consolidating a vast new empire (Benton and Ford 2016).

Third, the demise of slavery coincided everywhere with the rise of a new kind of authoritarian imperial state whose guiding purpose was, arguably, the manufacture and management of new kinds of unfree people across vast expanses of ground. Within plantation societies of the Caribbean and East Indies, unfree workers in the post-emancipation era included former slaves enveloped by legal regimes that diminished their newfound rights. Unfree people on nineteenth-century plantations were also indentured immigrant workers, who came by the hundreds of thousands, often from elsewhere in the empire (India, Sierra Leone), with contracts that reduced them to bonded laborers. Finally, convicts figured prominently in the nineteenth-century unfree labor force, in the West Indies and beyond. Punitive labor, often by so-called natives, became a convenient substitute for chattel slavery and immigration.

The intra-African slave trade outlasted the abolitionist era in the Americas and flourished in the late nineteenth century (Klein 1998; Mesnard *et al.* 2013). Indeed, the collapse in slave exports toward the New World increased African reliance on slaves while the Indian Ocean trade and the Arab overland trade expanded. Slave caravans sent approximately 15,000 slaves per year out of the kingdom of Wadai in modern-day Chad toward the Libyan coast, whence slaves were exported to Constantinople, Smyrna, Cyprus, and even Albania (Seddon 2000). In 1905, the English journalist E.D. Morel noted that the trade through Tanganyika continued to flourish with slaves purchased by Arab merchants in exchange for salt (*Westminster Gazette*, December 22, 1905, as cited in Bourne *et al.* 1997).

Unfree Africans were on the move in imperial Africa for reasons other than their eventual export. The European conquest of sub-Saharan Africa was the work of native armies composed of slaves and former slaves who (in a Homeric mode) claimed African female captives as war booty. Their looted wives soon trailed the army, sometimes three or four to a man (Clayton 1988). From 1817 until the 1850s, the French created several Senegalese companies of slaves (tirailleurs sénégalais) "liberated" (purchased) and then subjected to fourteen years of compulsory military service (Rodet 2014) (Figure 5.2). Likewise, the Germans colonized East Africa by way of the askari, a Schutzgruppe or fighting force comprised originally of Sudanese slaves, whom the Germans deployed for their scorched earth tactics and vaunted as the "bravest blacks" (Moyd 2014: 48) (see Kent in this volume).

Within Asian, East Indian, and Caribbean plantation societies, members of the imperial labor force—slaves, convicts, and immigrants—resembled one another despite their diversity of origin. Slaves within Africa were purchased by recruiters and passed off in European colonies as free immigrants. Immigrant recruiters were often former slave traders and the immigrants traveled aboard slave ships (Dorsey 2004). Immigrants might even labor alongside slaves on arrival, as was the case for Chinese in Cuba and South Asians on the Mascarene

FIGURE 5.2: Rélégués (recidivists) at the Camp Saint Jean du Maroni in French Guiana (early twentieth century). Public domain.

Islands of Réunion and Mauritius (Anderson 2000; Carter 2000; Allen 2015). Immigrants moved around and got shorn, measured, and documented by methods developed by prison administrators (Anderson 2009). Convicts became immigrants at the end of their sentences in some places (Anderson 2012). And immigrants—from Africa or Asia—became convicts whether because of petty offenses or because of crimes tantamount to resistance—the murder of overseers, the burning of cane fields (Delisle 2001; Dorsey 2004). As Walter Rodney observes of immigrants to post-emancipation British Guiana, "for those who went to prison, the distinction between convict labor and indentured labor was erased, because they performed their hard labor on the estates" (Rodney 1981: 40).

The unfreedom that characterized much imperial mobility after slavery's formal demise—at least in British and French colonies—extended well beyond the case of indentured workers. Britain deported approximately 164,000 convicts to Australian colonies between 1787 and 1868 when the gold rush largely brought an end to the system. Despite the discredit of convict transportation by Victorian moral reformers, this practice nonetheless endured as a punishment for colonial convicts, who wound up at penal sites in Burma, the Straits Settlements (Mallaca, Singapore, Penang), Mauritius, and the Andaman archipelago in the Bay of Bengal.

The French, too, deported political and common criminals on an increasingly wide scale in the nineteenth century. Crackdowns on the insurrectionary left in 1848, 1851, and 1871 led the French government to deport thousands of socialists, anarchists, and communists. In 1852, after overthrowing the Second Republic, President Louis Napoleon (who soon became Napoleon III) founded a penal colony in French Guiana into which more than 20,000 felons disappeared before he fled, at the fall of his regime, in 1870 (Spieler 2012). The new Third Republic not only emptied felons into the empire but also consigned recidivists (called relégués)—usually repeat petty offenders—to perpetual imperial banishment (Figure 5.3). Imperial relegation, a disappearing act for the lumpenproletariat, also applied to imperial subjects: Antillean recidivists languished in exile in French Guiana while Indochinese ex-convicts wound up in New Caledonia (Price 2008). Approximately 60,000 people—including both

FIGURE 5.3: Photograph of tirailleurs sénégalais first published in *Les colonies françaises: petite encyclopédie coloniale*, vol. 1, edited by M. Maxime Petit. Paris: Larousse, 1902. Courtesy The New York Public Library.

common and political prisoners—entered French colonial prisons in French Guiana and New Caledonia during the second half of the nineteenth century (Toth 2006; Sanchez 2013).

Convicts on the move were not merely inmates of far-flung prisons but also agents of conquest. In Angola and elsewhere in Luso-Africa, settlers who engaged in slaving raids were often Portuguese and Brazilian criminals banished from their home societies. Their offenses ranging from murder to treason. Once in Africa they became "the face of Portuguese colonialism" (Candido 2013: 126). Beginning in the 1830s with the conquest of Algiers, the French army (and soon the navy) oversaw the creation of a host of new punitive regiments including the legendary infanterie légère d'Afrique known informally as the Bat'Af or bataillons d'Afrique. As crack troops known for brutality, the Bat'Af saw action throughout the nineteenth-century empire—at Dahomey, Morocco, Indochina, Formosa, Tunisia; as historian Dominique Kalifa notes, their repute hinged on their astounding metamorphosis in active combat; what counted as deviant outlawry in garrison towns and society more generally became, at the outbreak of imperial war, unrivaled dash and courage in the face of enemy fire (Kalifa 2009).

A variety of circuits linked the imperial movement of convicts to systems of bodily control within European societies. The nineteenth-century medical case study of Albert Dadas inadvertently reveals the close link between European policing mechanisms and the sort of coerced movement that became visible on imperial soil (Tissié 2005). Before toppling, as an incorrigible deserter, into a punitive work battalion in French Algeria, Albert moved around Europe for reasons that quite often had little to do with his alleged malady, called fugue— an uncontrollable desire to travel combined with blackouts (where am I?) that seizes the patient with a force comparable to post-hypnotic suggestion. Let us take, for instance, Albert's 1878 arrest in a Paris train station. Found asleep and lacking papers, he is jailed and then expelled with a *feuille de route* (a police passport tracing an itinerary) that shunts him back to Bordeaux, his home town. Veering from the assigned path, he is "arrested and imprisoned because I didn't have papers," and rerouted back to Paris, whence he came (64). And so it continues: lost papers, arrest, police passports with compulsory routes running him out of town, new rounds of wandering, until Albert enlists in the army, which alters the legal meaning of vagabondage. After deserting twice, he is sentenced by Court Martial to forced labor in Algeria "in the camp called the Iron Doors" (79). Released with a punctured eardrum, he gets rerouted to Bordeaux's Saint André hospital thanks to another indigent passport. There Tissié finds him, weeping on his bunk. In *Les voyageurs aliénés*, now a classic work, the psychiatrist evokes Albert as a sentimental colorblind illiterate masturbator with deformed retina and average cranial dimensions, subject to intense migraines, who has forgotten the words for purple and pink; the modern reader of Tissié's work cannot help but remark the role of the police in delivering up Albert for medical scrutiny. Though written to chronicle the life of a deviant—the world's first case of fugue—the tale of Albert is also a story about the violence of the imperial state.

LIBERALISM, GENOCIDE, IMPERIAL MOBILITY

A staggering number of Europeans immigrated to colonies during the second half of the nineteenth century of whom most spoke English. Some 1,270,000 settlers from Britain and Ireland resettled in Australia in the two decades following the 1851 Gold Rush. As James Belich notes, the city of Melbourne arose from scratch in the nineteenth century to become the colony's banking center with a boom-time population of 500,000 in 1891—on the eve of a major economic depression—that exceeded that of Madrid (Belich 2009). French Algeria began in 1830 but increased considerably after 1870, when Germany absorbed most of Alsace and a small portion of Lorraine (Sicard 1998), while miniscule arthropods, called phylloxera, ravaged French vineyards, bringing national wine production to a halt (Gale 2011).

Convicts aside, European settlers during the nineteenth and early twentieth centuries did not encounter anything like the coercion or lethal force that befell Africans and Asians in imperial plantation societies. In colonies to which Europeans arrived without constraint and remained without compulsion, violence targeted native groups.

Emptying the earth in order to re-people it would result in forms of population movement—flight, deportation, child abduction, expulsion from shrinking native reserves—that many contemporary scholars now describe as genocide (Madley 2004). Indigenous people responded with diverse forms of resistance including warfare (Guiart 1968; Reynolds 2006; Muckle 2010) and apocalyptic tribal self-destruction (Price 2008).

Officials and frontiersmen, together with armchair fellow travelers, described aboriginal erasure as a cosmic inevitability (Legassick 2006; Jacobs 2009; Veracini 2010), or a convenience enabling the spread of liberal democracy (Sessions 2011; Curthoys 2014). For the utilitarian Jeremy Bentham (1748–1832), the vanishing of inferior peoples counted as a mark of human progress. "When one permits oneself to dream of the future of the human race, one is led to hope that barbarous, ill-governed or depraved races will disappear little by little to make space for the establishment of the best race (espèce), of that portion of the human family (genre humain) in possession of superior intelligence and sagacity."[3]

There is little to separate the early nineteenth-century racial fantasy of Jeremy Bentham from the writings of Friedrich Ratzel (1844–1904), the fin-de-siècle inventor of Lebensraum, a concept later embraced by National

Socialists. According to the geographer Ratzel, human groups or races, in common with non-human species, needed to expand the space they occupied or else die out; the geographical reach of a given race was a mark of its evolutionary success. In the near term, Ratzel's prescriptive theory of racial expansion inspired the 1904 killing of 60–100,000 Herero in German South West Africa (modern-day Namibia) to clear a place for volkisch pastoralists and enrich them with confiscated cows (Smith 1980; Sarkin 2011).

As bookends to the nineteenth century, the genocidal reveries of Bentham and Ratzel help to situate the views of Alexis de Tocqueville, the liberal politician, during the conquest of Algeria (Grandmaison 2005; Pitts 2006).[4] Read in light of Anglophone imperial writing in the early nineteenth century, Tocqueville's brutal remarks on the replacement of Algerians by immigrant Frenchmen were as conventional as they were distasteful. When Tocqueville floated the option in 1841 of "replacing old inhabitants with the conquering race," he did not merely prescribe a method of domination but also sketched one under way. While deporting refractory elites, the imperial government despoiled the population, transferring land—minus the occupants—to European settlers. Many new settlers to Constantine in the early 1870s were obliged to hole up in temporary lodgings—tents, jails, abandoned villages—while awaiting the post-harvest exodus of locals from their land (Fischer 1999). Soon thereafter, the hills and valleys of Kabylie were made over as export wineries (Baroli 1992: 121).

Native removal schemes tended to be "systematically disavowed violence" linked to a myth of vacant earth (Veracini 2010: 79). Thus nineteenth-century visitors to British East Africa described the Rift Valley as an "almost untouched and uninhabited country" that abounded with "great herds of cattle" and large "flocks of sheep and goats" (Hughes 2006, 24). Absent from this diagram of Britain's future "white highlands" were Maasai people, whom the imperial government soon despoiled and moved to new enclaves that doubled as big game reserves.

In 1921, a British imperial official recalled the 1912 Maasai relocation scheme as a rescue project aimed at preserving a race marked for extinction (Tignor 1976). He was not alone in pitching native removal schemes as humanitarian endeavors. The tendency in frontier societies to depict coerced movement and extinctive violence as benevolence was perhaps most explicit in Australia's Aborigines Protection Acts (1886–1911). These acts aimed to shunt so-called full bloods to native reserves (O'Malley 1994) pending extinction, while priming mixed children in special orphanages for eventual procreation with white people (Jacobs 2009). This racial hygiene project, which aimed to "breed out the color" by extinguishing Aborigines over successive generations enjoyed the approved of liberals, ethnographers, and feminists of the day (Wolfe 1999), though later Australian feminists would campaign against it (Paisley 2000).

Advocates of native removal schemes did not envisage these policies as a violation of western legal norms; instead they insisted on the inapplicability of western law to unevolved savages. In every imperial frontier society of the nineteenth century, European settlers depicted the natives they displaced as subhuman evolutionary failures (Bensa 1988; Wolfe 1999). To justify the cantonment of Kanak people in New Caledonia on newly delimited "tribal territories," a French pamphleteer alleged that the Kanak should not—could not—be "administered as French citizens" in having "no law" of their own and "no private property" (Feillet 1900). To vary the famous phrase of Prudhon, where there was no property, there could not be theft.

IMPERIAL MOBILITY IN THE INDUSTRIAL AGE

In 1848, British manufacturers envisaged trains linking Bombay to Indian cotton districts as "nothing more than an extension of their own line from Manchester to Liverpool" (Aguiar 2011: 15). First in India and then throughout nineteenth-century empires, the railway served the economic interests of European elites by whisking raw materials onto steamboats and enabling European goods to reach new markets.

The railroad from Dakar to Saint Louis (Senegal) became vital to industrial production in France. Peanut and palm oil became candles, lit up factories, and served as machine lubricant. Tropical forests vanished into household products. The oil of Senegalese palms became *savon de Marseille*. Trees from the Lever family's concessions in the Belgian Congo became English domestic soap (Coquery-Vidrovitch 2003). With the outbreak of war in 1914, the very trains that had whisked raw materials from inland sites in Asia and Africa interior to coastal ports became extractive in a different sense. Together with the steamship and the telegraph, the imperial railway enabled huge levies of colonial troops and requisitioned laborers (Stovall 1998; Stibbe 2009; Costello 2015). Between 1914 and 1918 the imperial railway thus played an unanticipated role in remaking European war.

In common with railroads everywhere, though perhaps more extremely, imperial railways depended on lethal forms of mobility during their phase of construction. Unlike national railroads, at least prior to the First World War, imperial railroads seemed to produce even more lethal forms of mobility upon completion. During the Indian famine of 1876–8, which killed some 5,500,500 people, the government of the Raj exported a record quantity (6.4 million bushels) of grain by rail, while creating a small number of ill-supplied food distribution camps at points remote and inaccessible to the population, resulting in veritable death marches (Davis 2001). In India, the rail became an accessory to famine by delivering colonial food crops to global consumers, destroying native livelihoods, promoting monoculture—in the form of cotton—and reducing the peasantry to a heavily indebted, landless rural proletariat. The rail whisked grain away from places where people died for lack of food and lack of money to buy it with (Laxman 1997).

Imperial trains were never peacetime tools of capitalism. In Rudyard Kipling's eponymous novel, the urchin Kim arrives to Lahore's "fortlike train station" at night, which his companion, the lama, calls "the work of the devil" (Figure 5.4). The Indian rail was in its first phase of construction at the outbreak of the 1857 Sepoy Rebellion (Kerr 2007). The timing of rail construction in India brought its military function to the fore. Alongside the importance of trains in moving troops, the fortlike architecture of early stations, remembered by Indian-born Kipling, proclaimed those buildings' secondary purpose as defensive redoubts against natives. After the 1870s, however, the military function of the Indian rail ceased to be visible in station design, which became distinct for its theme-park Oriental Indo-Islamic-Venetian magnificence. In the same period, the railway staff down to the waiting room attendants donned paramilitary uniforms and assumed supra-legal repressive powers against undisciplined natives, degenerate whites, and hypothetical pestilence. No wonder nationalists compared the rail to a demon looming over India. In a final twist, the rise of nationalist sentiment in India led imperial administrators to

FIGURE 5.4: Lahore Railway Station. Photographed by William Henry Jackson (1843–1942). Courtesy Prints & Photographs Division, Library of Congress.

entrust this role to a staff composed overwhelmingly of Anglo-Indians; toward that end, they removed Anglo-Indian children from orphanages for retraining, with whom they sought to forge a railway race (Bear 2007).

In French North Africa, military concerns did not merely shape the construction of the rail but rather animated the project altogether. The ministry of war oversaw the construction of Algeria's first train line, from Alger to Blida, using military engineers and *la main d'oeuvre militaire* ("military workers"), a term that covered army convict labor. In the wake of an 1881 insurrection at Bou-Amema in southern Oran, the ministry of war oversaw the rapid construction of a railway to the foot of the insurrection, at Mecheria, using Spanish laborers along with deported French convicts who dragged their balls and chains around work sites. In North Africa, the military character of the train stations remained conspicuous in their architecture through the end of the nineteenth century in step with French expansionist efforts. A journalist for *L'Illustration* evoked a Saharan station in 1889 by noting "four carved bastions flanking all sides, its central wall pierced by holes defending, in a sense, the vast interior enclosure containing the railroad material . . . in case of alert, all the engines can be rolled into the interior, like a tortoise withdrawing into its carapace, and hence protected from the depredations of indigenous marauders" (Beju *et al.* 1992) (Figure 5.5).

FIGURE 5.5: Postcard of fortified train station at Ben Zireg, Algeria (*c*. 1906). Public domain.

Beyond their economic and military importance, imperial railways transformed European and colonial societies in unexpected ways. Steam travel not only enabled regional tourism and pilgrimages by colonial subjects within their own countries, but also shrank the distance, in practical terms, between colonized people and the imperial center. Earlier, during the age of sail, Indians in England (except for the occasional prince) were nannies and stranded sailors—called lascars—unable to find a place on a homeward ship (Visram 1986). The railway and steamship, by contrast, made it possible to move back and forth with relative ease. England became a destination for Indian tourists and a temporary home for Indian students, male and female, who weathered religious and caste constraints to travel there (Hay 1989).

As Antoinette Burton remarks, "subjects gain[ed] subjectivity precisely by moving in and through" empire (Ballantyne and Burton 2009: 10). The new ease of roundtrip travel turned England into a space of cultural exchange and political engagement for an educated elite that included future social reformers and nationalist leaders (Burton 1998). In England, they moved freely among vegetarian theosophists (Gandhi), leftists, and Irish nationalists. The first prime minister of India, Jawaharlal Nehru, encountered prejudice at Harrow and Cambridge, where he was banned from the Officer Training Corps. Apart from his youthful brushes with exclusion, Nehru traced his political awakening to George Bernard Shaw, campus Marxism, and the pamphlets of Sinn Fein. In England, colonial subjects freely engaged in radical politics. Indian students in 1907 paraded through London to commemorate the 1857 mutiny—which they openly called a nationalist rising. The Indian National Congress was born on English soil (Lahiri 2000). The Indian railway, which was built to serve English military and commercial needs, played a key role in the emergence of radical consciousness and anti-imperial critique.

MOBILITY AND THE IMPERIAL SUBJECT: CONTAGIOUS BODIES ON THE MOVE

In the twentieth century, tropical medicine became a celebrated feature of the imperial project as the scientific expression of the civilizing mission. Yet the relationship of imperial expansion to tropical disease cannot be understood as a tale of intrepid Pasteurians carrying science to the bush (Peckham 2013). In the late nineteenth and early twentieth centuries, imperial expansion in Africa and Asia produced epidemics of cholera, rinderpest (a cattle disease), and bubonic plague while contributing immensely to the spread of sleeping sickness and malaria. It would be folly to claim that all diseases affecting Asians and Africans in the nineteenth century arose exclusively from European empire-building. The point is simply that new methods of population control emerged out of the need on the part imperial governments to manage epidemic disease at times of intense mobility. Confronted with the morbid effect of their very presence, imperial authorities developed new methods for inspecting and isolating bodies on the move well before it became a matter of treating them.

In *Heart of Darkness* (1899), Josef Conrad's gothic yarn about the Congo Free State, a rusty steamer moves ever so slowly down the Congo River toward Kurtz, an imperial middle manager turned ivory potentate. Kurtz loses his mind before losing his life: we discover him at a jungle compound in moribund delirium, born aloft by cannibals. Yet the book's protagonist is arguably neither Kurtz nor the steamboat captain, but rather a mental and physical affliction whose symptoms duplicate those of sleeping sickness, human trypanosomiasis, which raged in the late nineteenth-century Congo (Dempsey 2013).

As a parasitic illness borne by tsetse flies, sleeping sickness existed in pockets of Africa for centuries. Yet the new rubber and ivory trade together with military service, imperial forced labor, and the advent of steam travel shunted Africans from fly-free areas into infested ones while helping infected tsetse to travel swiftly around the continent. According to one German doctor, the flies traveled by rail and steamer (Neill 2012: 105). Belgian, English, and German imperial officials looked to similar methods to contain the disease. In East Africa, where the disease hit hardest, hygienic measures included depopulation, quarantine, and game destruction. In modern-day Uganda and Kenya, "No native [was] allowed to travel by railway without having a medical certificate as to his freedom from sleeping sickness." All European empires created facilities to contain afflicted people, wreathed in barbed wire, which the English called "suitable camps," the Belgians called "lazarets," and the Germans called Konzentrationslager (Neill 2012: 110–12). In the Belgian Congo, even non-infected Africans traveled by water in movable cages (Neill 2012: 124).

As in the case of sleeping sickness, the global bubonic plague pandemic at the turn of the twentieth century inspired movement-related protocols that reveal the increasing centrality of racial classification and hierarchy to European imperial regimes. The plague is likely to have spread from India to British South Africa via steamers laden with forage grain (and hence rodents) for the region's commercial herds. In consequence, so-called coloreds—a category that included Indian immigrants, biracial people, and the indigenous Khoisan—were banned from rail travel whereas whites were not (Echenberg 2002; Dube 2012).

In French Indochina, the risk of malaria for colonial inhabitants worsened after conquest, during the phase of deforestation, road, rail, and canal-building that the French called *la mise en valeur*. In Indochina, la mise en valeur coincided with the mass migration of tens of millions of people from India and China to various points in Southeast Asia. Malaria killed between forty and seventy percent of immigrant coolie railway workers in Indochina. French efforts to combat malaria unfolded with a veneer of efficiency and in practice involved the haphazard dispersal of quinine while imperial authorities, citing cost, scoffed at the "promotion of mosquito nets and glass windows" (Monnais 2013: 210). In contrast to conditions in revolutionary Haiti and Latin America, malaria in nineteenth-century Asia could hardly be described as a weapon of the weak against mobile conquerors.

For indentured immigrants from South Asia, the link between imperial mobility and constraint became manifest in the travel formalities that British authorities imposed on plantation workers. Before their departure for the Caribbean or British Malaya, Indian immigrants faced the indignity of the emigrant camp, an isolation regimen spurred by news of past horrors at sea—ghost ships ravaged by cholera—and also, less nobly, by the need to allay doubt about where the blame lay when coolies return starving and wretched from stints abroad. Next came quarantine on arrival: coincident with the fin-de-siècle pandemic of bubonic plague, Tamil immigrants to Singapore and Penang faced detention at insular depots for up to three weeks before reaching Malayan plantations (Amrith 2013). The quarantining of immigrants did not betoken a concern with workers' health; the isolation regime existed to protect European colonists from alien infection. The same habit of mind turned segregation into a norm of imperial urbanism, as cities became divided worlds, with airy European sectors sealed from collapsing old towns, whose insalubriousness, while arising from mere neglect, was ascribed to congenital racial deficiency—the exotic filth of native races.

With the movement of European soldiers overseas for conquest and defense, troop sex became a concern of imperial governments, prompting efforts to manage the bodies of native women. Imperial sex regimens for white bodies on the move had contradictory aims. In Asia, the British government sought to preserve white military bodies from infirmity. Racial hygiene became a public service for agents of empire. And yet the policing of sex in and around garrisons also leant an official character to sex with native girls. Sex regulation built a structure for the routine transgression of racial boundaries. In North Africa, the French government created *quartiers réservés*—state-administered urban sectors for troop sex—or *bordels mobiles de campagne*, mobile bordellos, which France oversaw in the role of pimp and hygiene police (Taraud 2003; Taraud 2015).

French imperial efforts to police venereal disease extended and modified an existing national framework for managing sex workers. British imperial authorities, on the other hand, pioneered a system that predated similar measures on domestic soil and entailed a far more robust use of police power than legislators would have countenanced at home. Where domestic Contagious Diseases Acts applied only to streetwalkers in garrison towns, imperial Diseases Acts were colony wide and included the oversight of bordellos (Levine 2003). In Hong Kong, the British government taxed all whorehouses in the city while inspecting only those with foreign clients. As Philip Howell notes, British imperial sex regulations "were more ambitious, more thoroughgoing and more extreme than to be found in the domestic Contagious Disease Acts" (Howell 2009: 189).

The fear of contagion denotes a feeling of imminent physiological peril from a source that threatens to elude confinement at any instant. The link between empire-building and contagion was never a mere medical problem for it concerned the moral and racial identity of colonial occupiers. Inevitably, in the age of steam power, the threat of succumbing to random deathly metamorphosis in imperial settings became a trope that redounded upon the home country. In the Sherlock Holmes stories of Arthur Conan Doyle, the British Empire is the source of crime and freakish anatomical accident. Colonies are the origin of unusual poisons, killers, licentious schemers, blackmailers, disfiguring ailments, and an essence that inverts evolution, turning man into ape. The colonies are not merely a domain of racial otherness but also produce otherness: they create altered specimens of Englishness. In "The Disappearance of Lady Frances Carfax," the Right Honourable Philip Green returns in the form of "a savage"; in "The Devil's Foot," Dr. Leon Sterndale, an African explorer, is known about London for "[his] huge body, [his] craggy and deeply seamed face with fierce eyes." Ultimately the three Holmes collections by Doyle, himself a physician (like Watson), read like medical casebooks, if only obliquely. They describe the physiological remaking of England by empire.

CONCLUSION: NON-PLACES OF EMPIRE

By way of conclusion, the story of imperial mobility invites a rethinking of how we picture the present in relation to the past. At the very least, the history of people on the move from the American Revolution to the Great War (and beyond) gives the lie to popular and scholar notions of globalization and modernity. The anthropologist Marc Augé gives the name *non-lieu* or non-place to the kinds of travel-related spots that remove and isolate modern people on the move, which he pictures in terms of airport waiting rooms, recharging stations, metros, TGVs, taxis, and economy plus seats. Non-places refer to these impersonal bubbles of rootless experience—corporate, vinyl, climate controlled, perfumed by air fresheners. Supermodernity, for Augé, describes the fragmentation of cultures, as technology remakes time and space and a person's life comes to consist of anonymous itinerancy through these blank spots.

Imperial mobility produced its own repertoire of non-places, which looked nothing like Augé's leatherette oases of individualism. A sample list would include places like coastal baracoons and slave ships, emigrant camps, sleeping sickness lazarets, plague quarantine sites, and *bordels mobiles*. The modern form of state authority that Michel Foucault calls biopower, involving control over the life forces and bodies of peoples, developed precociously and most acutely in Western empires (Stoler 1995); it did so, quite often, through the act of moving people around. The imperial non-place, which arose from human mobility, was a privileged site for the exercise of biopower. In the case of slaves and former slaves, immigrants, troops, criminals, and conquered peoples, the imperial management of human mobility hinged on the exercise of this sort of control, however imperfectly.

From The Revolutionary Era to the Great War, Western imperial rule centered on the management of population flows, which meant orchestrating movement and constraint simultaneously. And yet the accelerated mobility of people across empires, or between colonies and the home country, was not only about coercion. Movement also meant flight and liberation. It brought forth diasporic communities and hybrid cultures. Mobility in the age of steam power created new spaces of thought and politics—sites from which to imagine a postcolonial world.

CHAPTER SIX

Sexuality

1800–1920

ESME CLEALL

INTRODUCTION

There were two kinds of sex in colonial discourse: sex between one man and one woman that occurred within monogamous, Christian, marriages, between people of the same ethnic background, in utmost private, for the purposes of reproduction. And sex that was not confined to these tightly policed boundaries. Sex for pleasure, same-sex sex, interracial sex, extra-marital sex, and sex for money, among many other sexual practices, were illicit, exotized, and altogether unacceptable. These two kinds of sex are reflected in the three arguments that I make in this chapter.

First, I argue that sexuality was a discourse of otherness: sexual activity that might broadly be defined as "legitimate" and "illegitimate" were mapped onto an "us" and "them" binary. Indigenous people were sexually other and it was their sexuality that helped define their otherness. As Sander Gilman argues, by the eighteenth century "the black, both male and female, becomes ... an icon for deviant sexuality" and this worked in two directions: what it meant to be sexually other came to be racialized and those who were racialized came to be seen as sexually different (Gilman 1985: 81). Discourses of sexuality were closely bound up with the gendered ideology of colonialism. Enlightenment thinking suggested that the social position occupied by women was a core indicator of civilization (Wilson 2007: 14–46; Hall 2007: 46–77). Writers such as the British historian and East India Company civil servant James Mill argued that "[a]mong rude people, the women are generally degraded; among civilized people they are exalted" (Mill 1817: 293). At the apex of civilization were European, Christian women gendered by emergent evangelical discourses of the familial. At the bottom of the hierarchy, Mill wrote, lurked many "degraded" women ranging from those in southern Africa where "the women are reckoned unworthy to eat with the men," to those in India where Hindu women occupied a position of which a "state of dependence more strict and humiliating . . . cannot easily be conceived" (Mill 1817: 293–4; Cleall 2012: 26).

Second, I argue that this otherness was fragmented: there were lots of ways of being sexually other. What the "degradation" Mill and others spoke of entailed oscillated between women's oppression and women's "disorder" with sexuality a key signifier of each. In India, a dominant discourse developed that cited women's oppression as a key justification for colonial intervention. In the early nineteenth century, *sati* was increasingly used to imagine Indian women's victimized state (Mani 1998). Over the following decades, similar concerns about Hindu women's oppression were reconfigured around other tropes from the child bride, to the zenana woman. Women who were "unrestrained" by patriarchal structures could, however, be equally challenging to colonial expectations, and were typically seen as "uncivilised," and potentially subversive (Hunt 2002: 1; Herndon 2002: 79–91). While colonial discourse could operate as an oppositional formation—there were "proper" ways of constructing a family and "disordered" ones—the "other" was always fragmented, and contained within it, oppositions of its own (Cleall 2012: 25–7). A wide variety of indigenous sexual practices were seen to be "other" from child marriage to polygamy.

Third, I argue that a lot of effort, discursive, judicial, and reformist, was put into policing the boundaries between "good" sexuality and "bad" sexuality, keeping them separate and consolidating the first articulation here. What Ann Laura Stoler calls the "management of sex" in the Dutch East Indies was a high concern to all the major European colonial regimes (Stoler 1995: 7). As Stoler puts it, "The regulation of sexual relations was central to the development of particular kinds of colonial settlements and to the allocation of economic activity within them. Who bedded and wedded whom in the colonies of France, England, Holland and Iberia was never left to chance" (Stoler 1995: 47). This meant that the sexual relationships of Europeans in the colonies was just as much a site of concern as that of indigenous peoples. And, perhaps, most importantly of all, the interracial relationships between colonizers and colonized was an issue of central concern that needed to be discouraged and prevented. As the French theorist Michel Foucault suggested, sexuality is an especially "dense transfer point for relationships of power," serving as a "lynch-pin" through which many personal dynamics are informed (Foucault 1990: 103). Drawing on Foucault, Stoler has explained that this was no less so in a colonial environment where discourses about sexuality were prolific.

Sexuality was an important colonial discourse and sex was an important experience and practice that was shaped by colonial contexts. It often signified and embodied relationships of power that were uneven and, while frequently confirming these discrepancies, also had the power to subvert them. Sexuality spoke to the deeply enmeshed intersectional logics of race, class, and gender and to the tendencies of colonial regimes to police the intimate lives of their subjects and actors.

FANTASY AND REPRESENTATION

The language of race, gender, and sexuality were intimately entangled (De Groot 2000: 53). Just as transgressive sexuality was racialized, so were attitudes toward race sexualized, at least from the early modern period on (Morgan 2005: 54–67). At the same time, the language of gender was mapped onto racial distinctions with European read as "masculine" to the feminized colonial other (McClintock 1995: 55).

In using the language of "penetration" and "rape" to discuss the European exploration and exploitation of the "virgin" territories of empire, the very processes of colonization were imbued with sexualized metaphors. What Anne McClintock discusses as the "porno-tropics" in the western imagination—"a fantastic magic lantern of the mind onto which Europe projected its forbidden sexual desires and fears"—affected both the presentation of the landscape and the people who inhabited it (McClintock 1995: 22). Landscape, or "nature," read as female, was to be "discovered, entered, named, inseminated and, above all, owned" by the masculine colonizers (McClintock 1995: 31). Erotic images of "exotic" others circulated in "Orientalist" discourse, through European travel writing, art and literature (Said 1978/2003; Ali 2015: 33–46) (Figure 6.1).

The European empires became sites of homosexual as well as heterosexual fantasy and practice (Aldrich 2003). In French Indochina, homosexuality was seen as a "typically Asian practice," while in Algeria it was considered to be a "peculiarity of the Arabs" (Yee 2001: 269; Dunne 1994: 29). And as Robert Aldrich has demonstrated, homosexual practices among indigenous cultures in places as wide-ranging as Polynesia and North Africa, attracted the fascinated attention of European travel writers, while spaces of empire also provided the opportunity for same-sex sexual relations for Europeans both with indigenous people and within the colonial army itself (Aldrich 2002: 201–18).

Female sexuality was also particularly frightening. As Ann McClintock writes "women figured as the epitome of sexual aberration and excess. Folklore saw them, even more than the men, as given to a lascivious venery so promiscuous as to border on the bestial" and in the colonial setting this tendency was further exaggerated (McClintock 1995: 22). Ideas about colonized women's "excessive"

FIGURE 6.1: Jean-Léon Gérôme, *The Snake Charmer*, c. 1879. Credit: Universal History Archive/Getty Images.

sexuality became embodied in specific women of color taken to Europe for display and examination.

The most famous example of such women was Sara (or as she was known by her Cape Dutch owners Saartjie) Baartman the so-called "Hottentot Venus" who was taken to London in 1810 and then to France where she was exhibited before medical professionals and a voyeuristic public until her early death in 1816 (Crais and Scully 2008) (Figure 6.2). The primary draw was her prominent buttocks which were highly sexualized and pathologized as an example of the steatopyia (protruding buttocks) that had been widely reported by travelers to the Cape. Her genitalia were also a source of fascination for both the French and British. Her elongated clitoris was seen to exemplify what had become known as the "Hottentot Apron" and seen as an example of "primitive" genitalia. As Sander Gilman writes, Baartman was exhibited less as a woman than as a "collection of sexual parts" and this is reinforced by the fact that, after her death and dissection her reproductive organs were preserved as "scientific curiosities" (Gilman 1985: 88). Yvette Abrahams sees Baartman's display as "the turning point toward exhibiting the savage as raw sexuality" and thereafter, the genitals of both black men and women were seen as anatomically different from those of white Europeans (Abrahams quoted in Levine 2006a, 127).

The processes by which "race" and "sex" became intertwined occurred differently across colonial sites. Titillating images of bare-breasted Polynesian

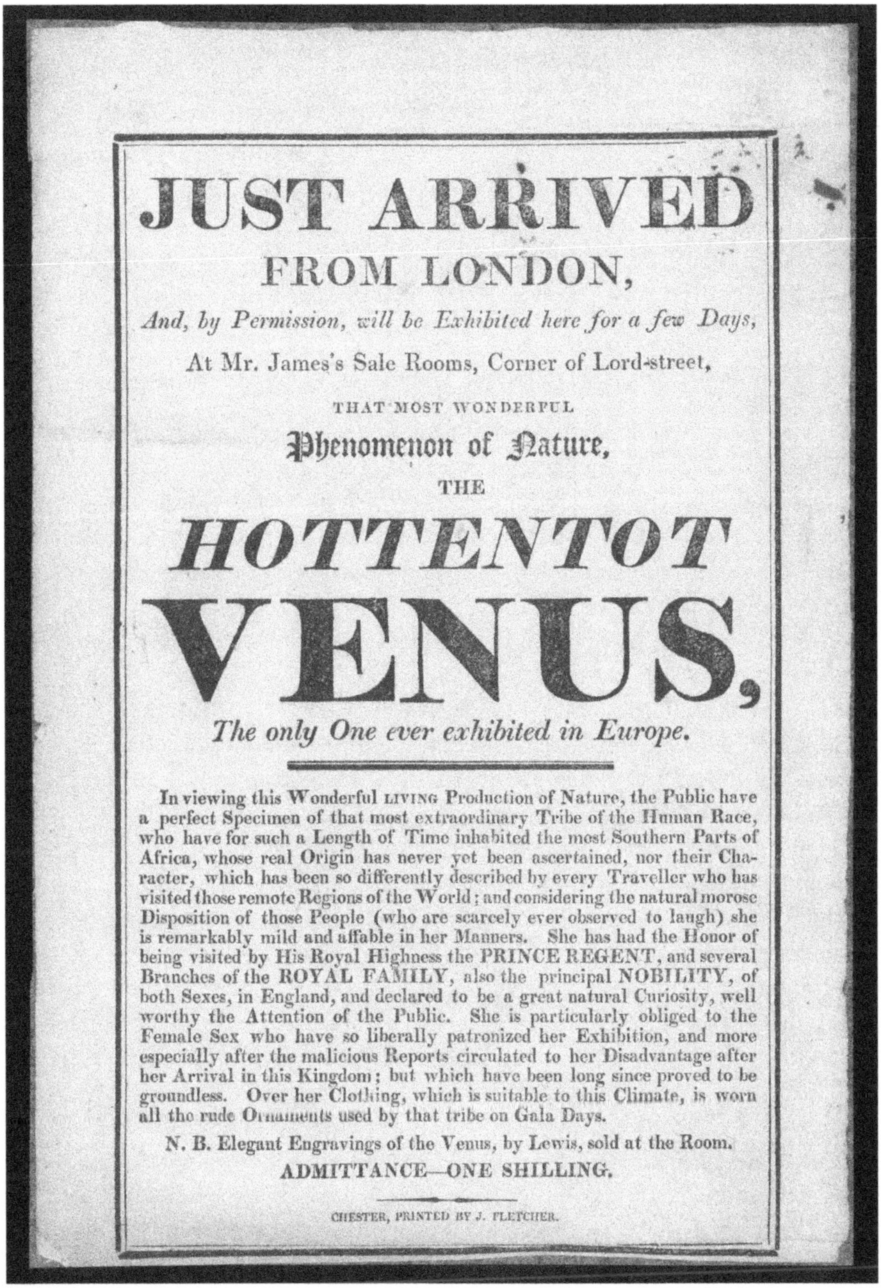

FIGURE 6.2: Poster advertising the "Hottentot Venus." Courtesy of Wellcome Images under Creative Commons licence CC BY 4.0: https://creativecommons.org/licenses/by/4.0/

women, for example, imagined to be "sexually available," differed from those of secluded, yet also sexually charged, depictions of the Indian zenana (Cleall 2012, 25). Erotic images of African and Asian women differed markedly and were defined relationally to one and other, with Asian people further up the racial hierarchy (Bhattacharya 1998: 22–35). Yet both relied on assumptions about the sexualization and commodification of non-European women and both drew on tropes of disordered sexuality. So did images of Bengali men as effeminate, African men as sexually aggressive, and Indochinese men and women as "androgynous" (Sinha 1995; Yee 2001: 270–5).

CULTURAL IMPERIALISM

Changing the sexual behavior of indigenous peoples was a key element of the "civilising missions" that characterized a range of European missions from the British, to the French and Portuguese, and encompassed a range of activities from inculcating domestic values, to encouraging the adoption of commercial trade, to western education and Christian proselytization (for the Portuguese example see Bandeira Jerónimo 2015). Often these "civilising missions" had gendered dynamics. As Rebecca Roger demonstrates in the case of nineteenth-century colonial Algeria, the training of girls and women was key to the French "civilising mission" (Rogers 2011: 741–59).

Missionaries were one such agent that identified and attempted to "correct" sexual "deviance." Missions had an ambivalent relationship with the formal axes of empire, which changed according to time and place (Copland 2006: 1025–54; Porter 2004; Stanley 1990; Daughton 2008). In French Algeria, for example, proselytization was explicitly prohibited, while in colonial Bechuanaland, Scottish missionary John Mackenzie was actively involved in the extension of British rule. Swiss and Norwegian mission societies, hardly insignificant in the numbers of Protestant missions, operated independently from their own nations' national influence though often within the boundaries of another European power's colonial interests. Despite these complexities, however, missionaries shared with other colonial actors a tendency to embody images of sexual otherness in the sexual practices of actual Africans, Asians, Native Americans, and Australasians. Horrified by what they saw as the sexual degradation of indigenous others, particularly women, across the non-western world, missionaries were determined to control the sexuality of those they sought to convert. From India, to Polynesia, to Australasia, the Americas, and Africa, they encountered a range of sexual practices they believed incompatible with Christian life. "[M]issionaries knew better ways, it seemed, to do almost anything," Patricia Grimshaw writes of American missionaries, and much of their critique revolved around issues of sexuality and gender. "They proclaimed prevention of pregnancy a sin," "wives bore too many babies or gave them away uncaringly to relatives," "mothers breastfed for intervals that were too long or too short," the "early betrothals should be done away with . . . and their choice of marriage partner should be divested of kinship considerations," on the other hand, "young people should not be given unfettered choice," adolescents in Polynesia and New Zealand seemed to have "too much liberty at far too young an age," while, everywhere, pre-marital sex was "denounced as disgraceful" (Grimshaw 2007: 271–2). Bridewealth and dowry arrangements were read as harboring forms of sexual slavery, and even virginity, highly prized in nineteenth-century Europe, could be suspect in the colonies as missionaries wrote of Ndebele women "doomed to perpetual virginity" in King Mzilikatzi's "hareem" (Cleall 2012: 37). In German East Africa, missionary influences in the gender order have been argued to have been so pervasive as to have left a powerful legacy of gender inequality (Montgomery 2017: 225–68).

One of the problems that missionaries faced was that even if indigenous people were prepared to convert to Christianity, many of them wanted to retain their traditional sexual practices. Forcing converts to give up polygamous marriages proved a particular sticking point in Africa, while the continued marriages of newly converted Christians to partners who intended keeping their traditional faith was seen as pre-emptive of "backsliding" in India. Sexual relationships were a key site where missionaries agonized over an all too unclear boundary between "heathenism" and "Christianity." There were no easy answers to questions as to what was to be done with second or third wives, whether children could be circumcised, whether new converts could live communally or whether Christianity demanded the absolute privatization of marriages and whether tom-toms might be played at a Christian wedding. As I have argued elsewhere, "in posing such questions, missionaries engaged with the intangibility of difference; in attempting to answer them they erected boundaries to define it" (Cleall 2012: 54–5).

At the same time, missionaries constructed "ideal" families, whose sexuality was contained within the boundaries of Christian marriage, reproduction, and private walls (Figure 6.3). The ideal family reoccurred as a trope in missionary writing formed around a sexual bond yet divested of any obvious sexual overtones. Converted families could perform this role but, among Protestant missionary societies, most frequently it was represented by the missionary family itself as the embodiment of domestic ideology.

Ideas of "cleanliness" and "purity" permeate the image and as Karina Hestad Skeie notes in the case of Norwegian Missions in Madagascar, so too did images of the house and the home (Skeie 1999: 72). But at the center of the family was the marital bond which, among other things, Protestant missionaries saw as an important distinction between their practice and the celibacy of Catholic missions. Many Protestant missionary societies considered marriage a "task" that it was advisable to complete before departure. Women would act as a

FIGURE 6.3: Hawaiian missionary family, 1878. Card from A.A. Montano's New Photographic Gallery, Honolulu. Public domain.

"helpmeet" to the day-to-day running of the mission and, during the frequent periods when a male missionary was away from their station, or incapacitated by sickness, acted on his behalf (Hall 2002: 91–2, 96).

In missionary literature, such marriages were sentimentally represented as exemplars of compatible gender relations, though, as in Jane Eyre's caustic assessment of the view that "God and nature intended you for a missionary wife," these representations were not universally shared (Brontë 1847: 356). Catholic missionaries, meanwhile, were constructed by their Protestant counterparts as suspiciously celibate and more relaxed in their attitudes toward indigenous sexual practices.

EUROPEAN WOMEN AND THE "MYTH OF THE DESTRUCTIVE FEMALE"

Sexual relationships between European missionaries and indigenous people had the power to disrupt neat binaries though, again, how this occurred was contingent on time and place. While, later in the nineteenth century the missionary couple were held up as an exemplary sexual partnership, Emily Manktelow has demonstrated that, in the early days of missionary activity, interracial marriage was actually encouraged by the London Missionary Society (LMS), one of the largest British Protestant organizations (Manktelow

2014: 135–59). Relationships with indigenous women, that is those that were sanctioned by marriage vows, were thought to be of pragmatic value, helping to integrate the missionary into the society of the South Seas, where many early LMS missionaries were based. At the same time, such a policy meant avoiding the need to bring European women, who were perceived as "both a sexual and a physical liability," into the foreign mission field (Manktelow 2014: 139). The changes that led the LMS as a society to turn against these practices are both complicated and instructive for thinking about broader shifts in sexual attitudes. Manktelow suggests that in the South Seas a series of "scandalous events" including "backsliding" and non-Christian marriage led to the cession of the practice of integration. As Elizabeth Elbourne has explored, the early Cape Colony also had a tradition of LMS relationships with women of color including the marriages of James Read, John Barlett, Michael Wimmer, and Johann Heinrich Schmelen to Khoisan women (Elbourne 2008: 197–232). Some interracial relationships were openly constructed as "disordered," perhaps most famously, the Dutch missionary Johannes Van der Kemp's marriage to Sara Janse, who, besides being from Madagascar, at the time of marriage was only thirteen years old and enslaved (Van der Kemp had purchased her freedom himself). But others seem to have been tacitly accepted (Elbourne 2008: 220–1). Over time, however, sexual scandal engulfed many of these missionaries. A generational shift spelled the end of missionary marriages to women of color and ideologies requiring greater "social and sexual distance" between "black" and "white" were increasingly adopted (Elbourne 2008, 197–232).

This can be seen as part of a larger shift or a turn away from interracial marriages following a period of greater "freedom" and a "toleration" of such relationships in the eighteenth century. There is a long tradition of scholarly work, that Margaret Strobel discusses as "the myth of the destructive female," where the arrival of the European woman has been associated with the hardening of racial attitudes and subsequent deterioration of race relations in places as diverse as British India, Malaya, Papua, Fiji, the Solomon Islands, and Africa (Strobel 1991, 2). Interestingly, these arguments seem to transcend different imperial nationalities. Before the arrival of European women, scholars have suggested, there was a "golden age" of interracial love and relationships, where solitary European men formed intimate sexual attachments with indigenous women (or in some renditions of the narrative, men). One famous example of such a relationship is that between the British Resident James Achilles Kirkpatrick and the Muslim Noblewoman Khair un-Nissa (Dalrymple 2002). It was the "insular whims and prejudices" of European women, Percival Spear famously asserted, that "widened the racial gulf" in eighteenth-century India while writing of British Africa, L.O.H. Gann and Peter Dunignam have stated that "it was the cheap steam ticket for women that put an end to racial integration" (both quoted in Stoler 2002: 32). Though these writers have suggested that the trouble women spelled in the spaces of empire can be located in their inherent racism, other explanations as to why the arrival of European women should have led to this hardening of racial attitudes have consistently returned to the sexual dynamics of colonial relationships. Some have claimed that women disrupted the intimacies between European men and indigenous women that had, apparently, been beneficial to colonial rule facilitating greater cultural awareness on the part of the colonizer (Strobel 1991: 1). Thomas Beildelman, writing on colonial Tanganyika, has suggested that the desire of indigenous men European women were thought to have excited, and the vulnerability of the wives and daughters themselves, necessitated the chivalrous protection of European men and greater practices of segregation (Stoler 2002: 32–3). Taking a slightly different perspective, Ashis Nandy has claimed that the reason white women in colonial India "were generally more racist than their men" was because "they unconsciously saw themselves as the sexual competitors of Indian men, with whom their men had established an unconscious homoeroticized bonding" (Nandy 1988: 9–10).

In reality, the relationship between the arrival of European women and the shift in racial attitudes was much more complicated. As Stoler puts it in the case of the Dutch East Indies, "the arrival of women was tied to other plans" often coinciding with strategies of political stabilization (Stoler 2002: 33). "Sometimes," she argues, "their presence was encouraged precisely to enforce the separation between Asians and whites" (Stoler 1995: 33). Of the British Empire, Strobel also points to the coinciding between their arrival and in the intensified appropriation of indigenous labor, a growth of evangelical Christianity, and the increased numbers of Europeans of all genders (Strobel 1991: 2). And of course the shift did not mean that interracial relationships came to an end. Interracial relationships continued throughout all colonial interactions and varied considerably across time and place evoking, as Owen White explains in the French case, questions of citizenship, paternity, and social identity (White 1999). "Relationships between colonizers and colonized continued in many forms," operating on what Woollacott describes as "a spectrum running from marriage, through concubinage, to prostitution, and ultimately rape," importantly, "the spectrum should be viewed as a loop, with evidence that women's experiences ran in both directions" (Woollacott 2008: 320).

While the idea of a "golden age" before the arrival of European women does not seem to apply to the Australian case, as Angela Woollacott points out, here, as elsewhere in the settler colonies there was a distinctive culture of masculinity linked with the imbalance in the sex ratio (there were hugely more European men than women in Australia at the beginning of the nineteenth century and this did not even out until the beginning of the twentieth century) (Woollacott 2008: 320, 315). As Marie-Paule Ha explores, similar gender imbalances occurred in the French colonies, which only toward the end of the nineteenth century, started to encourage female migration to the colonies as a solution to both "concubinage," "forced celibacy" overseas, and an overrepresentation of women back home (Ha 2013: 222–5). What R.W. Connell discusses as "frontier masculinities" developed in many of the settler colonies, characterized by male homosocial bonding, harsh conditions, and the experience of physical violence (Connell 1995: 185–95).

ENSLAVEMENT

Slavery and its legacies structured sexual relationships in the Caribbean. The marriages of the enslaved were often unrecognized both by slave owners and abolitionists because of abolitionist concerns about divorce within African families (Bush 1990: 99). Refusing to recognize loving bonds, sexual or otherwise, conveniently absolved slave owners from having to think about the pain inflicted during indiscriminate separations of close family members through sales (Bush 1990: 100).

Sexuality was a tool to control the black population, "emasculat[ing] black men" and "terroris[ing] black women" (Hall 2014: 35). Enslaved women who attempted to resist the sexual advances of their owners were liable to severe reprisals. Those who complied, on the other hand, were sometimes subjected to vengeful punishments by jealous wives (Bush 1990: 113). For colonial society, isolated incidents of rape were not, however, as threatening as the long-term relationships white men forged with their enslaved "housekeepers." Relationships of concubinage were so widespread as to comprise the very social fabric of Caribbean society. Assessing the degree of agency which enslaved women had in such relationships is very difficult. Certainly many enslaved women were raped by their owners and overseers. But sometimes, to some extent, women were able to exercise agency and, as Bush suggests "Black women, too, despite their racial and sexual inferiority, could at times manipulate white men to their advantage" (Bush 1990: 111). We should be aware of the "subtle and complex framework of sexual relations" that characterized slave societies (Bush 1990: 114). Through sex, and in particular through long-term sexual relationships, an enslaved woman might exert power denied to her elsewhere. The children of these liaisons occupied a highly ambiguous position. Some were entirely disowned by their white fathers. But others were treated more favorably and sometimes recognized as the legal heir. Depicting enslaved women as "scheming jezebels" was a means to exonerate white men from their relationships with black women (or, at least, to plant the blame firmly on the latter), at a time when race was becoming increasingly important to constructions of European identities (Altink 2005: 279). But this did not stop mixed-race relationships being highly problematic for the planter class. The planter elite proved unable to reproduce itself meaning that, unlike in North America, the Caribbean never became a settler society (Hall 2014: 35). Abolitionists were particularly alarmed by the degree of sexual "corruption" in the Caribbean, with systems of concubinage "at the heart of [the abolitionist] critique of slavery" (Hall 2002: 112). As Catherine Hall has argued, women activists in particular used the predatory sexuality of "corrupted white men," the "enforced separation of mothers from children," and the failure to support the families of the enslaved as key evidence in underlining the immorality of slavery (Hall 2014: 35–6). The attempted destruction and denial of black families through the sale of close kinship members, the rape of black women, and refusal to recognize marriage, has had lasting consequences (Hall 2014: 35).

VIOLENCE AND RAPE

Rape and sexual violence were not just confined to systems of slavery but were filtered through sexual relations in many European empires (see also Kent and Fitzpatrick in this volume). If, following the work of Shani D'Cruze, sexual violence is not read as deviance but as "an integral part of the maintenance of historically located patriarchal power relations," then its widespread prevalence in colonial settings demonstrates not only the ubiquity of violence in the colonial sphere but its complex intersection with race and gender structures (D'Cruze 1992: 337). As is discussed earlier, rape operated as a power-tool in enslaved societies including at the Cape of Good Hope where rape has been seen as a means of controlling the enslaved and reproducing slave populations (Scully 1995: 337; Ross 1979: 421–33). British soldiers were reported to attack Indian women (Cleall 2012: 145). And, in Australia, European men demanded access to Aboriginal women, bartered for money, food, and goods (Woollacot 2008: 321).

Only some incidents of sexual violence were given the particular meaning of "rape." That most rape that occurred was of indigenous and enslaved women by white men, did not enter colonial "rape scripts" which continued to focus on the rape of European women by colonized men (Paxton 1999). Rape inside marriage was not recognized. And in the courts in both Britain and the colonies, ideas about "chastity," class, age, and circumstance meant that many rape cases were dismissed out of hand (Kolsky 2010: 1093–111). Further, as today, there were huge difficulties reporting and resultant silences in the reporting of rape due to the stigmatizing differential between "chaste" and "unchaste" women (Paxton 1999: 9). In a context when rape was not only highly taboo in the metropole, but was loaded with the additional ideological and symbolic overtones of a colonial setting, rape became "dangerously overdetermined" (Paxton 1999: 10).

By far the most common way in which rape was imagined was of an unprovoked assault on a white woman by a black man. This was known as the "black peril" referred to across Africa, or "yellow peril" in societies that saw high levels of Chinese migration. It has been widely demonstrated that these panics and anxieties had no statistical relationship with actual incidences of assault by men of color (Stoler 2002: 58). Indeed, the gap between actual rapes and fear of rape was so extreme that it has been treated by some historians as a form of "psychopathology," or "a complex paranoia" (McCulloch 2000: 5; Pape 1990: 701). We need to be careful not to repeat the historical silencing of raped women in completely dismissing their claims. But it is clear that the report of actual rape, as well as rape fantasies, and transgressions of social space perceived in a colonial context as "attempted rape," were escalated and exploited for political ends (Stoler 2002: 58). In Southern Rhodesia they helped to secure the more rigid demarcation of segregation, and across the various European empires they performed important ideological work in othering men of color as depraved sexual predators.

The relationship between "black perils" and the widespread rape of black women by white men is complex. Sometimes rape has been read as a metaphor for a generalized crisis. Some historians have read the relationships between black and white perils as a process of projection (McCulloch 2000: 9). Although little discussed, the "white peril" that swept Southern Rhodesia, in the wake of the 1896 War of Resistance was used to subordinate the black population at the same time as fears about "black peril" took hold of the settler imagination (Pape 1990: 710–14). Both served to do important ideological work. As John Pape argues, "The phenomena that the settlers called 'black' and 'white perils' were an essential factor in building and maintaining a white and male supremacist society" (Pape 1990: 700).

Although these fantasies took different forms at different moments and on different colonial sites, there were some striking similarities between them. Rape became a powerful way of conceptualizing colonial resistance (Ware 1992: 38, 40). During the so-called Indian "Mutiny" of 1857–8 there were widespread fears about the rape, violation, and murder of white women by Indian men (Figure 6.4). Although subsequent investigations found no evidence of this, the "memory" of sadistic sexual violence against white women and the trauma it invoked lived on not least in the novels that immortalized events at Kanpur (Brantlinger 1988: 199–224). Such images fed into constructions of the "Oriental" man as sexually depraved. According to Nancy Paxton, "the novels about the Indian Uprising of 1857 popularized and circulated a new rape script, which assigned Englishwomen to the place of rape victims," thus inverting earlier representations of colonial rape as being primarily about the metaphorical rape of the land and the people by colonizing Englishmen (Paxton 1999: 25).

The "White Mutiny" over the so-called "Ilbert Bill" in the early 1880s was another example of where the specter of the rape of a white woman by an Indian man served to do powerful ideological work (Sinha 1995: 33–69). The question as to whether Indian magistrates might try European subjects, including

FIGURE 6.4: The British Lion's Vengeance on the Bengal Tiger, *Punch* cartoon 1857. By John Tenniel, 1820–1914. Credit: Universal History Archive/UIG via Getty images. During the Indian Rebellion, Indian soldiers, represented here by the Tiger, were constructed as a sexual threat to European women.

over sensitive subjects such as marriage, divorce, and rape among Europeans, quickly descended into a discussion of the hypothetical scenario whereby a white woman, raped by an Indian man, was forced to testify in a court dominated by Indian men. The public outcry over such a situation soon revealed deeper anxieties about the sexual threat Anglo-Indian women felt that they lived with not only in public, but in their homes and very intimate quarters where they could be assaulted by lascivious servants (Dussart 2013). Similar concerns about domestic servants characterized fears about the "black peril" in southern Africa. Meanwhile, the idea of white women having consensual relationships with men of color was so unpalatable to the colonial imagination that such relations were often read as rape regardless of mutual consent.

REPRODUCTION

Relationships between white men and indigenous women of all sorts, while widespread, threatened the social order of colonialism which relied on a clear-cut division between colonizer and colonized (see Chattopadhyaya and Fitzpatrick in this volume). So did mixed-heritage children and wider communities of "Cape Coloureds," "mulattos," "métis" and "Eurasians." Discursive work needed to be done to seal the breaches that they represented. And sexuality was a site at which the boundaries between races were imposed, redrawn, and scrutinized. There were many ways of denying the legitimacy of certain relationships and excluding them from colonial society. Hannah Roberts, for example, has explored the way in which a discourse around "miscegenation" reveals "a disciplinary process through which interracial sex was placed firmly in a context of sex and vice rather than reproduction and family" (Robert 2001: 69). Such a maneuver facilitated the marking of Aboriginal women and children as "targets of intervention by the state," and making possible policies such as the removal of mixed-heritage children (Robert 2001: 71).

Over the course of the century mixed-heritage children also increasingly spoke to ideas about "degeneration": the idea that the racial "stock" was somehow being depleted, diluted, and compromised, and again this seems to have happened across a range of Western empires. Discourses of degeneration often concentrated around sexuality, perceived as a vulnerable site through which the dangers of a colonial location could take hold. Not only were interracial relationships problematic, but reproduction between white colonizers in the "tropics" could generate children who had a dubious relationship with the metropole. The intimate relationship between European infants and indigenous wet-nurses was one area of concern (Stoler 1995: 145–6). Fluency in indigenous languages was another. And all contributed to the pattern whereby white children were increasingly educated back in the imperial metropole, where it was hoped that their European credentials could be firmed up, despite the long, painful, and disruptive separations this represented to family life. They could then return to the colonies as colonizers after the dangerous period of adolescence had passed.

Reproduction was in and of itself a highly contested issue that, increasingly, became a matter of imperial concern. Under the Third Republic, French officials saw in the empire a possibility to use the empire to help "repopulate" the metropole, as Marie-Paule Ha explores (Ha 2013: 225–6). In Britain, the unhealthy "quality" of potential recruits to the Second South African ("Boer") War was perceived as an alarming warning as to the deteriorated quality of British "stock" (see Stock in this volume). In its wake, concerns about reproduction escalated. As Anna Davin has demonstrated, motherhood and child-rearing became an imperial concern and British levels of reproduction were anxiously compared with that of other "imperial races": the French, the Germans, and the Japanese. Eugenic marriages, education, and ideologies of natalism and maternalism were suggested as methods to address the crisis with many such policies aimed at women in particular and with clear class connotations (Davin 1978: 9–65). So too did discourses about disability, and in particular anxieties around the proliferation of a "feebleminded" population, contribute to understandings of who could and should reproduce. Across western Europe, new developments in birth control, perceived as a threat to "good," reproductive sexuality, were argued over and could be harnessed for both purposes of women's liberation and eugenistic endeavor. In weighing and measuring babies, regimentalizing domestic duties, and scorning "non-productive" women, the various European states increasingly intervened in issues of childhood and procreation.

STATE REGULATION, RESISTANCE, AND FEMINISM

In fact sexuality was always policed physically by the various European metropolitan states, as well as discursively, from prosecuting (some) incidents of rape, to regulating marriage, to outlawing sex between men (Phillips 2007: 143). Homophobic practices were exported to the colonies, and alongside other legislation intended to restrict sexual activity (Phillips 2007: 136–53). Sex-work was regulated, in different ways, across the European empires.

One example of where the British colonial state stepped in to regulate sexuality was over the Contagious Diseases (CD) Legislation passed in the first instance in 1864 (see Speiler in this volume). Alarmed by the rates of sexually transmitted infections among British soldiers and sailors, the British government took measures to "regulate" and control sex-work. Women working as sex-workers were required to register as "prostitutes" and to undergo regular examinations with the intention of identifying cases of sexually transmitted diseases (Levine 2003: 1). Between the 1860s and the 1880s, such legislation quickly spread throughout many of the colonies.

Philippa Levine's work on the CD Acts, which has argued that "[p]rostitution was a critical artefact of colonial authority, a trade deemed vital to governance but urgently in need of control," demonstrates among other things the importance of sexuality more widely in thinking about the politics of colonialism (Levine 2003: 227). It both reveals and created ways of policing gender and race hierarchies: the European sex-worker, while destabilizing, was nonetheless "fixedly superior" to her "colonial counterparts" and the definitional shifts adjudicating between British and "native" values and practices, were "powerful indices of the ways that the taxonomy of language served the ends of colonization and its deep commitment to a radicalized and gendered vision of the world" (Levine 2003: 227). The differential application of CD legislation in metropolitan and colonial contexts, and indeed between the colonies, not just reinforces the imperative to consider sexuality in the Age of Empire as occurring in one "analytic frame" that stretched from metropole to colony, but asks us to look at the complex intersection between colonialism, race, and sexuality on different colonial sites. In tracing the application of CD Acts between Hong Kong, India, Queensland, and the Straits Settlements, Levine has demonstrated how, unlike in Britain where such acts were confined to garrison towns and justified through military necessity, in the colonies CD legislation was thought also to "bring to heel sexual disorder amongst colonised people" (Levine 2003: 2). Further, as Richard Phillips points out, the reach of the CD Acts, while widespread, was not universal and the significant omissions of its application, notably to British Africa, speaks to the forging of different forms of colonialism and to the specificities of imperial sites (Phillips 2006: 112–35).

Unsurprisingly, the CD legislation met with considerable resistance from British feminists who recognized in the legislation a double standard, whereby women, blamed for carrying sexually transmitted diseases were forced to undergo examination, detention, and forced treatment, while the male clients of sex-workers escaped without censure. The internal examination, and use of the speculum especially, became a focus of particular ire with some finding the procedure so disturbing that it became known as "instrumental rape." Josephine Butler (Figure 6.5) was at the forefront of such protests in her campaign, which

FIGURE 6.5: Josephine Butler, *c*. 1885. Credit: London Stereoscopic Company/Getty Images.

gained force in the 1870s and led to the repeal of the CD Acts in England in 1886. Butler was also influential in mobilizing other feminist challenges to sex-work regulation in France, Belgium, and Switzerland (Machiels 2008: 195–205). Not only were their actions successful in practical terms, but campaigners managed to change the discourse around sex and sex-work.

Indigenous people were also active in both pushing for and against legislation regarding the policing of sexuality. One of the most controversial issues was the 1891 Age of Consent Act which raised the age of consent in India from ten to twelve years of age. The trial of Hari Mohan Maitee in Bengal in 1890 over the death of his child bride, Phulmoni, after brutal intercourse, was much publicized and a pivot point for the British mood of opinion. Maitee, a man of about thirty-five, was found innocent of rape as the current age of consent legislation stood at ten years of age, though he was found guilty of the more minor crime of causing "bodily harm" (Sinha 1995: 143). The legislation was read as a major affront to Hindu masculinity, particularly in Bengal where opposition to the Bill was at its strongest (Sinha 1995: 138–80). Indeed, it is seen as marking the start of a new era in the history of Indian Nationalism (Sinha 1995: 139). The most controversial elements of the Bill were the marital rape clauses and the refusal of the legislation to distinguish between the age of consent for married and unmarried girls. As Himani Bannerji has demonstrated, the sexualized body of the Indian woman or girl was at the heart of this discourse, there was almost "no mention" of her agency or volition in consenting to sexual intercourse (Bannerji 1988: 34). Opposition on the grounds of interference into the patriarchal structure of the Indian family found considerable sympathy among the British who were facing their own challenges to the patriarchal public sphere in the form of feminist challenges to the CD Acts and the feminist and purity campaigns for the British Criminal Amendment Act of 1885 (Sinha 1995: 153).

Feminism was an emergent theme across the period. As well as involvement around the social purity campaigns this period also saw the rise of other feminist campaigns from the efforts to improve women's education and access to the legal and medical professions to campaigns around divorce and property laws in Britain, France, Switzerland, Belgium, and Germany (Schröder 1995: 368–90). In Britain, successes included the Custody Act of 1839, the Matrimonial Causes Acts of 1857 and 1878, and the Married Women's Property Acts of 1870 and 1882. The campaign for the vote was led by women across the British Empire and involved considerable struggle including petitions, protests, and some militant tactics. Women first won the vote in New Zealand in 1893, South Australia in 1895, across Australia uniformly in 1902 for white women, in Canadian Federal elections in 1918, and only belatedly in Britain itself in 1918, for middle class women over the age of thirty, and in 1928 for all Englishwomen. Gender and race intersected in these campaigns. In Australia, Aboriginal women did not get the vote on the same terms as white women until 1962, while the fact that Maori women obtained the vote before their English counterparts was seen as so outrageous it was used in part as evidence in the British suffrage movement (Lake 1999).

At the same time, the attempt to "raise" the position of women of color could also be used by white feminists as a means to consolidate and extend their own place in the imperial hierarchy. The "plight" of the "Hindoo" woman was something of a cause célèbre for British women who, in mobilizing around *sati*, child marriage, and other issues were able to cast themselves as not only "liberated" but "civilised" (Midgley 2007: 65–92). As Antoinette Burton has demonstrated, it was not a coincidence that British feminism germinated at the same time as the British Empire flourished. The actions of British feminists were complicit with wider imperial goals (Burton 1994). Evoking the concept of "sisterhood," British women forged imaginative lines of connection with women of color that concealed structural inequalities. Motherhood was presented as a universal experience with which women across the globe could identify but was understood in profoundly Eurocentric ways. The need for "lady doctors" to "rescue" Indian women from the enclosed zenanas where they were forbidden to see male doctors, both facilitated the entry of women into the medical establishment and consolidated the spread of western reformist interventions into the zenana and biomedical practice (Burton 2011: 151–73). In the African and Pacific German colonies too, women who saw themselves first as German and then as female participated in colonial activities from nursing to missionary work (Wildenthal 2001). These processes of "imperial feminism" continue to shape the way in which the category of "woman" is constructed and contested today (Mohanty 1984: 333–58).

From a different perspective the histories of sexual emancipation and colonial emancipation may be argued to be linked. In his work on sexuality in the French colonies, Robert Aldrich suggests that the stigmatized position that homosexual French men occupied at home, could lead to identification and sympathy with the victims of colonization abroad, including support for anti-colonial resistance (Aldrich 2002: 217).

CONCLUSION

"The expansion of Europe," Ronald Hyam famously wrote, "was not only a matter of 'Christianity and commerce,' it was also a matter of copulation and concubinage" (Hyam 1990: 2). He argues that the British Empire provided an "unrivalled field" of "sexual opportunity" unavailable in the metropole, that it "unfroze restraint" and that without "sexual relaxation" the trials of running an empire would have "been intolerable" (Hyam 1990: 211, 90, 89). Hyam's rosy assessment of imperial relations has been rightly criticized by feminist scholars for its glossing over of the hugely exploitative dynamics of sexual practice (Berger 1988: 83–98; Voeltz 1996: 41–4; Bradford 1992: 209–14). His assertion that "sexual interaction between the British and non-Europeans probably did more long-term good than harm to race relations" fails to acknowledge that the "opportunities" he identifies for white male imperialists were had at the expense of others, not least indigenous women (Hyam 1990: 215). In turn Hyam has dismissed the work of feminist historians as "hugely over-preoccupied with rape" (Hyam 1988: 91). In this essay, I have painted quite a different picture of the sexual politics of empire where violence was indeed a recurrent and formative factor. What I have tried to do is to argue not so much that the European empires were sites of sexual freedom but that through the policing of sexuality, both discursively and through instruments of the state, difference was created, re-inscribed, and defended in colonial discourse. Sexuality was prolific in colonial discourses and while, as Robert Aldrich points out, much more work has been done on sexuality in the British and French cases than in the Belgium, Dutch, Italian, German, Spanish, or Portuguese empires, early indications suggest that this seems to be generally true across the European empires (Aldrich 2013). European empires were imagined as sites of sexual fantasy and lived as places where sexual relations were seeped with and contributed to the complex dynamics of colonial rule.

CHAPTER SEVEN

Resistance

Choices in Empire, 1780–1920

JENNIFER E. SESSIONS

Nineteenth-century resistance fighters figure prominently in the political cultures of postcolonial states. Men like the Algerian religious and military leader, Abd al-Qadir, who fought against European invasion two centuries ago, are national heroes today. Their portraits grace museum walls and outdoor murals; their names appear on street signs and public squares; stories of their military feats fill the pages of school textbooks and are recited at public holidays. These celebrations are meant to show what historian Terence Ranger called the "connexions between 'primary resistance movements' and modern mass nationalism" in opposing Western imperial domination: early armed resistance to conquest and rebellions against colonial rule laid the foundations for later, organized independence movements (Ranger 1968a,b). This connection can be seen vividly in the Algerian village of Aïn Torki, site of a small uprising against the French in 1901. Today, a set of three painted panels in the center of town portray Abd al-Qadir, who fought the French from 1832 to 1847, the leader of the 1901 revolt, and a nameless fighter of the Algerian War of Independence (1954–62). The panels, identical in format and style, are meant to show that Algerians never ceased fighting against French imperial domination, from the nineteenth-century period of conquest to the twentieth-century war of liberation (Figure 7.1).

Half a world away, in the Upper Midwest of the United States, another community celebrates Abd al-Qadir in service of a very different myth of anti-imperial resistance. Elkader, Iowa was founded in 1836 on land seized from the

FIGURE 7.1: Commemorative panel depicting Abd al-Qadir in Aïn Torki, Algeria, in 2016. Credit: Jennifer Sessions.

Sauk and Meskwaki peoples, but got its name a decade later when town fathers read about the exploits of the Algerian *amir* and saw parallels between Abd al-Qadir's *jihad* against the French and the American War of Independence from the British Empire. As the local tourist office now explains to visitors, Abd al-Qadir "fought desperately to drive out the French just as the colonists in America fought to drive out the British" (Northeast Iowa Tourism Association 2012). There is a deep irony in Euro-American colonists, whose presence in the upper Midwest was made possible by the expulsion of Native peoples, identifying with a man who fought to prevent European settlement in North Africa. But the founders of Elkader also ignored their namesake's imperial ambitions as much as they overlooked their own expansionist aspirations. As we will see, Abd al-Qadir's war against the French went hand-in-hand with a struggle for dominance in the central Maghreb, just like the fight for independence from Great Britain fueled American settlers' westward expansion into Native North America.

The naming of Elkader, Iowa embodies one of the main themes of this chapter: the contradictory character of resistance in the long nineteenth century. Especially in the first half of this period, between 1775 and 1850, anti-imperial resistance often fed the building of new empires. This critical period of transition in Western empires saw the "first decolonizations" in the Americas (Bayly 1989; Fisch 2015), as well as long struggles against European expansion in Africa, Asia, and Oceania. As soon as they had achieved their own independence, however, new settler nations, founded on the principles of self-determination, joined enthusiastically in the pursuit of continental and overseas empire. Resistance was always shaped by local circumstances, but was also embedded in broader global developments that could undermine as well as abet anti-imperial efforts.

This paradox reflects the difficulty of defining resistance in nineteenth-century empires.[1] The sorts of actions and behaviors categorized as "resistance" have varied along with historians' views of empire itself. For those, inspired by twentieth-century nationalists, who saw empire as a primarily political phenomenon, resistance meant armed struggles and organized movements for political independence. But broadening the understandings of empire has also meant broadening the range of activities recognized as resistance. Historians of slavery and of colonized societies point to labor conflicts and other, everyday actions that undermined colonial economies and hierarchies using what political scientist James Scott calls the "weapons of the weak" (1985). The field of postcolonial studies, which emerged in the 1980s and 1990s, takes language, culture, and social relations as fields of colonial power. From this perspective, cultural expressions or social practices that blurred distinctions between colonizer and colonized, celebrated cultures disdained by imperial "civilizing missions," or simply made colonized voices heard, could challenge imperial rule. If imperial discourses denied the agency of colonized and enslaved people, then subaltern agency, however micro in scale, constitutes a form of resistance.[2] Attention to the violence of colonial conquest, especially in the context of settler colonialism and its efforts to eliminate aboriginal people altogether (Wolfe 1999; Wolfe 2006; Veracini 2010), further expands definitions to encompass the very survival of indigenous peoples and their cultures.

Given these difficulties, rather than drawing a clear line between "resistance" and "acceptance" or "collaboration," it makes more sense to think about the "choices" (Sweets 1986) that subject peoples made and the strategies they adopted to contest imperial rule. Of course, there were always constraints on those strategies and choices. Within colonial societies, different individuals and groups had access to different material, institutional, and cultural resources. They often had different interests, too. If imperial states relied on flexible "repertoires of rule" to incorporate and manage their diverse populations (Burbank and Cooper 2010), it is helpful to take a similarly elastic view of resistance as a range of responses to incorporation and differentiation. On closer examination, even forms of resistance that fit the narrowest definition of armed struggle in pursuit of political autonomy turn out to contain multiple strategic choices. But as such, they also operated in a kind of feedback loop with strategies of imperial rule and dynamics of imperial expansion. This chapter, by mapping out these wider "repertoires of resistance" over the course of the long nineteenth century, emphasizes the ways that the Age of Empire emerged from the Age of Revolution.

Extending the chronological scope of the nineteenth century back into the closing decades of the eighteenth becomes especially necessary when we consider the ways that repertoires of resistance were conditioned by culture. Just as this chapter seeks to avoid stark oppositions between collaboration and resistance, so too it cautions against overdrawing distinctions between "cultural" and other approaches to imperial histories. The strategies and choices made by individuals and groups within nineteenth-century empires were always embedded in and shaped by what Kirsten McKenzie terms, "ways of thinking and being" (see Introduction, this volume). This was no less true of armies, treaties, and politics than of the art, ideas, religion, or daily life more familiar to cultural historians. Culture itself became an arena of contestation, but repertoires of resistance also drew on symbolic vocabularies and practices grounded in historical actors' cultural worlds. In the process, they transformed those vocabularies, generating new "ways of thinking and being" and new horizons of possibility for action. Considering repertoires of resistance in this sense, as political cultures, pushes us to recognize the fundamental impact of the Age of Revolution on the political imaginaries of the Age of Empire.

FIRST DECOLONIZATIONS

The most successful resistance movements of the long nineteenth century came at the very beginning of the period. Between the 1770s and 1820s, a wave of armed rebellions swept the Americas, dramatically reshaping the New World empires of Great Britain, France, Spain, and Portugal. Textbooks today describe these Atlantic uprisings as national "revolutions," but they were first and foremost revolts against imperial systems based on mercantilist trade restrictions and forced labor (Adelman 2008). They began as resistance movements *within*, rather than *against* European empires. What historians now call the "Age of Revolution" opened with efforts to reimagine imperial arrangements, not defiant claims to independence. In British North America, Iberian Central and South America, and the French Caribbean, colonial populations first tried to renegotiate their political and economic subjugation to European metropoles.

Creolized settlers, free people of color, enslaved Africans, and Native Americans turned to both familiar and novel modes of protest to press for rights as imperial subjects. Only when these efforts failed did they take up arms in pursuit of independence and what reluctant revolutionaries called, often with little appreciation for its ironies, "the empire of liberty."

Both native people and newly arrived white colonists had contested European domination from the time of Christopher Columbus's landing in the New World in 1492. But resistance intensified dramatically at the end of the eighteenth century, when the Spanish, Portuguese, French, and British all undertook significant reforms to stabilize their American empires. Increasingly strained by the costs of imperial defense, European governments imposed new taxes and customs duties, tightened restrictions on trade, and consolidated their control over colonial administration. The goal of these measures was to bolster European monarchs' claims to imperial grandeur and to geopolitical predominance in the Atlantic world. But they came at the expense of American-born colonists' influence in local affairs. To creole elites, who saw themselves as an integral part of larger imperial polities, colonial reform looked more like an unjust demotion to second-class status (Adelman 2006; Elliott 2006; Burbank and Cooper 2010).

When the British Parliament passed the Stamp Act of 1765 and then the Townshend Acts of 1767, for instance, North American colonists appealed to King George III to defend their rights as "freeborn Englishmen" (Bailyn 1967). Calling themselves "patriots," they demanded that Parliament respect constitutional guarantees against taxation without representation. In Spanish America, merchants and creole elites also presented themselves as "loyal vassals" of the king in complaints about the increased power of *peninsulares* from Spain in colonial affairs (Adelman 2006: 41). Like their counterparts in North America, they used traditional mechanisms, including petitions and royally sanctioned bodies like commercial guilds, to voice their discontent with increased taxation and commercial reforms. Even those who took up arms against reforming royal administrators in the 1780s stressed their undying loyalty to the monarchy. Participants in the 1781 Comuneros Revolt in New Grenada chanted "Death to bad government and long live the king!" as they marched against rising taxes, prices, and administrative "tyranny," while the largest Indian revolt in the colonial New World, the Túpac Amaru rebellion of 1780–3, began with the appearance of a mysterious placard on the wall of a Peruvian customs house proclaiming, "'Long live our great monarch—long live Carlos III and may all duty-collectors die'" (Adelman 2006: 49–50).

In the French Caribbean, colonists were similarly resentful of mercantilist trade restrictions and administrative curbs on local prerogatives. White planters and free people of color declared their patriotic attachment to the king in protests against restrictions on slave-owners' authority or expanded civic obligations. When free colored planters in Saint-Domingue refused to join a new colonial militia in 1769, they nonetheless assured white elites and royal officials "that they are faithful subjects of the King and good citizens" (quoted in Garrigus 2006: 133). In some cases, these appeals worked. British colonists won the repeal of the Stamp Act, for instance. But when they did not, colonists developed new strategies to push for changes to imperial regimes. The experience of these increasingly violent actions gave rise to new "American" identities and, ultimately, to revolution.

The Boston Tea Party perfectly illustrates this expanding political imaginary (Breen 2004; Carp 2010). By the end of the eighteenth century, tea had become a potent symbol of both Britishness and imperial injustice in British North America. Men and, especially, women prized tea-drinking as a sign of gentility and a pretext for social gatherings. But they resented the British East India Company's monopoly on tea imports and Parliament's heavy taxation of the quintessentially imperial beverage. From the 1760s, colonists began to attack customs officials, write pamphlets and newspaper articles, and petition authorities on both sides of the Atlantic. They also developed a new kind of consumer-based resistance: a widening boycott on the import and consumption of tea and other British consumer goods. As an anonymous "Woman" wrote in a Massachusetts newspaper, "in the present case the use of tea is considered not as a *private* but a *public* evil; . . . it is made a handle of to introduce a variety of public grievances and oppressions amongst us" (quoted in Carp 2010: 306).

It was to enforce this non-importation movement that colonial patriots, some dressed as "Mohawk" Indians and calling themselves the Sons of Liberty, overran three East India Company ships and dumped their precious cargo into Boston Harbor on December 16, 1773 (Figure 7.2). The harsh British response to this popular violence—closing Boston Harbor and shutting down local assemblies—spurred the colonists to call the First Continental Congress. The Congress delegates limited themselves to renewing the boycott and petitioning for reconciliation with, not separation from, Britain, but the British answered with force. British troops fired the opening shots of what would become the Revolutionary War, setting in motion the events that culminated in the Declaration of Independence in July 1776.

This unprecedented step, followed by the American colonists' even more unexpected military victory over the British army in 1783, added a powerful new weapon to the arsenal of creole resistance. Boosted by the French example after 1789, revolution and independence now became thinkable as responses to colonial frustrations. Spanish colonists initially rallied to King Ferdinand VII in his struggle against France during the Napoleonic Wars (1799–1815). But when they were not accorded equal representation in the Cortes (parliament) of 1810 or under the liberal constitution of 1812, radicals in Spanish America began to call for free, independent republics of their own. Over the next decade,

FIGURE 7.2: Colonial Patriots dressed as "Mohawks" dumping tea into Boston Harbor, engraving c. 1846. Courtesy Prints & Photographs Division, Library of Congress.

secessionist revolts broke out across South and Central America. By 1828, when Uruguay obtained its independence, all that remained of Spain's American empire were the Caribbean islands of Cuba and Puerto Rico (Adelman 2006; Elliott 2006). Brazil followed a different trajectory, but there too, efforts to maintain imperial ties collapsed when Portuguese liberals refused to accord the colony political influence proportional to its economic, demographic, and territorial dominance. The king, Dom Pedro I, fled Napoleon's invasion of Portugal, moving his capital to the "Tropical Versailles" of Rio. In 1822, he himself proclaimed the independent Empire of Brazil, rather than accede to Portuguese revolutionaries' demands for his return and the restoration of metropolitan administrative and commercial privileges (Bethell 1985; Paquette 2013).

The American wars of independence were not straightforward struggles between colonists and European rulers. Many in colonial societies opted for the monarchy, sparking internecine conflicts between patriots and loyalists (Jasanoff 2011). Revolutionary movements also split along lines of race and class. In Venezuela, the first Spanish colony to declare independence in 1811, the new independent republic collapsed into civil war within a year. The conflict pitted republicans, dominated by wealthy *criollos* (white descendants of Spaniards), against royalists supported by Indian peasants and *pardo* (people of mixed white, African, and Indian descent) pastoralists, who saw the king as their protector. In New Spain, an 1810 peasant rebellion of Indians and mixed-race *castas* launched by Catholic priest Miguel Hidalgo alienated creole elites (Figure 7.3). Hostile to Hidalgo's vision of social revolution, including the abolition of Indian tribute payments and ethnic distinctions, they joined with

FIGURE 7.3: Father Miguel Hidalgo proclaiming the independence of Mexico in 1810, engraving based on an 1830 lithograph. Courtesy New York Public Library.

Spanish-born *peninsulares* to crush the revolt. As historian J.H. Elliott writes, "their fear of social upheaval, as in Peru after the revolt of Túpac Amaru, proved stronger than their dislike of *peninsulares*" (2006: 381). Simón Bolívar was finally able to liberate Venezuela for good in 1821 by raising an army of creoles, mulattos, and slaves to whom he promised freedom in exchange for military service.

Bolívar was not the only American general to recruit slave fighters by offering them emancipation. The colonists and the British had both done the same in North America (Frey 1991). (British authorities also threatened to encourage a slave revolt in an effort to intimidate the southern colonies into loyalism.) This strategy for raising troops points to a final critical aspect of the first decolonizations: their dramatic limitations when it came to enslaved people and Native Americans (Davis 1999; Calloway 1995). Creole and settler revolutionaries succeeded only with the help of black slaves and indigenous allies, but largely excluded them from republican polities after independence. Like Boston's Sons of Liberty, settlers declared themselves the rightful Americans and constructed their new nation-states accordingly.[3]

STRUGGLES FOR FREEDOM

The most dramatic reimagining of the Atlantic empires' racial and political hierarchies arose from the slave revolt that began in the French Caribbean colony of Saint-Domingue in August 1791 and ended with the founding of the independent black republic of Haiti in 1804.[4] Forged by a coalition of African- and American-born laborers wielding a powerful combination of traditional modes of slave resistance and new revolutionary idioms, the Haitian Revolution was the only successful slave revolution in the New World and the most radical of the great Atlantic revolutions:

> By creating a society in which all people, of all colors, were granted freedom and citizenship, the Haitian Revolution forever transformed the world. It was a central part of the destruction of slavery in the Americas, and therefore a crucial moment in the history of democracy, one that laid the foundation for the continuing struggles for human rights everywhere.
>
> (Dubois 2004: 7)

It also paradoxically set in motion a chain of events that transformed and reinvigorated Western imperial ambitions around the globe. In the short term, the Haitian Revolution inspired enslaved people and bolstered emerging anti-slavery movements. But defeat in Saint-Domingue also led France to sell the Louisiana Territory to the United States, opening up vast new areas to slaveholding and European colonization. In the longer term, the blow the

Haitian revolutionaries struck to colonial slavery led European imperialists to imagine new, enduring forms of empire based on white emigration and settlement.

On the eve of the revolution, Saint-Domingue, on the island of Hispaniola, was the most valuable colonial territory in the Americas (Dubois 2004). The largest exporter of sugar and coffee in the world, it produced forty percent of the sugar and sixty percent of the coffee consumed in Europe. To power its eight thousand plantations, more African captives—some 685,000 between 1700 and 1791—were sent to Saint-Domingue than to any other American society than Brazil. Harsh labor (especially in sugar production), malnutrition, disease, and mistreatment took the lives of up to one-tenth of these enslaved workers annually. But by 1791, Saint-Domingue's half-million slaves still vastly outnumbered its 30,000 white colonists and 25,000 free people of color, or *gens de couleur*, many of them the children of white masters and enslaved women.

Enslaved men and women fought back against the dehumanization of bondage with classic forms of slave resistance, including shirking work and sabotaging equipment, running away, or *marronage*, poisoning masters, and outright rebellion (Craton 1982; Thornton 1998). Some used European legal systems to challenge their mistreatment or even their enslavement (Peabody and Grinberg 2007). The importation of thousands of captives, primarily from West Africa, gave rise to new black cultures combining African and European traditions. Religious belief systems mixing West African spirituality with Christianity played an especially important role in slave revolts, the most dramatic and, for whites, frightening form of slave resistance.

At a more personal level, slaves cultivated and treasured family ties as a critical source of social support against the physical and psychological hardships of enslavement. "Nations," or groups based on shared African geographical or ethnolinguistic origins also provided social organization and mutual aid. But some slaves sought refuge in suicide, during and after the Middle Passage. Historian Carolyn Fick notes that "slave women often resorted to abortion and even infanticide as a form of resistance rather than permit their children to grow up under the abomination of slavery" (1990: 48). In 1791, this existing repertoire was combined with new revolutionary ideals to create an explosively powerful new weapon: slave revolution.

Resistance to French policies came from other quarters, as well. White planters protested against royal reforms instituted in the mid–1780s to clamp down on slave abuse, smuggling, and locally elected colonial councils (Ghachem 2012). They were joined by lower-class whites, known as *petits blancs*, who jealously guarded their racial privilege against *gens de couleur*, many of whom owned substantial property, including slaves, plantations, and urban real estate. *Gens de couleur*, for their part, identified with French colonists and resented the racism that increasingly excluded them from full equality with whites. They lobbied the colonial ministry for changes to discriminatory racial codes, particularly mandatory service in the local police and militia responsible for policing slaves (Garrigus 2006).

Like their continental counterparts, these more privileged members of Saint-Domingue society initially expressed their complaints through existing channels and in the language of patriotic loyalty. White colonists and *gens de couleur* insisted they were devoted subjects of the king as they appealed to Paris for relief from "abusive" local officials. As the wealthy colored indigo planter and lobbyist Julien Raimond wrote to the colonial ministry in 1784, for instance, *gens de couleur* "were truly attached to the state by their religion, their possessions and by their feelings of patriotism" (quoted in Garrigus, in Geggus and Fiering 2009: 59), and thus deserved royal recognition.

The outbreak of revolution in France in 1789 added new practices to these traditional modes of protest. Whites and free men of color submitted *cahiers de doléances* (grievance lists) and elected deputies to metropolitan assemblies, formed local bodies to debate colonial reforms, and established committees to represent their interests in Paris (Dubois 2004; Ghachem 2012). In these forums, colonists, especially *gens de couleur*, proclaimed themselves "Patriots" entitled to equal rights under the Declaration of the Rights of Man and the Citizen issued in August 1789. Radical poor whites also adopted the "Patriot" label to denounce equality for *gens de couleur*. They used new colonial assemblies to push for stricter enforcement of laws discriminating against free people of color.

When Paris failed to resolve the question of free colored citizenship (an impossible task), legal expressions of discontent escalated into extralegal violence. In 1791, free men of color, led by a wealthy merchant named Vincent Ogé, and then poor whites revolted. Ogé and his comrades were quickly captured and executed, while poor white Patriots seized the capital, Port-au-Prince, killing the royal commander and forcing the government to flee. In May 1791, the National Assembly in Paris finally took action, voting to recognize some free men of color (property owners with free parents) as citizens. This compromise went too far for *petits blancs* and not far enough for *gens de couleur*, however, and fighting broke out between these two groups in the southern part of the island. It was in the midst of this unrest that black slaves launched a carefully organized mass revolt in the north. Horrified, the National Assembly first rescinded the May 1791 law and then, hoping to enlist them to fight against the slave rebels, extended full citizenship to all free blacks and free men of color.

The slave revolution that began on August 22, 1791 amplified familiar slave resistance tactics. The conspirators used habits of sociability among elite slaves, especially slave drivers, to disguise nighttime planning sessions as "dinners." At the final meeting, probably on the night of August 21, they gathered to seal their plan in a religious ceremony inspired by West African traditions, where assembled rebels swore an oath of secrecy and then drank the blood of a sacrificed pig. Religion played a critical role in the insurrection that began the next night, too (Dubois 2004). Insurgent troops marched on plantations and towns to the sound of African music and chants; slave fighters wore fetishes and carried talismans against enemy fire; rebel leaders staged religious ceremonies that incorporated Christian elements. Insurgents killed masters and overseers, as well as slaves who refused to join the revolt, burned plantation buildings and cane fields, and smashed sugar-manufacturing equipment. They targeted, "in short, every material manifestation of their existence under slavery and its means of exploitation" (Fick 1990: 97).

The ideology that helped make the slave revolt into a full-blown revolution drew on both French and African political ideas. Like revolutionaries in France, ex-slave leaders in Saint-Domingue insisted that their goal was "liberty," sometimes explicitly citing the "rights of man." But they also invoked King Louis XVI and declared themselves to be *gens du roi* (king's men) (Thornton 1993; Dubois 2004). Some even called for the restoration of the monarchy. Thanks in part to earlier imperial reforms, many slaves saw the king as a benevolent, paternal figure who defended them against their masters' cruelty. Saint-Domingue, like other slave colonies, had seen periodic rumors about royal emancipation decrees frustrated by colonial elites (Geggus 1997). As recently as August of 1791, rumors had circulated of a royal decree forbidding use of the whip and giving slaves three days off per week. As historian John Thornton shows, African-born slaves had visions of kingship rooted in military strength and social harmony that they translated into the new revolutionary context. This helps to explain why one rebel leader, Macaya, informed a French envoy "I am the subject of three kings: of the King of Congo, master of all the blacks; of the King of France who represents my father; of the King of Spain who represents my mother" (quoted in Thornton 1993: 181).

Macaya's inclusion of the King of Spain points to a last critical innovation in slave resistance in Saint-Domingue: international diplomacy. The outbreak of the French revolutionary wars in 1792 quickly drew Britain and Spain into the conflict in Saint-Domingue. This development presented insurgents with new opportunities and new choices.

Most important, war paved the way for the abolition of slavery. Both the Spanish, based in eastern Hispaniola, and the British saw the Saint-Domingue revolt as an opportunity to undermine French power in the Atlantic. Authorities in Spanish San Domingo offered unofficial support to the ex-slave rebels before beginning to openly recruit members of the ex-slave armies into their own ranks. Rebel commanders Jean-François and Biassou went over to the Spanish side with some 10,000 fighters, giving Spain a valuable auxiliary against France and reinvigorating the ex-slave forces. The British first blockaded and then, in September 1793, invaded the French colony. White planters, hoping to preserve slavery, forged an alliance with the invaders. "Turning to the enemy was a reasonable and a pragmatic choice for the planters," historian Laurent Dubois notes. "In the end, however, instead of saving slavery, it created the conditions for its final destruction. In making themselves traitors to the Republic, they opened the way for slaves to become citizens and defenders of France" (2004: 154).

Faced with this triple threat, revolutionary commissioners sent from Paris to restore order did what Simón Bolívar and other American leaders did: they offered slaves freedom in exchange for military service. In June 1793, commissioners Léger Félicité Sonthonax and Étienne Polverel promised that any enslaved man who took up arms for France would be freed and accorded full citizenship rights. Then, on August 29, 1793, they issued a far more radical general emancipation decree. Declaring "the French Republic wants all men to be free and equal with no color distinctions," the decree called upon liberated slaves to "defend the interests of the republic against kings" (in Dubois and Garrigus 2006: 122–3). This was an unprecedented step, but it was also a pragmatic decision in the context of the ongoing war for control of Saint-Domingue (Popkin 2011). And in practice, it was as much a recognition of slave rebels' self-liberation as it was an extension of French revolutionary principles to the colonies. When Parisian legislators voted in February 1794 to formally abolish slavery in all French territories, they were essentially ratifying an emancipation the Saint-Domingue rebels had already won for themselves.

French ideas did help convince the revolutionary government to accept universal liberation and the citizenship of former slaves, however. The radicals in power in Paris in 1794 welcomed colonial delegates carrying news of the emancipation decree. "It is time that we rise to the height of the principles of liberty and equality," one deputy declared (in Dubois and Garrigus 2006: 130). Indeed, Sonthonax and Polverel had been chosen for the Saint-Domingue mission because of their earlier criticisms of slavery and sympathies for the emerging French abolitionist movement.

The first French anti-slavery group, the Société des Amis des Noirs (Society of the Friends of Blacks), had been founded in Paris in 1788. It was part of a broader movement that developed in Europe and America at the turn of the nineteenth century. Abolitionists organized first and most extensively in the United States and Britain, where non-conforming Protestant sects built critical networks of anti-slavery activism. The Society of Friends, or Quakers, had publicly opposed slavery and the slave trade since the seventeenth century. American Quakers were the driving force behind the first US abolition society, organized in Philadelphia in 1775. British Quakers submitted the first anti-slavery petition to Parliament in 1783, and founded the first British abolition group, the Abolition Committee, or Society for the Abolition of the Slave Trade, in 1787. Women, in particular, played a key role in the Anglo-American anti-slavery movement well into the nineteenth century. They led consumer boycotts of sugar and other goods produced by slave labor, funded anti-slavery speakers and programs to aid enslaved people, and joined mass petition campaigns to push for legislative action to end slavery in the 1830s (Midgley 1992). Ex-slaves were also critical anti-slavery campaigners. Men and women like Oloudah Equiano, Mary Prince, Frederick Douglass, and Sojourner Truth wrote and spoke about their experiences of bondage, providing great moral weight to arguments against slavery and powerful intellectual claims to black freedom (Quarles 1969; Yee 1992; White 1999).

Western abolitionists were inspired by a mix of Enlightenment and Christian ideas about the unity of humankind and the evils of absolute authority, as well as the first stirrings of liberal economic thought (Davis 1999; Hall 2002; Brown 2006; Blackburn 2011). They criticized New World slavery as morally and politically corrupting, as well as economically inefficient. But early abolitionists also had limited ambitions. They focused their efforts on ending the slave trade, which they considered especially appalling. The trade was outlawed under a British-imposed international agreement of 1807, and then confirmed by the Peace of Paris that ended the Napoleonic Wars in 1815.

Only in the 1820s and 1830s did abolitionists begin to take aim at the institution itself, and even then, they moved with caution when it came to the liberation of enslaved blacks. Some worried about the economic consequences of emancipation and slave-owners' property rights. Others held racist ideas about Africans' supposed lack of civilization and thus advocated "gradual" emancipation, with mandatory waged labor and religious instruction to "prepare" them for freedom. The violence of the slave revolt in Saint-Domingue reinforced these anxieties about black freedom and citizenship.

In Saint-Domingue itself, emancipation was followed by a period of protracted international and internal struggle. The leadership of a mixed-race ex-slave, Toussaint Louverture (Figure 7.4) helped to turn these contests toward independence (James 1938). After fighting with the Spanish, Louverture joined the French when the abolition decree was ratified in May 1794. A skilled politician and military leader, he rose quickly to command French military and diplomatic operations against Spain and Britain, while fighting local rivals for power within the colony. In 1801, he grasped the opening created by Napoleon Bonaparte's seizure of power in France to draft a new constitution naming himself governor-for-life. This document reiterated the abolition of slavery, but it also imposed sharp limits on the freedom of emancipated blacks, requiring ex-slaves to continue working on plantations in order to restore sugar and coffee production (Dubois 2004).

Toussaint Louverture sought to redefine Saint-Domingue as an autonomous territory within the French empire, but this new arrangement proved too

FIGURE 7.4: Toussaint Louverture, engraving by Marcus Rainsford, 1805. Courtesy Schomburg Center for Research in Black Culture, Manuscripts, Archives and Rare Books Division, The New York Public Library.

radical for the French political imagination. In 1801, Napoleon dispatched a military expedition to retake control of the island. On arrival in 1802, the expedition's commander had Louverture arrested and deported to France, where he died in prison a year later. At the same time, in May 1802, Napoleon repealed the revolutionary abolition law and re-established slavery in the French colonies.

These measures, combined with French efforts to disarm ex-slaves, sparked renewed fighting. Ex-slaves began to flee plantations and desert to the enemy. Over the following year, decimated by desertion, brutal combat, and disease, the French expeditionary army disintegrated. By December 1803, when Napoleon finally gave up, only 8,000 of his original 43,000 European soldiers remained. On January 1, 1804, Louverture's lieutenant Jean-Jacques Dessalines, who had ruthlessly imposed his authority on former slave soldiers, declared Saint-Domingue to be the independent nation of Haiti. Dessalines addressed his fellow citizens in language that emphasized both freedom from slavery and new revolutionary conceptions of liberty:

> It is not enough to have expelled the barbarians who have bloodied your country for two centuries; it is not enough to have restrained those undying factions that one after another mocked the specter of liberty that France dangled before you. We must, with one last act of national authority, ensure forever the empire of liberty in the country of our birth; we take any hope of re-enslaving us away from the inhumane government that for so long kept is in the most humiliating stagnation. We must, at last, live independent or die (Dessalines 1804).[5]

Independence did not bring peace to Haiti. The new country was riven by civil strife and ex-slaves found themselves subjected to a new forced labor regime, despite constitutional guarantees against the restoration of slavery. But the very existence of an independent black state posed a powerful threat to racial hierarchies and white domination around the Atlantic world.

Colonial and slave-owning interests worked to fend off this threat. Great Britain, home to the most influential abolitionist movement, did not end slavery in its colonies until 1833, and even then, the Emancipation Act required a period of "apprenticeship," during which slaves would continue working for their masters. It also provided a sum of twenty million pounds (equal to over two billion today) to compensate slave owners for the loss of their human property. France finally abolished slavery for good after the Revolution of 1848 brought to power a radical government including one of the few French abolitionists to advocate immediate emancipation, Victor Schoelcher (Figure 7.5). But France, too, went to great lengths to compensate planters for their lost land and human property. In 1825, the restored French monarchy imposed a crippling, 150-million-franc indemnity on the new Haitian Republic in exchange for diplomatic recognition. By the end of the nineteenth century, half of the Haitian budget was going to France and to French banks to cover service on loans taken out to pay this sum (Dubois 2012).

Newly independent creole republics in the Americas proved equally resistant to emancipation (Blackburn 2011). In Simón Bólivar's Venezuela, the white, commercial elite that retained power after independence relied on slave labor to power the country's cacao and coffee plantations. They also feared the prospect of a political and social alliance between emancipated slaves and the non-white *pardos* who made up the majority of the population. Black slaves who had not traded military service for emancipation thus remained in bondage in Venezuela until 1854, when slavery was finally abolished. Although Mexico,

FIGURE 7.5: Religious ceremony celebrating the abolition of slavery in Martinique in 1850. Courtesy J. Paul Getty Museum Open Content Program.

the Federal Republic of Central America (later Nicaragua, Honduras, Costa Rica, Guatemala, El Salvador, Panama, and Belize), Chile, and the Dominican Republic abolished slavery in the 1820s and Uruguay did so in 1842, abolition in the rest of South America waited until the 1850s and 1860s. Brazil resisted pressure to end the slave trade until 1850, and indeed Brazilian independence actually spurred a boom in slave exports from Portuguese enclaves in Central Africa. Almost 2.5 million captives were shipped to Brazil between 1800 and 1850, and Brazil did not abolish slavery itself until 1888.

In the United States, it took a brutal civil war (1860–5) to put a legal end to slavery. Here, the period between the Haitian Revolution and the American Civil War saw a dramatic expansion of slavery. This was one of the greatest paradoxes of the revolutionary era. The victory of ex-slaves in Saint-Domingue pushed Napoleon Bonaparte to negotiate the sale of the Louisiana Territory to the United States in 1803, opening up vast new spaces to slaveholding (Dubois 2007). An influx of refugees from Saint-Domingue, including slave owners and their slaves, and free people of color, into US cities pushed Americans to reaffirm their commitment to slavery (White 2010).

The expansion of slavery in the United States was only one of the ways that the Haitian Revolution reshaped Western empires. It hardened the resolve of slave owners, but it also inspired slaves to fight for their freedom throughout the nineteenth century. The example of Saint-Domingue was an important factor in slave revolts in Cuba in 1812, Barbados in 1816, Demerara in 1823, and Jamaica and the United States in 1831 (Ferrer 2014; Clavin 2010). In the process, the Haitian Revolution also prompted Europeans and Americans to develop new visions of empire. Repressing slave resistance was costly, and abolitionist pressure was increasing. Together, these forces drove a momentous shift in Western imperial imaginaries toward white settlement in the middle decades of the nineteenth century.

EMPIRES OF LIBERTY

The first decolonizations broke imperial bonds but did little to alter colonial societies' reliance on forced labor and racial hierarchies (see Chattopadhyaya, Spieler, and Fitzpatrick in this volume). White elites included non-whites—Indians, people of mixed race, and, more rarely, blacks—as "Americans" when they wanted to oppose intervention from overseas. But at home, they distanced themselves from and marginalized the non-white masses (Gobat 2013). Equally important, they used their newfound autonomy to launch new imperial conquests. As modern nationalism took hold in both Europe and its former American colonies, empire-building came to be seen as one of the hallmarks of the modern nation-state. For Haitian revolutionaries, the "empire of liberty" meant a new era of freedom for a nation of formerly enslaved people. For Western imperialists, the phrase signaled renewed conquest and the subjugation of millions of Native Americans, Africans, and Asians.

Through much of the century, these conquests aimed at the acquisition of land for white colonists (Weaver 2003). In Anglophone North America, United States independence and, later, home rule in Canada were followed by accelerated westward expansion. In shaking off British control, American colonists had also shaken off imperial controls (however limited) on white settlement in the interior of the continent. Tensions continued between eastern elites and frontier settlers after independence, but expansion into Indian Country became key to US national identity. As President Thomas Jefferson wrote in 1809, the new country was destined to build "such an empire for liberty as she has never surveyed since the creation." This belief in inevitable continental domination, later called Manifest Destiny, drove American colonization policy throughout the century. The United States laid claim to ever-expanding swathes of Native territory and forcibly removed people from land coveted by white settlers.

Similar convictions underpinned a dramatic extension of settler colonization by European powers, which increasingly saw emigration and settlement overseas as solutions to both the moral problem of colonial slavery and the domestic social problems associated with industrialization and urbanization (Bell 2007; Sessions 2011). Between 1815 and 1930, some sixty million Europeans left the continent for other shores. Half of them went to the booming United States, but the majority of the rest went to new or expanding settler colonies, including French Algeria, British Australia, Canada, Kenya, and South Africa, or German Southwest Africa and Tanganyika (Baines 1991).

Indigenous populations in all of these places were subjected to similar policies designed to strip them of their land and stamp out their cultures, including languages, religions, and economic ways of life. Settler colonialism aimed to eliminate native people and replace them with immigrant settlers. The realization of these goals varied with the density of white settlement and the vulnerability of local people, especially to imported diseases. But this basic logic has led some historians to consider settler colonialism to be genocidal (Wolfe 2006; Veracini 2010).

The genocidal impulses of settler colonialism confronted indigenous people with new and terrible choices. Native peoples could fight back against expropriation and removal, try to negotiate (relatively) favorable treatment, harass settler farms and villages, withdraw beyond the frontier of settlement, or do their best to stay put and reach some sort of "accommodation" with the colonial state. Each of these choices carried risks, however: military defeat and loss of life, the betrayal of treaty terms, collective punishment for raids, conflict with the people on whose lands they sought shelter, or cultural assimilation. And regardless of the choices, colonization was accompanied by brutal violence. Both physical and cultural, that violence could be directed outward to expel foreign invaders but also inward to crush local rivals or enforce local hierarchies.

Periods of conquest carried the most uncertainty, as well as the greatest array of possible choices. Imperial invasion often disrupted existing balances of power. The resulting unrest and power vacuums created opportunities for aggressive or ambitions locals. In North America, for example, tribes like the Sioux and the Comanche built their own empires at the margins of European expansion (Ostler 2004; Blackhawk 2008; Hämäläinen 2008). So too did leaders in Algeria, where we can see the range of strategies deployed in response to French conquest in the middle decades of the century.

At the beginning of the nineteenth century, Algiers was formally part of the Ottoman empire. Its governors paid tribute to the sultan, but in practice enjoyed significant autonomy from Constantinople and depended heavily on local auxiliaries to exercise their power. When the restored French monarchy ordered the invasion of Algiers in 1830, in an effort to counter its deep unpopularity at home, these diverse local powers responded with both "acts of resistance" and "attempts at accommodation" (McDougall 2017: 50). The governor in Algiers, Dey Husayn signed a capitulation agreement on July 5, 1830 and went into exile, but Ahmad, bey of eastern Constantine province, determined to continue defending Ottoman authority. The bey of central Titteri province opted for accommodation, agreeing to accept French suzerainty. And in the west, Hassan Bey accepted defeat and fled to Egypt. Ordinary people responded in similarly diverse ways. Civilians abandoned Algiers to escape bombardments and fighting, while the city's elites pressed for peace and order. Some Jewish and Muslim notables maneuvered to advance their own interests, putting themselves forward as intermediaries between the French and the local population. Others imagined new political arrangements that would accord Algerians "the right to enjoy freedom and every advantage enjoyed by the nations of Europe" (Hamdan ben Uthman Khoja, quoted in McDougall 2017: 53).

French king Charles X's political gambit failed, and he was overthrown shortly after Husayn capitulated. But his successor adopted a policy of "total" conquest and settlement colonization, dramatically increasing French pressure on Algerian politics and society. The European settler population grew rapidly, reaching 125,000 by 1850, while the war devastated Algerian society. As French military operations and colonization expanded, requisitioning, property seizures, and brutal violence affected ever-greater numbers of people. The precolonial population of about 4 million fell by almost half, to 2.3 million, by the mid-1850s, before slowly beginning to recover (Kateb 2001). Tribal leaders responded to the catastrophe differently. Some revolted, alone or in regional alliances; some offered cooperation in return for recognition of their local privileges; some emigrated to places beyond the reach of French arms, whether in the Algerian hinterlands or in neighboring Morocco and Tunisia (Clancy-Smith 1994). Some seized on the collapse of the Ottoman state to throw off regional authorities or to raise their own status within local hierarchies of power.

The most famous of these leaders was Abd al-Qadir ibn Muhyia al-Din al-Hasani, who espoused all of these strategies in a protracted struggle against the French in the 1830s and 1840s (Danziger 1977; McDougall 2017). In 1832, religious and political leaders in west-central Algeria elected the young scholar-warrior to lead a *jihad* against both foreign invasion and domestic disorder. As *amir al mu'minin* (commander of the faithful), Abd al-Qadir drew on his spiritual authority (his father was the regional head of a powerful Sufi Muslim brotherhood) and military prowess to legitimize his authority. For fifteen years, he fought and negotiated with the French, while building his own modernizing state. He used promises of justice and threats of collective punishment to command tribal allegiance and raise troops for war against the French army. At other times, the *amir* turned to diplomacy, signing treaties with the French in 1834 and 1837 that recognized his sovereignty in western Algeria and allowed him to consolidate his power over the tribes. When the military tide began to turn in the early 1840s, an alliance with the sultan of Morocco provided Abd al-Qadir military aid and then, after the defeat of his armies in 1844, a haven. Only when that alliance failed—the sultan became increasingly wary of Abd al-Qadir's popularity and ambition—was the Algerian leader forced to leave Morocco and, in December 1847, to surrender to French authorities. But even after his imprisonment in France, later exile in Syria from 1853, and death in 1883, Abd al-Qadir offered Algerians a symbolic rallying point against outside domination.

As colonization advanced, religion continued to provide a powerful resource for subject peoples in Algeria and elsewhere. Nineteenth-century Algeria saw no fewer than fifteen millenarian revolts led by local holy men claiming to be the *mahdi* or *mawl al-sa'a* (master of the hour), messianic figures whose arrival heralded the end of time (Haddad 2010). Other religious leaders chose "paths of accommodation." In Muslim North and West Africa, the *shaykhs* of Sufi brotherhoods carved out a certain degree of autonomy for themselves by acceding to French rule and steering their followers away from armed resistance (Clancy-Smith 1994; Robinson 2000).

Religious revivals and reform movements informed resistance, but also provided a way to cope with conquest by revitalizing indigenous societies. In North America, for example, the Plains Sioux maintained their spiritual practices despite a US government ban on Native religions and efforts to assimilate them to American ways of life through schools, police, courts, and missionary churches. In the 1880s, Sioux embraced the syncretic millenarian religion known as the Ghost Dance (Ostler 2004). The Ghost Dance was inspired by a prophecy of the Northern Paiute visionary Wovoka (Jack Wilson) that if Indians lived cleanly, put aside their martial ways, and performed extended circle dances, the dead would return to life and white control over the West would evaporate. Wovoka preached anti-militarism, but the movement signaled Indians' refusal to surrender to cultural assimilation. Its inherently anti-colonial implications were reflected in the alarmed response of settlers and US government agents, who arrested chiefs and, most notoriously, massacred the Miniconjou band of Lakota Sioux at Wounded Knee Creek in 1890, in their efforts to halt the dancing.

Especially in settler colonies where assimilation policies, including the forcible enrollment of indigenous children in state-run and missionary boarding schools (Jacobs 2009), aimed to extinguish indigenous cultures, religious revival was one of many cultural responses to colonization. Women often played a key role in the conservation, transmission, and adaptation of Native cultural practices. For instance, even after most members of the American Kiowa tribe moved from the southern Plains to a reservation in Oklahoma in 1867, Kiowa women passed beadwork techniques and patterns down to new generations of girls, while also developing new designs to cater to a growing market of white tourists (Rand 2008) (Figure 7.6). Despite the powerful forces arrayed against them, native people everywhere found creative ways to adapt to changing circumstances, preserving existing political, social, economic, and cultural practices and cultivating new ones. In the so-called empires of liberty that

FIGURE 7.6: Two Kiowa women at the 1898 Trans-Mississippi and International Exhibition in Omaha, Nebraska, photographed by Frank Rinehart. Courtesy Boston Public Library.

transformed the globe in the nineteenth century, these acts of survival and creation themselves constituted a powerful form of resistance. As Native American journalist Ruth Hopkins recently put it, even today, "Every Native born into this world is a victory against colonialism & attempted genocide. You are the resistance" (Hopkins 2015).

CONCLUSION

Resistance is always a slippery, multiform phenomenon in imperial history. But in the long nineteenth century, as Europe's early modern Atlantic empires collapsed and spawned new imperial imaginaries, its ambiguities were particularly sharp. Taking a narrow view of resistance as the pursuit of political sovereignty, the most successful resisters of the period were the creole settlers who seceded from Britain, Spain, and Portugal between 1770 and 1830. But the Age of Revolution gave rise almost immediately to a new Age of Empire, as newly emancipated settler republics launched their own empire-building projects. Despite the dramatic victory of slave revolutionaries in Haiti, colonists elsewhere used their independence to defend slavery and conquer native territory. The westward expansion of the United States was only one part of a global explosion of white emigration and settlement from the mid-nineteenth century onward. By 1900, European colonists in Algeria, South Africa, Australia, and elsewhere were agitating in their turn for greater autonomy within their respective empires, in order to more strictly enforce racial hierarchies and settler privileges (Reynolds and Lake 2008b). This growth of settler colonialism, along with the more familiar economic exploitation associated with the New Imperialism of the late nineteenth century, called forth new responses from the peoples displaced and brought under western domination. As the repertoires of empire shifted, so too did colonial subjects' repertoires of resistance.

CHAPTER EIGHT

Race

MATTHEW P. FITZPATRICK

INTRODUCTION

Just prior to the First World War, Germany's Colonial Secretary Wilhelm Solf led an (in the end failed) attempt to insert racial criteria into Germany's citizenship laws (Gosewinkel 2003, 303–9). Attempting to persuade the Reichstag's recalcitrant Social Democrats and Catholic Centre Party deputies of the merits of a race law, Solf argued that the experience of other powers in colonial sites such as Brazil, the Dutch Indies, and British India had revealed the political dangers of unrestricted racial mixing and formal political racial equality. In particular, Solf argued, the United States had demonstrated precisely how allowing non-whites citizenship rights could lead to, in his mind, perverse political outcomes:

> Gentlemen, the 13th Amendment of the Constitution of the United States and Lincoln's Emancipation Edict are portents of warning to all colonising nations . . . The recognition of the Negro as a white citizen . . . has led in America to enormous consequences. Now the Negro is free! He can even become President, if he is not lynched first! (*Hilarity*) . . . Gentlemen I urge you to allow the naked facts to work on you. You are sending your sons to the colonies. Do you wish that they bring back black daughters-in-law to you, to your homes? Do you want them to lay woolly-haired grandchildren in cradles for you? (*Hilarity*) Much worse; . . . would you like white girls to return with Hereros, with Hottentots and Bastards as husbands? No, gentlemen, let these facts work upon your instincts as Germans, as whites! The entire German nation will thank you, if you have no other consideration than this: we are German, we are white and we want to remain white. (VdR 1912, 1648–9)

Paradoxically, at the time of this speech Solf enjoyed a reputation as having been one of the most humane, liberal, and indeed anti-racist of Germany's colonial governors. Not only had Solf previously argued that it was "tasteless and lacking in racial tact to use skin color as the criterion for making legal distinctions," he had given both of his children Samoan names, and while governor he had presented himself to Samoans as a Samoan chief (Steinmetz 2007, 351–4). His liberal stance on racial issues as governor of Samoa in the late nineteenth and early twentieth centuries had seen him lambasted by the nationalist-liberal German press as presiding over an interracial "colonial swamp" (BA Berlin R1001/3066, 133).

In many ways, Solf personifies the contradictions of racialized imperial encounters at the end of the nineteenth century. These encounters ranged from an acceptance of intercommunal and (in the language of the day) interracial approaches to trade, marriage, law, and cultural practices, through to a strong commitment to racial separation, social exclusion, domination and, in some cases, genocidal elimination. Notwithstanding the overarching, material logic of imperial conquest and displacement, which offered absolute limits to the scope for building intercommunal cultural ties, many colonial sites, indeed many colonists, oscillated between the two poles of interracial co-operation and racial exclusion, with some even integrating elements of both approaches simultaneously. These varying cultures of race and racial relations in the long nineteenth century's age of imperialism is the subject of this chapter. After looking at the emergence of racial theory in the colonial metropoles of Europe, this chapter will examine the degree of colonial heterogeneity, to see how differing cultures of racialization functioned in a variety of imperial settings.

DISCOURSES OF RACE AT THE IMPERIAL METROPOLE

Understanding precisely how "race" was understood and used in nineteenth-century imperial sites is difficult, because of the range of interchangeable synonyms that were used to describe it. Not just in English, the terms "nation," "people," and "race" were all used to describe a sprawling set of intermingling understandings regarding cultural, political, religious, linguistic, and phenotypical differences. These terms, so carefully parsed in the twentieth century, were less carefully used by nineteenth century scholars and were often virtually synonymous in standard usage. By the time the nineteenth century had begun, the word "race" was already frequently being used to describe clearly cultural differences, while "nation" and "people" were often used to describe a hierarchical ordering of peoples on the basis of observable phenotypical differences.

At the level of metropolitan high culture, the Enlightenment thinker Immanuel Kant has been credited by some as having "invented" race, or at least its Eurocentric encoding, with his 1775 essay "On the Different Races of Men" (Bernasconi 2001; Bernasconi 2002; Larrimore 2008). This claim, however, should be treated with care, given that as early as 1734 France's Enlightenment thinker Voltaire had offered a vehemently racist theory which posited that black Africans were a different and inferior species to Europeans. So too the central philosopher of the Scottish Enlightenment, David Hume, had argued in 1753 that he considered "negroes and in general all the other species of men . . . to be naturally inferior to the whites" (Poliakov 1982). Nonetheless, it is true that Kant postulated the biologically essentialist position that observable, racial differences dictated or at least predicted behaviors. In the early 1780s he also argued that the enslavement of non-Europeans was permitted, because "[Native] Americans and Negroes cannot govern themselves. Thus they serve only as slaves" (Kleingeld 2007; Mikkelsen 2012).

Kant's views on race did not go unchallenged, with Johann Gottfried Herder emerging as Kant's most formidable critic. At issue between them was Kant's insistence that race and human progress were linked, and that it was only through serving "progress" (defined in European terms) that humans could be separated from lower animals. Herder, on the other hand argued that no "comparative, context transcending evaluative judgements can be made since every culture has to be understood on its own terms" (Mertel 2014, 397). Seemingly devoid of a guiding teleology for social development, Herder's concept of the human condition infuriated Kant, who offered a bitter and racialized critique of Herder's apparent cultural relativism. To counter Herder, Kant critiqued the cultural state of the peoples of the Pacific (who had come to the attention of Europeans during the age of exploration) through the lens of an Enlightenment belief in monolinear global progress. Given the Eurocentric framing of his notion of progress, Kant unsurprisingly found Pacific cultures wanting:

> Does [Herder] really mean that if the happy inhabitants of Tahiti were never visited by more civilized nations, and were destined to live in their quiet indolence for thousands of centuries, one could give a satisfactory answer to the question why they bothered to exist at all, and whether it would not have been just as well that this island should have been occupied by happy sheep and cattle as by happy men engaged in mere pleasure.

More tellingly, Kant argued elsewhere along the same lines that, "the world would not lose anything if Otaheite perished" (Berry 1982, 52).

Like Kant, Georg Wilhelm Friedrich Hegel also differentiated between Europeans and non-Europeans, albeit in cultural rather than overtly biological terms. Echoing Kant, Hegel argued that the world was divided between the cultured peoples of history (*Kulturvölker*), and natural peoples outside history

(*Naturvölker*). His culturally chauvinist world history dictated that "civilised nations" were entitled to "regard and treat as barbarians other nations which are less advanced than they are . . . in the consciousness that the rights of those other nations are not equal to theirs" (Guha 2002, 35–42). Despite his knowledge of the slave revolution in Haiti in the 1790s and the first years of the nineteenth century, and his immersion in contemporary ethnological literature on Africa, Hegel persisted in his view that a long apprenticeship in civilization was necessary before the slavery of "non-historical" Africans could be ended (Bernasconi 1998; Buck-Morss 2000). Deeply dismissive of African culture as a whole, Hegel nonetheless repeatedly stressed individual cultural adaptability to European norms and rejected intrinsic biological difference as an explanation for social variation (Bonetto 2006).

Following in the wake of Kant, Voltaire, Hume, and Hegel, however, a host of other more explicitly racial thinkers emerged around the globe who steadily built up a corpus of biologically racist theoretical works that gradually displaced the often more culturally framed discussions of the Enlightenment. One such thinker was the German Johann Friedrich Blumenbach, who, while following the Bible in arguing for a single human species, posited the existence of five different racial categories within it (Blumenbach 1865). Building on this (and other Blumenbach-inspired ethnologists such as Britain's James Cowles Prichard), the mid-century French novelist and biological racist Arthur de Gobineau wrote his highly influential "Essay on the Inequality of Human Races" which popularized pseudo-scientific notions such as the potential for racial degradation through race mixing, the superiority of the Aryan racial type, and the centrality of blood purity to human progress (Gobineau 1983).

In the racial battleground of the United States, Josiah Nott re-tooled Gobineau's work (which he said had afforded him "much pleasure and instruction" [Nott 1856]), in order to preach his own brand of polygenesis, asserting that "the Anglo-Saxon and Negro races are, according to the common acceptation of the terms, distinct species" (Nott 1843, 254) (Figure 8.1). Gradually, entire academic disciplines such as ethnology, anthropology, and biology began to incorporate the new science of biological racism into their work, creating a discursive edifice that not only referred to the phenotypical markers of Europeanness (particularly whiteness), but linked these to older, cultural notions of world historical progress and civilizationary hierarchies. This idea, that Europeans were innately superior vessels for the progress of world history, offered European imperialists philosophical cover for the material rapacity of their global empires.

Other landmark figures of European biological science which had a colonial afterlife are well known: works such as Charles Darwin's *The Descent of Man*, plus the gradual acceptance of Mendelian genetics offered the intellectual building blocks for anthropologists such as Eugen Fischer to postulate the need

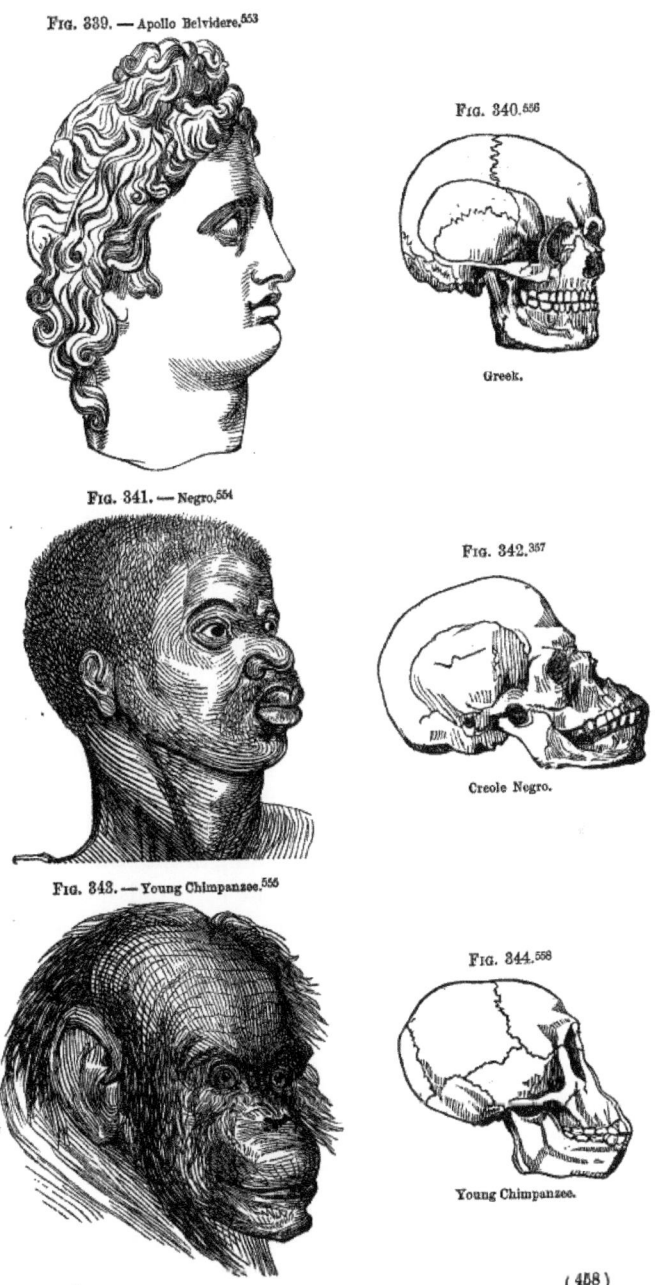

FIGURE 8.1: "Racial types" as per Josiah Nott and George Glidden's work *Types of Mankind*, 1854. Courtesy University of Michigan library.

for active state control over the racial profile of colonial populations (Weindling 2010). Cesare Lombroso's concept of degeneration and atavistic regression in his 1876 *L'uomo delinquente* would also play its part, although perhaps more in the analysis of Europe's own underclasses than in the colonies (Lombroso 1876). Importantly, however, the gestation period for such innovations was a long one, with Fischer not applying this mid-century, metropolitan biological science to his fieldwork in German Southwest Africa until 1908. Far from inspiring new racial directions in colonial management, his publications in 1913 and thereafter came too late to be of use to German colonists, who had lost their colonies in the First World War. Arguably, anthropological science was guided by observed colonial practices and cultures of racialized rule, rather than the other way around (Fischer 1913).

Nevertheless, the intellectual shift towards biological racism in European humanities disciplines such as anthropology and ethnology was discernible much earlier than in politics. One scholarly symptom of this was the collection of the remains of indigenous people which were sent to Europe for study by physical anthropologists. These stolen remains were measured, compared, and contrasted in an attempt to designate interrelationships, but also to establish a human hierarchy. In some instances, such as the 1904 Herero-Nama wars in German Southwest Africa, genocidal colonial warfare and the collection of human remains overlapped, with the remains of deceased inmates of the German concentration camps sent to Germany to facilitate this "scientific" study of racial types (Zimmerman 2003).

Perhaps the most extreme version of an overtly biological view of race prior to the First World War came at the very opening of the twentieth century, with Alfred Ploetz. In his 1904 introduction to the first edition of his new journal, *Archive for Racial and Social Biology*, Ploetz proposed a philosophical basis for racial thought. "The old dualistic view, that in our body there is a free spirit that is scarcely constrained from unfurling its wings by bodily life and attains ultimate freedom in the spiritual heights of pure spirit once the physical has been extinguished, no longer has a place in the modern mind . . . Today we base ourselves more and more on the basis of monism, the unity of the spiritual and the physical" (Ploetz 1904, 2–3).

According to Ploetz, philosophical monism offered a new ontological basis for answering questions of race. For Ploetz, the old dualist assertion of a divide between the mind and biology had erroneously led some to postulate that it was possible to transcend biology through an intellectual or spiritual shift. Dualists, he argued, had assumed that belonging to a nation or civilization was a matter of making a cultural, even spiritual commitment. Such views were indeed popular in the 1880s, with Moritz Lazarus and (plagiarizing Lazarus) Ernst Renan having both argued that nations were primarily a product of a nationalist sensibility rather than biology (Lazarus 2008; Renan 1990). For monists such as Ploetz, however, social belonging was strictly a matter of biology and race. On this basis, he argued that the only form of transcendence possible in the new secular world came in the form of a "life carrying" race that could perpetuate the biological materials of its constituent parts into an enduring collective. According to this view, the individual found existential meaning through his or her contribution to the species being of the racial whole, not through cultural expressions of belonging:

> What is the enduring corporeal carrier of life? It is not the individual, whose form of life decays. It belongs with a multiplicity of similarly shaped individuals, who bind themselves together and give birth to new individuals from and alongside them, in order to maintain the living form over time. This multiplicity of like individuals . . . represents in a morphological sense the actual enduring life bearer that we morphologically call 'race' (Ploetz 1904, 5–6).

The relationship between race and society, according to Ploetz was that: "Race provides the biological base for society" with society constituting "a part-phenomenon within the race." According to Ploetz, it was the role of practitioners of racial hygiene to ensure that individuals did not hinder the development of the race, by passing on their defects to the next generation (Ploetz 1904, 24–6).

LOCALIZING CULTURES OF RACIALIZATION

The metropolitan shift from a cultural to biological understanding of race continued up to and beyond the First World War (Bernasconi and Lott 2000). Yet it is important to note that such biologically bounded theories of race were far more prevalent in the academy than society at large and were not necessarily central to frontier imperial practice in the nineteenth century. Notwithstanding the familiarity that some educated colonial authorities had with metropolitan philosophies of race, the historical record of racialized encounters in imperial settings reveals improvised approaches to racial questions that accorded with the needs of the settler population rather than doctrinal or philosophical purity; both in terms of how individuals lived their lives and how colonial governments administered their territories.

To be clear, all nineteenth-century empires were racialized, in the sense that phenotypical differences held a locally understood socio-political significance. Yet precisely what the significance of race was in different empires or different colonial sites within an empire did not remain constant. Despite their structural family resemblances and their shared metropolitan centers, different colonies, even within the same empire approached the question of race very differently.

As a result, understanding how race functioned in Western empires requires close, individual attention to the differing cultures of race and racialization in each individual colonial site over time. Not only were there well understood differences in the possibilities for racial relations in settler colonies, plantation colonies, and extraction point trade colonies, there were also other highly individuating features that require consideration. These include the colony's location, scale, density of population, the cultural similarity or dissimilarity of the colonizers and the colonized, the pre-existing social relations of the colony, the relative political, military, or economic strength of the colonizers and the colonized, as well as the value of the colony in strategic, economic, demographic, or political terms to the imperial power that controlled it.

Beyond this, global and regional contexts changed markedly throughout the century and how race functioned in a particular colony in 1800 was not the same as in the same colony in 1900. While the nineteenth century more or less saw the formal end of the slave trade and slavery, it also saw the upswing in so-called "Kanaka" labor (and the concomitant practice of "blackbirding," or kidnapping laborers) in the Pacific, as well as the sprouting of semi-free "coolie" labor from China and East India, albeit it on a more modest scale than African slavery (Speedy 2015; Cullen 2012). Some colonies had flared into open racial warfare during this period; perhaps most famously in Tasmania's and Queensland's "Black Wars" from the 1820s and 1830s, the mid-century American expansion into California, and the Anglo-Māori New Zealand Wars; yet others simply did not (Clements 2014; Madley 2016). While empires always enacted forms of structural domination designed to advantage the imperial power of the colonizers, the role that race played in establishing and maintaining the structural inequalities of any given empire is best understood at the level of the particular colonial site rather than through the type of universal discourse proffered by Kant, Gobineau, or Ploetz, even if various colonizers in particular sites declared that how they were operating reflected a set of universally accepted principles regarding racial difference.

This understanding, that race might best be examined through local cultures of racialization in specific imperial sites rather than through metropolitan discourse analysis, has recently re-emerged after almost three decades of scholarly focus on overarching questions related to race and empire, work that has sought what Ann Laura Stoler once called "the implicit racial grammar" of imperial order (Stoler 1995, 12). Perhaps unintentionally, this earlier work on imperial discourse often fused the multifarious ways that "race" functioned into an overarching, epochally distinct structure of racism that Michel Foucault might have called an "episteme" or "discursive formation" (Foucault 2002a, xviii–xxiv; Foucault 2002b, 69–75). More recently, however, scholars have started to shift away from this universalizing approach, towards studying the heterogeneity of racializing processes that neither conformed to the discursive regimes of the metropole nor necessarily mirrored simultaneous developments in other colonies of the same empire, or in the colonial sites of other powers. Bart Luttikhuis (for example) has convincingly critiqued Stoler's insistence that "'European' identity in the Indies was a *racial* identity." It would be a mistake, he argues, to take race as "the *a priori* starting point for the deconstruction of historical categories, even when 'race' was a term mostly shunned at the time." For Luttikhuis, Stoler's approach "has a tendency to link all discriminating practices to the concept of race, blinding itself to the possibility that other categories may sometimes predominate." Quite effectively, he argues against dissolving all forms of imperial hierarchy into the category of "race," encouraging historians to study "*which* discriminatory categories dominated in *which* situations and for what reasons" (Luttikhuis 2013, 540–1).

With this in mind, historians are inching forward empirically, engaging in what Iris Clever and Willemijn Ruberg have called "praxiography" (Clever and Ruberg 2014), a historiographical practice that encourages the close study of individual cultures of race. This new work begins from the jarring ontological starting point offered by Linda Martin Alcoff that "race is real" (and that it has been experienced historically in concrete sites as real), while the social encoding of visible physical differences is certainly not fixed (Alcoff 2005). Indeed, it is this lack of fixity in the social encoding of phenotypical difference that makes the study of individuating cultures of race so important. Following Arun Saldanha too, this new attempt to "reonotologise" race (Saldanha 2006) is shifting away from the study of metropolitan theories of race, towards fine grained, even microhistorical analyses of particular, local colonial cultures of racialization; charting "phenotypical encounters" in imperial space.

While the emphasis is shifting towards heterogeneity, and the material, local conditions that encoded bodily differences with social, economic, and political meaning, (and ensured that the culture of racialization remained congruent with the prevailing material conditions of a specific colonial situation), some generalizations nonetheless remain handy shortcuts. Alan Lester has argued that settler colonies and slave economies were far more likely to generate "innatist" notions of racial difference than other imperial sites, because a rejection of universal human characteristics matched the political and economic requirements of dispossession and/or enslavement (Lester 2012). Going further, Patrick Wolfe posited that unlike other forms of colony (such as plantation colonies, mercantile entrepôts, or resource extraction points) settler colonies were predicated on the displacement and elimination of indigenous people, and were therefore "structurally eliminationist," even "structurally genocidal"(Wolfe 2006). Notwithstanding the record of genocide in some settler colonies such as German Southwest Africa, colonial Queensland, and the frontier plains of the US, even this claim of a genocidal structure overplays the regularity of the mechanics of settler colonialism, given that some colonies actively sought to preserve indigenous peoples as an invaluable and inexpensive labor force (Rowse 2014). Both of these positions, however, tend to confirm Wolfe's larger point that while cultures of racialization might have varied from colonial site to colonial site, the range of possibility was in the final analysis circumscribed by the overarching logic of Europe's attempt to globalize "industrial capitalism" through their empires (Wolfe 2002).

As Wolfe pointed out, as important as it was, race was "but one among various regimes of difference that have served to distinguish dominant groups from groups whom they initially encountered in colonial contexts" (Wolfe 2001). Avoiding using race as a totalizing explanation for the various forms of colonial domination requires attention to the individual colonial sites in order that the heterogeneous roles of race as a category of domination might be discerned. Accordingly, it is instructive to seek out this variance and explain how the messy record of lived experience in polyethnic empires followed different, if sometimes overlapping, paths of racial experience. This enables a clearer description of the function of race in a variety of colonial settings, emphasizing just how malleable the concept of race was.

In line with this emphasis on multiple cultures of racialization, the rest of this chapter surveys examples of how raced, embodied subjects navigated the power differentials of empire in particular contexts, showing that "race" and "racism" were not so much discursive constructs as products of specific cultures of racialization which injected different social weightings to embodied interactions that foregrounded phenotypical difference. In this way, the variety of histories of how race straddled the interface of bodies, subjectivity and social structures becomes much clearer.

RACE AND IMPERIAL LABOR

At base, the relationship between the nineteenth century's colonizing and colonized lands was transactional; a transfer of surplus from the colonized to the colonizers (Frank 1998). This transfer was generally facilitated by the loss of indigenous sovereignty and a reordering of the politico-economic priorities of the colonized territory towards the interests of the imperial power and its local representatives. As nineteenth-century commentators as varied as Friedrich List and Karl Marx acknowledged, this transfer of wealth often meant harnessing the resources and, in particular, labor of those in extra-European lands (and "underdeveloped" regions on the periphery of Europe) to serve the metropolitan centers of the global economy (List 1971, 228; Marx and Engels 1971, 84). As the examples of slavery, blackbirding, and indentured coolie labor make clear, labor relations in imperial settings were often viewed in particularly racialized terms, leaving a heavy imprint on the development of local systems of colonial hierarchy.

An integral part of the process of extracting labor was assessing different colonized peoples around the world in accordance with their capacity and availability to undertake "work"; not in the sense of their ability to interact with their environment so as to provide for their own needs, but as understood within the context of European labor practices as the capacity to sell or (in the cases of unfree labor systems such as slavery) to be coerced into offering their labor to produce surplus value for their colonial employers or masters. Crucially, at the imperial interface, such assessments were not based on phenotypical differences such as pigmentation alone, and a great deal of work went into differentiating between different populations of the same appearance, but with different work practices. Those non-European peoples that already had long histories as pastoralists, traders, or agricultural peoples were generally seen as capable of being "civilised" (that is trained to work) by the state, settler colonists, or missionary outposts; whereas those living in subsistence economies, particularly nomadic hunter-gathering peoples were often deemed likely to perish in the face of the new imperial strictures. In addition, nomadic peoples in settler colonies were often seen as far easier to displace, whereas hitherto settled peoples clung more stubbornly to their territories. Hence, in the colony of German Southwest Africa for example, the cattle-herding Herero were seen as a highly valuable labor force and prime candidates for training to work, at the same time as their refusal to concede their grazing lands was seen as a threat to the growing pastoral interests of the German settlers seeking new territory for their herds (Bley 1996). The San "Bushmen," on the other hand were generally seen as culturally incapable of adjusting to new demands, with one geographer commenting in 1878 that "how these most miserable of the miserable should come into the area of the missions and of civilisation remains a mystery" (Fitzpatrick 2008, 171). Despite living in territory too marginal for pastoral development, they were still hunted in "Bushman hunts" (Gordon 2009).

With the gradual end of the African slave trade in the early nineteenth century (and in some places such as Australia the end of unfree white convict labor in the middle decades of the nineteenth century), the economies of settler, plantation, and mercantile colonies demanded new sources of labor. While in the main this need was met by drawing newly freed populations into an evolving wage economy, this need was also met in some areas by switching to sources of inexpensive semi-free, indentured, and free labor from the global south. In this context, the structural shift to "coolie" labor was made in many colonial sites where an indigenous workforce was seen as either incapable, unwilling, or too sparse to meet the economic needs of the colony. While some specious equations between race and certain industries were made, such as the notion that "black people had a special affinity for growing cotton" (Zimmerman 2010, 12–13), in many cases, the precise racial characteristics of labor was not as important as its price and availability. As unskilled laborers, the cheapest workers were often freed slaves making the gradual, uneven transition to wage labor. In other sites, indigenous labor was keenly sought after. Thus, Western Cape farmers employed both local free Africans alongside slaves, and then employed freed slaves once slavery had ended in the 1830s (Worden 1992). In Australia, dispossessed Indigenous people were also used as a cheap "reserve pool of labor," kept as a contracted precariat rather than waged laborers by European settlers who required just such an inexpensive, geographically immobile seasonal or occasional work force (Brock 1995; Castle and Hagan 1998). Elsewhere, however, such as in colonial Brazil, the end of slavery and the transition to wage labor after 1888 was more often viewed through the prism of race, as enabling the end goal of "whitening" Brazil. Here, the anti-slavery movement concerned itself not merely with the rights of African slaves, but also slavery's role in slowing white migration to Brazil (Triner 2005, 7).

Race worked curiously in the context of coolie labor. For example, when the British sought to create a tea industry in Assam (Northern India) in the late 1830s, the Chinese workers that were imported for their specialist knowledge considered themselves to be skilled labor and refused to undertake menial forest-clearing work, while the local Assamese understandably preferred to work their own fields rather than be drawn into permanent dependence through wage relations with the British. Accordingly, these more demanding sources of labor were replaced in later decades with a more pliant (that is economically dependent) Southern Indian coolie workforce (Sharma 2009). Elsewhere, some sixty years later, it was Chinese workers that were hired as coolies by German plantation owners who, lacking access to Indian labor, sourced Chinese workers for their plantations in Samoa and even New Guinea, where local Melanesians (who had long been recruited to work in the Australian cane fields) were also being brought into a ramshackle corvée labor system (Featuna'I Liua'ana 1997; Firth 1976). Availability and a desire to construct a lowly paid plantation and farm workforce, rather than perceived intrinsic racial characteristics shaped localized decision making about the complexion of the post-slavery labor market.

Proximity also played a role in racialized imperial labor markets, as in the case of so-called "kanaka" labor in the Pacific, where over 62,000 indentured laboring Melanesians were brought from surrounding islands to work in Australia, mostly in the sugar cane fields of Queensland (Figure 8.2). With varying degrees of consent, this movement of unskilled Pacific Islander labor continued into the early twentieth century. Those engaged in the illegal kidnapping or "blackbirding" of Melanesian laborers were pursued by Australian authorities as modern day slavers who kidnapped "Kanak" laborers and trafficked in human misery (Hunt 2007; Mortensen 2000); although more recent studies have cautiously reinstated a degree of Pacific Islander agency in

FIGURE 8.2: Pacific Islanders on Pineapple Plantation, Queensland, Australia. Photo courtesy of the National Library of Australia.

this racialized circular migration. Ultimately, the practice was stamped out not as a result of indignation regarding the exploitative conditions faced by Islander laborers, but by the effects of Australian unification in 1901, which saw the federal government push the Queensland government to implement policies (not unlike those of post-slavery Brazil) designed to create an all-white citizen labor force (Megarrity 2006; Shlomowitz 2005). Over time, most Pacific Islander workers were largely repatriated, albeit not always to their point of origin (Munro 1995).

INTERRACIAL IMPERIAL RELATIONSHIPS

As Stoler and Lora Wildenthal have made abundantly clear, beyond labor issues, race was also deeply connected to questions of sexuality and gender (Stoler 1995; Wildenthal 2001), although often in surprising ways that undermined official understandings of the "habitual" or "default position" of the colonizing European body (Merleau-Ponty in Alcoff 2005, 184). If any area of scholarship pertaining to the culture of racialization in imperial settings has been intensively studied in the past two decades, it is this interrelationship between race and sex (Ray 2013), an area of research spurred on by the huge strides in the field afforded by Stoler's work on miscegenation and the colonial attempts to control the emergence of so-called "half-castes." Again, however, it is important to remember that not only were attitudes to interracial sex different in different colonies (or within the same colony at different times), but that this sex took place in different contexts, ranging from state and church consecrated, life-long marriages, less formal co-habitation, and concubinage (some condoned, others discouraged), through to forms that were discouraged and controlled, such as prostitution and rape.

Interracial marriages and long-term interracial relationships were not uncommon in colonial settings, particularly in areas where the vast majority of colonists were male and the prospects of a return to the colonial metropole was remote. In many colonies, this was not merely a question of the desire for companionship but also about obtaining and retaining privileged access to land, resources, or valuable dowries. This amounted to a *de facto* recognition by colonizing men of the economic and social power wielded by some indigenous women, whose insider status and social access was of importance to their would-be spouses. This was the case in German Southwest Africa, where German men often married local women because, as the German governor Friedrich von Lindequist argued in 1906, "they often bring a herd of livestock, an oxen wagon and not seldom a farm into the marriage" (Walther 2002, 35). As Katherine Ellinghaus has pointed out, in the United States, the experience of couples in mixed relationships depended upon (and often reinforced) the local cultures of race, with Native Americans, for example, seen in the late nineteenth century as having been historically free and therefore worthy of more respect as partners than the descendants of black slaves. Local understandings of which interracial relationships might be condoned also betrayed the extent to which varying strategies of assimilation had affected the social mobility of indigenous peoples and, accordingly, the desirability of intermarriage (Ellinghaus 2006, 214–17).

As mentioned, much of the work coming after Stoler's study of miscegenation has foregrounded the extent to which mixed race offspring were conceptualized as a colonial problem. Undoubtedly Stoler is right in arguing that so-called "half-castes" were seen as undesirable in numerous colonies, particularly where European colonial hegemony was tenuous. This was not, however, monolithically the case (Stoler 2002, 51). In some colonies, it was simply assumed by colonists that over time, a mixed race population would be integral to the colony's longevity. Again in German Southwest Africa, until the Herero Revolt of 1904 radically altered race relations, so-called half-castes were seen by missionaries as playing an important role in binding Africans to the new German administration through an increasing number of familial ties (Becker 2004; Zimmerer 2002, 95), while in Samoa, German settlers were still arguing in 1911 for interracial marriages, on the assumption that "it will not be purely white children born here but children strengthened by a mixing with Samoan blood that will be in charge here in later years" (BA Berlin R1001/3066, 89). Damon Ieremia Salesa has also illustrated how for colonial authorities in nineteenth-century New Zealand, the strategy of "racial amalgamation" was consciously promoted not as a means of undermining the colonial project, but of stabilizing and furthering it. In fact, far from bringing racial amalgamation to an end, New Zealand's mid-nineteenth century racial wars "provided the settings through which racial amalgamation was reconfigured and revived, expanded and intensified" as a colonizing strategy (Salesa 2011, 27–37).

Concubinage too was a part of the sexual landscape of empire. In places such as Italian Eritrea, where, as Giulia Barrera has pointed out, racialized fears of the "black peril" in the form of interracial sexual mingling were not as prevalent as in other colonial sites (Barrera 2003, 86–7), the semi-formal institution of *madamismo* saw Eritrean women become partners to high-ranking Italian colonial officials and ordinary settlers alike. These instances of concubinage straddled the full range of relation modes from abusive and exploitative through to relationships of genuine mutual affection (Iyob 2000, 222–7; De Donno 2006, 400). As Ronald Hyam famously argued, British officials in India were similarly accustomed to keeping an Indian mistress in British India until the practice was complicated by the Indian Rebellion of 1857 and the arrival of white spouses (Hyam 1990, 118). In the Pacific, German Samoa too saw numerous, officially condoned *fa'a Samoa* relationships, which the governors and missionaries there wished to see not ended but upgraded to fully consecrated marriages, while Governor Albert Hahl of German New Guinea famously fathered a child by his Tolai wife (Conrad 2012, 119–20) (Figure 8.3). Interestingly, however, in German Samoa, the introduction of Chinese coolies saw Samoan men warn Samoan women that while relationships with Europeans were permitted, interracial unions between Samoans and Chinese workers were undesirable. Whether this was on racial grounds, a result of their class position as semi-free laborers, or simply the expectation that the Chinese were a transient population is unclear, although one source indicates that it grew out of a fear that the rise of Chinese-Samoan relationships (with Chinese outnumbering Germans 10:1) might threaten the future of the Samoans themselves (BA Berlin R1001/2760, 183, Fetuna'i Liua'ana, 34).

Interracial sexualized violence and rape were also prevalent in nineteenth-century empires. Overwhelmingly these involved the predations of Europeans upon the colonized, particularly in situations of domestic service and on the frontier when military operations were under way. There were, however, rare cases involving non-European troops being used in colonial conflicts; perhaps the most famous of these incidents were the sexual assaults on Chinese women perpetrated by Britain's Indian sepoys from the 37th Madras Native Infantry which sparked the Chinese uprising of Sanyuanli in 1841 (Thampi 1999, 409–10; Wakeman 1966, 16–17). While unchecked in many frontier sites, some more flagrant abuses were punished, such as the interracial sexual abuse of African men by a German farmer in Southwest Africa which saw him deported from the colony (Fitzpatrick 2015, 230).

FIGURE 8.3: Governor Hahl of German New Guinea with his Tolai partner and child, 1910. Credit: bpk/Ethnologisches Museum, SMB.

RACIALIZED COLONIAL WARS

Colonial warfare often radically altered the prevailing culture of racial interaction in a colonial site, greatly increasing the tendency towards dehumanizing the colonized. While it is often argued that the processes of racialization dehumanized the colonized in a way that gradually enabled murder, warfare, and even genocide, it more often occurred that situations of conflict and war—whether declared or undeclared—led to a concomitant radicalization of racial categories and racial thinking that was in peacetime unnecessary, or even counterproductive to imperial objectives. This shift in the local culture of race often played an important role in preparing soldiers psychologically for the task of killing an ostensible enemy.

An excellent example of this is the gradual transformation of the status of Filipinos in the letters of US soldiers during the Philippine-American War (1899–1902) which saw their civilizationary status drop markedly in the eyes of the Americans as they shifted from being "brother human kin" when they were viewed as victims of Spanish imperialism, to natives seeking independence, until they eventually became dehumanized enemies at war. For Filipinos too, the Americans' reputation as racial murderers increased as the conflict intensified, with the US characterized as a nation which had "mercilessly slain and finally exterminated the race of Indians that were native" and which had gone to war in 1861 "to suppress an insurrection of Negro slaves, whom [they] also ended by exterminating." For Filipinos seeking sovereignty from all imperial rule, death in war was seen as preferable to becoming "subject to a nation where . . . the colored man is lynched and burned alive indiscriminately" (Kramer 2006, 179–80).

So too in Australia, the violent radicalization accompanying Indigenous resistance to settler colonialism was marked by a cultural shift in local racial understandings where earlier the "color line" had been more permeable. Under these circumstances, the color-blind pretensions of formal legal protection for Australia's Indigenous first nations were no impediment to the increasingly genocidal logic of the Black War in Tasmania and the radical clearances on the frontiers of Queensland and Western Australia (Rogers and Bain 2016; Dwyer and Ryan 2016) (Figure 8.4). The same process of radicalized grassroots

FIGURE 8.4: Indigenous Australian Prisoners in Neck Chains, Wyndham, Western Australia. Photo courtesy of the State Library of Victoria.

racialization accompanied the exterminatory "modern conquista" conflicts in Brazil waged by militias called the "*bugreiros*" against the Xokleng and the Kaingang, who came to be labeled as "*Bugre*" (Ritz-Deutch 2015, 21–5). Similarly, during Britain's reconquest of the Sudan, the Mahdists massacred by the British at Omdurman in 1898 came to be described as "vermin" in the context of a campaign viewed as war of revenge by the "civilised" British for the death of General Charles Gordon in Khartoum at the hands of "barbarians" (Gordon 2015, 277–8).

Of course colonized people were on both sides of the military frontier, with indigenous troops used as locally available soldiers for colonizing armies. The colonial army offered a source of income to many ascari in Italian Eritrea (Barrera 2003, 85), and the same was true for Askaris in German East Africa (Figure 8.5), the Sepoys of British India, and of course the colonial troops used

FIGURE 8.5: Askari with the flag of the German Empire. German East Africa. Photo courtesy of the Bundesarchiv.

in French Africa (Thompson 1990). In Australia, shocking frontier violence against Aborigines was meted out by the British commanded "Black Troopers," while in the Belgian Congo, the local *Force Publique* under Belgian command carried out King Leopold II's homicidal extraction of the rubber quota, at the cost of millions of lives (Hochschild 1999, 127–9). Elsewhere in the British Empire, during the 1865 Morant Bay Rebellion in Jamaica the infamous Governor of Jamaica, Edward John Eyre, used both white British troops and black "Maroons" to violently suppress the uprising (Bilby 2012).

IMPERIAL RACIAL LAWS

Of course, military campaigns were often presented as actions designed to uphold colonial law and order. Given their role in the codification of political and juridical norms, colonial laws were both an official record of the prevailing culture of racialization in any given colony, as well as a blunt intervention by the colonial state into the regulation of the behavior of those under their jurisdiction. In colonial settings, laws pertaining to race were far from uniform and generally arose as interventions meeting specific local needs. These interventions provided differing legal solutions to the question of how to stabilize imperial rule, against a backdrop of contested and overlapping claims to jurisdiction and a desire to limit the legal scope for individual agency within a colonial state eager to consolidate its juridical hold over the territory (Benton 1999).

Colonial law has been profitably critiqued from two sides—because it forcibly homogenized all inhabitants (including indigenous people who had their own pre-existing frameworks of law) by forcing them to abide by European norms, or because by legally differentiating between colonizers and the colonized the law created a two-tier system which betrayed the principle of equality before the law. Both are simultaneously true and clearly no legal setting could have offered a satisfactory set of structures offering a legally just path for either the dispossession inherent to settler colonialism or the physical and epistemic violence it entailed. Yet, that this material dispossession itself was not necessarily primarily racially motivated, even when it proceeded from a Eurocentric understanding of space and property is clear from the promulgation and prosecution of many imperial laws.

In the nineteenth century, hard-edged racial laws in the twentieth-century sense were uncommon outside of ex-slave societies such as the United States. More often, what colonial laws sought to do was to establish separate jurisdictions for the colonizers and the colonized so as to enable a smoother path to dispossession. Often phrased as a form of respect for pre-existing indigenous forms of law and justice, legal differentiation was more regularly an attempt to ensure that citizenship and property rights were restricted to colonists from the colonial metropole. Far from being calibrated to offer legal equality within the colonial site, law formally structured the forms of imperial inequality that the colonizers found necessary for the construction and perpetuation of their colony. Rarely were explicit appeals to biological difference made in this differentiation; instead cultural, civilizationary differences were often foregrounded, with longstanding indigenous behaviors gradually criminalized, leading to a situation in which indigenous peoples were *de facto* rendered criminal unless they acquiesced and shifted into the subordinate roles designated for them by colonial administrators.

Examples of this type of law abound and include the Russian 1822 Statute of the Natives (*Ustav ob upravlenie inorodtsev*), the French *Code de l'indigénat*, and the German *Schutzgebietsgesetz* (1886). The first of these differentiated legally between "*inorodtsy*" ("aliens") and other subjects of the Russian empire. The category of "*inorodtsy*" was reserved for non-Russian peoples of the empire who were viewed as living in a manner distinctly different to Russians. Seen as living at a "low level of civilisation," they were viewed as existing under a "special relationship of trusteeship" with the Russian state, paying special taxes while their traditional forms of governance were left largely intact. Rather than resting on biological distinctions, the main marker of difference was nomadism (although the category did include some settled Tartars and Bukhtarmen). Although infrequently done, it was possible for individuals to shift out of this legal category through Russification; namely by becoming settled and converting to Orthodoxy. Crucially, in the west of the empire, the category also included Jews, clearly marking out their status as non-Russian outsiders. The vast majority, however, were the enormous number of conquered and colonized peoples of Central Asia. In fact, once all of the different *inorodtsy* were tallied in the 1897 census, it emerged that they were only a minority because Belorussians and Ukrainians were counted as members of the *russkii narod*, the Russian nation (Kappeler 2001, 169–71; Slocum 1998).

The French *Code de l'indigénat* similarly marked out clear legal differences between the colonizers and the colonized and sought to preserve indigenous forms of leadership, while leaving open the theoretical opportunity for individuals to "evolve" to a French way of life and in some cases French citizenship. In its radicalized 1881 incarnation it reconfirmed the rule of metropolitan law for French colonists, while ramping up a regime of forced labor and more or less arbitrary applications of punishment for indigenous, non-French peoples, making it far more difficult for them to cross the dividing line between French and native (Saada 2011, 229–30). Offering a malleable suite of powers, it enabled colonial rule at the discretion of local officials who were freed from metropolitan law codes. In its application, the *indigénat* differed markedly, depending upon whether it was being applied in Indochina, the Pacific, or Africa. The specific culture of race and race relations in these colonial sites mattered greatly (Mann 2000; Muckle 2010), however, far from mitigating systemic inequality, its very indeterminacy allowed for local, racialized short hands and colony-specific racial (and other) hierarchies of convenience to flourish without metropolitan control. Under these conditions, as Michael G. Vann, has argued, "colonial racism did not operate by homogenizing the non-whites into a single entity. Instead, several distinct categories existed into which the various non-whites fit" (Vann 2003).

Differential legal structures such as the *Code de l'indigenat* offered colonial officials scope for legal improvisations that favored the colonizers. Equally amenable to colonial ends, however, were colonial legal frameworks derived from British imperial law that assumed a notional equality before the law. Such legal regimes left no room for indigenous autonomy and instead subsumed indigenous people under the rubric of metropolitan legal norms of which they were entirely ignorant and to which they could not possibly hope to conform. These inflexible legal frameworks effectively criminalized local customs and behaviors and demanded that indigenous people conform to the practices and prohibitions of metropolitan powers. More broadly, they assumed that indigenous peoples would quickly adopt to not merely new legal regimes, but also to the intellectual patterns that sustained them.

In Canada, this deliberate attempt to minimize and gradually eradicate difference was facilitated by the 1857 Civilisation of Indian Tribes Act. This Act sought the same kind of racial assimilation as that of colonial New Zealand, implementing a policy of racial amalgamation, and withholding enfranchisement except for those deemed "sufficiently advanced" and "capable of managing their own affairs" (Bartlett 1978, 583; Salesa 2011, 37–42) Thereafter, the Canadian Indian Act of 1876 emerged, not merely as a law, but as Bonita Lawrence has argued, as a local form of "classification, regulation and control that ... indelibly ordered how Native peoples think of things 'Indian.'" By asserting a deeply restrictive legal definition of "Indian" as "pure Indian," the Act employed biological criteria not to exclude those with indigenous heritage from settler society, but instead to hasten their assimilation by forcibly shutting as many as 25,000 "non-status" indigenous Canadians off from their communities, deeming them ineligible for life on "native" reservations and demanding their Europeanization. Designed to accelerate racial mixing, its effects on the survival of a separate indigenous culture and community were both deliberate and devastating (Lawrence 2003, 3–4). Perhaps with such episodes in mind, James Patterson Smith has argued that "before the mid-nineteenth century most British commentary on race fell into the category of ethnocentrism rather than the more virulent biologically based racism that has given the twentieth century so many tragedies." Yet, as the Indian Act case illustrates, biological concepts of purity could be marshaled not to halt a local culture of racial mixing, but to accelerate it (Patterson Smith 1994, 136).

CONCLUSION

Beyond the obvious, structural point that empires were systems of domination that privileged the metropole over the periphery, what is striking are the differences rather than the commonalities between the cultures of racialization and the roles they played in the construction and maintenance of imperial hierarchies. Patrick Wolfe once argued that "there are no grounds for assuming that such striking disparities can be reconciled under a single category called 'race'" (Wolfe 2001, 867). This seems to be an important insight and one taken seriously by the new cultural histories of race and empire, which have shifted away from the study of nineteenth-century metropolitan discourse towards a praxiological interrogation of the differing cultures of racialization in different colonial sites. This praxiological method has illustrated just how malleable racial categories were, and how different the social and political encoding of phenotypical difference could be. It was this malleability that enabled different cultures of racialization to emerge in response to site-specific imperial imperatives.

These individual cultures of racialization were of course structured by the broader politico-economic imperatives of empire. They were also informed by metropolitan understandings and priorities. And it is still fair to say that race was an omnipresent category of identification in imperial sites. Yet the heterogeneity of the social, economic, and racial complexion of colonial sites means that the history and role of race in empire tends towards variegation rather than uniformity. Differing colonial cultures of racialization were a reflection of intrinsically local dynamics, of the interactions, exchanges, and degrees of frontier friction between differing communities of colonizers and colonized in different types of colonies, at different times and in different places.

NOTES

Introduction

1. British officer and his wife (EA1996.115), Ashmolean museum, Oxford, gouache with gold and silver on paper. The catalogue lists "Lahore, Punjab province (now Pakistan) *c.* 1850–1860" as the associated place and date of the image. In 1849 the British East India Company took control of the Punjab in the aftermath of the Anglo-Sikh wars and the fall of the Sikh empire. I am grateful to Robert Aldrich, Brad Manera, Jim Masselos, and Peter Stanley for their expertise in discussing the details of this painting. My thanks also to Miranda Johnson and Andrew Fitzmaurice for their suggestions, and to Robert Aldrich, Antoinette Burton, and Brad Manera for their comments on earlier drafts of this essay.
2. The officer's left arm shows traces of a chevron (point down) painted over—an incorrectly positioned signifier of sergeant's rank (unlikely in a European serving in India in this period) and possibly a corrected mistake on the part of the artist.
3. European, and particularly British, trade interests would see a resurgence in Central and South America in the era of New Imperialism, though not through formal colonization in the region.
4. Strongly influenced by the United States, the post-war League of Nations was in theory opposed to further imperial expansion. On the other hand, it was under pressure from the victorious European powers who wished to dismantle and appropriate the colonies of their rivals. The solution placed the colonial possessions of the defeated under a mandate system controlled by the League of Nations and administered by the victors.
5. On the distinctiveness of settler colonialism and historians' debates over its genocidal intentions see chapters by Jennifer Sessions and Matt Fitzpatrick in this volume.
6. It is perhaps worth spelling out that "new imperial history" was designated "new" by reason of its methodology and should not be equated with histories of the late nineteenth-century "New Imperialism" era.

7. "New" imperial history is of course no longer new. After several decades, as Alan Lester points out, "a different descriptor is now overdue" (Lester 2013, 86), and revisionist imperial history writing has itself evolved across this period. The turn away from high politics and economics is not as true as it once was. The cultural aspects of economics were an early focus in histories of commodities, trade, and lived experience. Formal (as opposed to interpersonal) politics and legal history has more recently enjoyed a resurgence among those working in the field. These scholars insist on the importance of viewing such structures through a cultural lens and see limitations in the historiographical division between "old" and "new" styles of imperial history (Howe 2010; Laidlaw 2012; McKenzie 2015).
8. Stoler's work is a reminder that not all pioneering scholarship in the field emphasized British imperialism, though her theoretical frameworks were taken up extensively by historians working on Anglophone topics.
9. For a study on related issues in French imperialism see (Ha 2014).
10. One of the earliest and most influential of the "new imperial" histories was Mrinalini Sinha's *Colonial Masculinity*, published in the Manchester series in 1995, the same year as MacKenzie published his own critique of Said's interpretation of Orientalism.

Chapter 5

1. Voyages Database. 2017. *Voyages: The Transatlantic Slave Trade Database.* http://slavevoyages.org/voyages/imssjv6t [accessed November 2, 2017].
2. This number is based on the statistic provided by Jenny Martinez of 80,000 intercepted people, compared with the number of slaves embarked aboard ships destined for Brazil or Cuba. Voyages Database. 2017. *Voyages: The Transatlantic Slave Trade Database.* http://slavevoyages.org/voyages/M5Dp9LPH [accessed November 2, 2017].
3. The text is in French and was redacted by Etienne Dumont. MS Bentham Box 177, University College, London.
4. For a critique of Le Cour Grandmaison's controversial book, see Gilbert Meynier and Pierre Vidal-Nacquet "Coloniser, Exterminer: de vérités bonnes à dire à l'art de la simplification idéologique," published in the online review Études coloniales http://etudescoloniales.canalblog.com/archives/2006/05/10/2311101.html (10 May 2006).

Chapter 7

1. For a useful overview of these ambiguities, see Cooper 1994 and Ostler 2004.
2. Key figures in this cultural turn are the postcolonial critic Edward Said and the Subaltern Studies school in South Asian history. See Said 1978 and Guha 1997. On discourse, see also Cohn 1996. Critical texts on voice and subjectivity are Mohanty 1984 and Spivak 1988. For more recent approaches to discourse and resistance in postcolonial studies, see Jefferess 2008.

3. This is to say nothing of women. American revolutionaries relied heavily on the contributions of women of all races and classes, but systematically refused them rights after independence (Kerber 1980).
4. The literature on the Haitian Revolution is important and expanding. Scholars continue to debate key aspects of the revolution, in particular the relative weight of African, American, and French influences. See, among others, James 1938; Fick 1990; Thornton 1993; Trouillot 1995; Dubois 2004; Dubois and Garrigus 2006; Popkin 2012; Geggus 2014. Geggus and Fiering 2009 and Sepinwall 2012 offer excellent collections of classic and more recent interpretations.
5. A slightly different translation is in Dubois and Garrigus 2006.

FURTHER READING

Adamson, Alan (1984), "The Impact of Indentured Immigration on the Political Economy of British Guiana," in Saunders, Kay (ed.), *Indentured Labor in the British Empire 1834–1920*, London: Croom Helm.
Adamson, G.C.D. (2015), "Colonial Private Diaries and their Potential for Reconstructing Historical Climate in Bombay, 1799–1828," in V. Damodaran, A. Winterbottom and A. Lester (eds), *The East India Company and the Natural World*, 102–27, Basingstoke: Palgrave Macmillan.
Adamson, G.C.D. and D.J. Nash (2014), "Documentary Reconstruction of Monsoon Rainfall Variability over Western India, 1781–1860," *Climate Dynamics*, 42: 749–69.
Adelman, Jeremy (2006), *Sovereignty and Revolution in the Iberian Atlantic*, Princeton: Princeton University Press.
Adelman, Jeremy (2008), "An Age of Imperial Revolutions," *American Historical Review* 113 (2): 319–40.
Aguiar, M. (2011), *Tracking Modernity: India's Railway and the Culture of Mobility*, Minneapolis: University of Minnesota Press.
Akyeampong, Emmanuel and Charles Ambler (2002), "Leisure in African History: An Introduction," *The International Journal of African Historical Studies* 35 (1): 1–16.
Alcoff, Linda Martin (2005), *Visible identities: Race Gender and the Self*, New York: Oxford University Press.
Aldrich, Robert (1996), *Greater France: A History of French Overseas Expansion*, Basingstoke: Macmillan Press.
Aldrich, Robert (2002), "Homosexuality in the French Colonies," *Journal of Homosexuality*, 41 (3–4): 201–18.
Aldrich, Robert (2003), *Colonialism and Homosexuality*, London: Routledge.
Aldrich, Robert (2013), "Sex matters: sexuality and the writing of colonial history," in
Alexander, Peter and Rick Halpern, eds (2000), *Racializing Class, Classifying Race: Labour and Difference in Britain, the USA and Africa*, London: Macmillan.
Ali, Isra (2015), "The harem fantasy in nineteenth-century Orientalist paintings," *Dialectical Anthropology* 39 (1): 33–46.

Allen, R.B. (2015), *European Slave Trading in the Indian Ocean, 1500–1850*, Athens, Ohio: Ohio University Press.
Allen, Richard (1999), *Slaves, Freedmen, and Indentured Laborers in Colonial Mauritius*, Cambridge: Cambridge University Press.
Allen, Theodore (1997), *The Invention of the White Race*, London: Verso.
Altink, Henrice (2005), "Deviant and dangerous: pro-slavery representations of Jamaican slave women's sexuality, c. 1780–1834," *Slavery & Abolition*, 26 (2): 271–88.
Ambler, Charles and Jonathan Crush, eds (1992), *Liquor and Labour in Southern Africa*, Pietermaritzburg: University of Natal Press.
Amin, Shahid and Marcel van der Linden, eds (1996), *"Peripheral" Labor? Studies in the History of Partial Proletarianization*, Cambridge: Cambridge University Press.
Amrith, S.S. (2013), "'Contagion of the Depot': The Government of Indian Emigration, in R. Peckham and D.M. Pomfret, *Imperial Contagions: Medicine, Hygiene, and Cultures of Planning in Asia*, 151–62, Hong Kong: University of Hong Kong Press.
Anderson, Clare (2000), *Convicts in the Indian Ocean : transportation from South Asia to Mauritius, 1815–53*, New York: St. Martin's Press.
Anderson, Clare (2009), "Convicts and Coolies: Rethinking Indentured Labor in the Nineteenth Century," *Slavery & Abolition* 30 (1): 93–109.
Anderson, Clare (2012), *Subaltern Lives: Biographies of Colonialism in the Indian Ocean World 1780–1920*, Cambridge: Cambridge University Press.
Anderson, Clare and Hamish Maxwell-Stewart (2014), "Convict labour and Western empires, 1415–1954," in Robert Aldrich and Kirsten McKenzie (eds), *The Routledge History of Western Empires*, New York: Routledge.
Anderson, K. (2005), *Predicting the Weather: Victorians and the Science of Meteorology*, Chicago: University of Chicago Press.
Anderson, W. (1992), "Climates of Opinion: Acclimatization in Nineteenth-Century France and England," *Victorian Studies*, 35 (2): 135–57.
Anderson, W. (2006), *Colonial Pathologies: American Tropical Medicine, Race, and Hygiene in the Philippines*, Durham, NC: Duke University Press.
Archer, Mildred (1992), *Company Paintings: Indian Paintings of the British Period*, London: Victoria and Albert Museum and Mapin Publishing.
Armitage, D. (2002), "Three Concepts of Atlantic History," in D. Armitage and M.J. Braddick, *The British Atlantic World 1500–1800*, New York: Palgrave Macmillan.
Arnold, D. (1996), *The Problem of Nature: Environment, Culture and European Expansion*, Oxford: Blackwell.
Arnold, D. (2000), "'Illusory Riches': Representations of the Tropical World, 1840–1950," *Singapore Journal of Tropical Geography*, 21 (1): 6–18.
Arnold, D. (2005), "Agriculture and 'Improvement' in Early Colonial India: A Pre-History of Development," *Journal of Agrarian Change*, 5 (4): 505–25.
Arnold, M. (1993), *Culture and Anarchy and Other Writings*, Avon: Cambridge University Press.
Atkins, Keletso (1988), "'Kafir Time': Preindustrial Temporal Concepts and Labor Discipline in Nineteenth-Century Colonial Natal," *The Journal of African History* 29 (2): 229–44.
Auerbach, Jeffrey A. (1999), *The Great Exhibition of 1851: A Nation on Display*, New Haven: Yale University Press.

Augé, M. (1995), *Non-Places: Introduction to an Anthropology of Supermodernity*, London: Verso.
Baber, Z. (2016), "The Plants of Empire: Botanic Gardens, Colonial Power and Botanical Knowledge," *Journal of Contemporary Asia*, 46 (4): 659–79.
Bailyn, Bernard (1967), *The Ideological Origins of the American Revolution*, Cambridge, MA: Belknap.
Baines, Dudley (1991), *Emigration from Europe*, Houndsmills: Macmillan.
Balachandran, G. (2012), *Globalizing Labor? Indian Seafarers and World Shipping, c. 1870–1945*, New Delhi: Oxford University Press.
Ballantyne, Tony (2002), *Orientalism and Race: Aryanism in the British Empire*, Basingstoke: Palgrave.
Ballantyne, Tony (2015), *Entanglements of Empire: Missionaries, Maori and the Question of the Body*, Durham: Duke University Press.
Ballantyne, Tony and Antoinette Burton, eds (2005), *Bodies in Contact: Rethinking Colonial Encounters in World History*, Durham: Duke University Press.
Ballantyne, Tony and Antoinette Burton, eds (2009), *Moving Subjects: Gender, Mobility and Intimacy in an Age of Global Empire*, Urbana: University of Illinois Press.
Bandeira Jerónimo, Miguel (2015), *The "Civilising Mission" of Portuguese Colonialism, 1870–1930*, Basingstoke: Palgrave Macmillan.
Bankoff, G. (2003), *Cultures of Disaster: Society and Natural Hazards in the Philippines*, London: Routledge.
Bankoff, G. (2006), "Winds of Colonisation: The Meteorological Contours of Spain's Imperium in the Pacific, 1521–1898," *Environment and History*, 12 (1): 65–88.
Bankoff, G. (2007), "Bodies on the Beach: Domesticates and Disasters in the Spanish Philippines 1750–1898," *Environment and History*, 13 (3): 285–306.
Bankoff, G. (2011), "The Science of Nature and the Nature of Science in the Spanish and American Philippines," in C. Folke Ax, N. Brimnes, N. Thode Jensen and K. Oslund (eds), *Cultivating Colonies: Colonial States and their Environmental Legacies*, 78–108, Athens, OH: Ohio University Press.
Bankoff, G. (2017), "Aeolian Empires: The Influence of Winds and Currents on European Maritime Expansion in the Days of Sail," *Environment and History*, 23 (2): 163–96.
Bannerji, Himani (1998), "Age of Consent and Hegemonic Social Reform," in Clare Midgley (ed.), *Gender and Imperialism*, 21–44, Manchester, Manchester University Press.
Barczewski, Stephanie (2014), *Country Houses and the British Empire, 1700–1930*, Manchester: Manchester University Press.
Barnett, C. (1998), "Impure and Worldly Geography: The Africanist Discourse of the Royal Geographical Society, 1831–73," *Transactions of the Institute of British Geographers*, 23: 239–51.
Baroli, M. (1992), *Algérie Terre d'espérances: Colons et immigrants (1838–1914)*, Paris: L'Harmattan.
Barrera, Giulia (2003), "The Construction of Racial Hierarchies in Colonial Eritrea: The Liberal and Early Fascist Period (1897–1934)," in Patrizia Palumbo, *A Place in the Sun: Africa in Italian Colonial Culture from Post-Unification to the Present*, Berkeley: University of California Press.
Bartlett, Richard H. (1978), "The Indian Act of Canada," *Buffalo Law Review*, 27.
Bay, Edna G. (1998), *Wives of the Leopard. Gender, Politics, and Culture in the Kingdom of Dahomey*, Charlottesville, University of Virginia Press.

Bayly, C.A. (1989), *Imperial Meridian: The British Empire and the World, 1780–1830*, London: Longman.
Bayly, C.A. (2004), *The Birth of the Modern World, 1780–1914*, Oxford: Blackwell.
Bear, L. (2007), *Lines of the Nation: Indian Railway Workers Bureaucracy, and the Intimate Histoical Self*, New York: Columbia University Press.
Beattie, J. (2003), "Environmental Anxiety in New Zealand, 1840–1941: Climate Change, Soil Erosion, Sand Drift, Flooding and Forest Conservation," *Environment and History*, 9 (4): 379–92.
Beattie, J. (2011), *Empire and Environmental Anxiety: Health, Science, Art, and Conservation in South Asia and Australasia, 1800–1920*, Basingstoke: Palgrave Macmillan.
Beattie, J. (2012), "Imperial Landscapes of Health: Place, Plants and People between India and Australia, 1800s–1900s," *Health and History*, 14, (1): 100–20.
Beattie, J. (2014), "Science, Religion and Drought: Rainmaking Experiments and Prayers in North Otago, 1889–1911," in J. Beattie, E. O'Gorman and M. Henry (eds), *Climate, Science and Colonisation: Histories from Australia and New Zealand*, 137–55, Basingstoke: Palgrave Macmillan.
Beattie, J. (2015), "A 'shock which . . . can be scarcely be understood': Health Panics, Migration and Plant Exchange between India and Australia, post-1857," in R. Peckham (ed.), *Empires of Panic: Epidemics and Colonial Anxieties*, 87–110, Hong Kong: Hong Kong University Press.
Becker, Frank (2004), "Die 'Bastardheime' der Mission. Zum Status der Mischlinge in der kolonialen Gesellschaft Deutsch-Südwestafrikas," in Frank Becker (ed.), *Rassenmischehen, Mischlinge, Rassentrennung: zur Politik der Rasse im deutschen Kolonialreich*, Stuttgart: Franz Steiner.
Beju, Pascal, L. Raynaud and J.-P. Vergez-Larrouy (1992), *Les chemins de fer de la France d'outre mer*, La Régordane-Éditions.
Belich, J. (2009), *The Settler Revolution and the Rise of the Anglo-World 1783–1939*, New York: Oxford University Press.
Bell, Duncan (2007), *The Idea of Greater Britain: Empire and the Future of World Order, 1860–1900*, Princeton: Princeton University Press.
Bell, M. (1993), "'The Pestilence that Walketh in the Darkness': Imperial Health, Gender and Images of South Africa, c.1880–1910," *Transactions of the Institute of British Geographers*, 18 (3): 327–41.
Benjamin, Roger, Ursula Prunster and Lynne Thornton (1997), *Orientalism: Delacroix to Klee*, Sydney: Art Gallery of New South Wales.
Bennett, B. (2011), "A Global History of Australian Trees," *Journal of the History of Biology*, 44 (1): 125–45.
Bensa, A. (1988), "Colonialisme, racisme et ethnologie en Nouvelle-Calédonie," *Ethnologie française*, 18 (2): 188–97.
Benton, L. and L. Ford (2016), *Rage for Order: The British Empire and the Origins of International Law 1800–1850*, Cambridge, MA: Harvard University Press.
Benton, Lauren (1999), "Colonial Law and Cultural Difference: Jurisdictional Politics and the Formation of the Colonial State," *Comparative Studies in Society and History*, 41 (3): 563–88.
Berg, Maxime, ed. (2015), *Goods from the East: Trading Eurasia, 1600–1800*, London: Palgrave Macmillan.
Berger, Mark (1988), "Imperialism and sexual exploitation: a response to Ronald Hyam's Empire and sexual opportunity," *Journal of Imperial and Commonwealth History*, 17 (October): 83–98.

Berland, A.J., S.E. Metcalfe and G.H. Endfield (2013), "Documentary-Derived Chronologies of Rainfall Variability in Antigua, Lesser Antilles, 1770–1890," *Climate of the Past*, 9: 1331–43.
Bernasconi, Robert (1998), "Hegel at the Court of the Ashanti," in Stuart Barnett (ed.), *Hegel after Derrida*, 41–63, London: Routledge.
Bernasconi, Robert (2001), "Who Invented the Concept of Race? Kant's Role in the Enlightenment Construction of Race," in Robert Bernasconi (ed.), *Race*, Oxford: Blackwell.
Bernasconi, Robert (2002), "Kant as an Unfamiliar Source of Racism," in Julie K. Ward and Tommy L. Lott (eds), *Philosophers on Race: Critical Essays*, Oxford: Blackwell.
Bernasconi, Robert and Tommy L. Lott (2000), *The Idea of Race*, Indianapolis: Hackett.
Berry, Christopher J. (1982), *Hume, Hegel and Human Nature*, The Hague: Martinus Nijhoff.
Bethell, Leslie (1985), "The Independence of Brazil," in Leslie Bethell (ed.), *The Cambridge History of Latin America*, vol. 3, *From Independence to 1870*, 157–96, Cambridge: Cambridge University Press.
Bhattacharya, Nandini (1998), *Reading the Splendid Body: Gender and Consumerism in Eighteenth-Century British Writing on India*, Newark: University of Delaware Press.
Bickers, Robert (2011), *The Scramble for China: Foreign Devils and the Qing Empire, 1832–1914*, London: Allen Lane.
Bilby, Kenneth (2012), "Image and Imagination: Re-Visioning the Maroons in the Morant Bay Rebellion," *History and Memory*, 24 (2): 41–72.
Bishop, Catherine (2015), *Minding Her Own Business: Colonial Businesswomen in Sydney*, Sydney: NewSouth Publishing.
Blackburn, Robin (1988), *The Overthrow of Colonial Slavery 1776–1848*, London: Verso.
Blackburn, Robin (2011), *The American Crucible: Slavery, Emancipation, and Human Rights*, New York: Verso.
Blackhawk, Ned (2006), *Violence Over the Land: Indians and Empires in the Early American West*, Cambridge, MA: Harvard University Press.
Blanford, H.F. (1880), "On the Barometric See-Saw Between Russia and India in the Sun-Spot Cycle," *Nature*, 21 (542): 477–82.
Bley, Helmut (1996), *Namibia Under German Rule*, Hamburg: Lit Verlag.
Blumenbach, Johann Friedrich (1865), *The Anthropological Treatises of Johann Friedrich Blumenbach*, trans. T. Bendyshe, London: Longman Green.
Bonetto, Sandra (2006), "Race and Racism in Hegel – An Analysis," *Minerva*, 10: 35–64.
Bonneuill, C. (2015), "The Geological Turn: Narratives of the Anthropocene," in C. Hamilton, C. Bonneuill and F. Gemenne (eds), *The Anthropocene and the Global Environmental Crisis: Rethinking Modernity*, 17–30, London: Routledge.
Borgonovo, John (2016), "Politics as Leisure: Brass Bands in Cork 1845–1918," in Leeann Lane and William Murphy (eds), *Leisure and the Irish in the Nineteenth Century*, Liverpool: Liverpool University Press.
Bose, Sugata (1993), *Peasant Labour and Colonial Capital: Rural Bengal since 1770*, Cambridge: Cambridge University Press.
Bourne, Kenneth, D.C. Watt, D. Throup and M. Partridge, eds (1997), *The Congo Free State 1863–1906*, British Documents on Foreign Affairs: Reports and Papers from the Foreign Office Confidential Print. n.p., University Publications of America.

Bradford, Helen (1992), "Sex, Lies and Englishmen," *South African Historical Journal*, 26 (1): 209–14.
Brantlinger, Patrick (1988), *Rule of Darkness: British literature and imperialism, 1830–1914*, Ithaca: Cornell University Press.
Braudy, Leo (2005), *From Chivalry to Terrorism. War and the Changing Nature of Masculinity*, New York: Vintage Books.
Breen, T.H. (2004), *The Marketplace of Revolution: How Consumer Politics Shaped American Independence*, New York: Oxford University Press.
Brereton, Bridget and Kevin Yelvington, eds (1999), *The Colonial Caribbean in Transition: Essays on Postemancipation Social and Cultural History*, Gainesville: University Press of Florida.
Brière, J.-F. (2008), *Haïti et la France 1804–1818*, Paris: Karthala.
Bright, Rachel (2013), *Chinese Labor in South Africa 1902–1910: Race, Violence and Global Spectacle*, New York: Palgrave Macmillan.
Broadbent, James, Suzanne Rickard and Margaret Steven (2003), *India, China, Australia: Trade and Society, 1788–1850*, Sydney: Historic Houses Trust of New South Wales.
Brock, Peggy (1995), "Pastoral Stations and Reserves in South and Central Australia, 1850s–1950s," *Labour History*, 69: 102–14.
Brontë, Charlotte ([1847], 1992 edition) *Jane Eyre*, Hertfordshire, Wordsworth Classics.
Brown, Christopher Leslie (2005), *Moral Capital: Foundations of British Abolitionism*, Chapel Hill: University of North Carolina Press.
Brown, Christopher Leslie (2006), *Moral Economy: Foundations of British Abolitionism*, Chapel Hill: University of North Carolina Press.
Brown, D.H. (2003), *Santería Enthroned: Art, Ritual, and Innovation in an Afro-Cuban Religion*, Chicago: The University of Chicago Press.
Buck-Morss, Susan (2000), "Hegel and Haiti," *Critical Inquiry*, 26 (4): 858–64.
Bulkeley, H. and Newell, P. (2015), *Governing Climate Change*, London: Routledge.
Bundesarchiv (BA) Berlin R1001/2760.
Bundesarchiv (BA) Berlin R1001/3066.
Burbank, Jane and Frederick Cooper (2010), *Empires in World History: Power and the Politics of Difference*, Princeton, Princeton University Press.
Burgess, Douglas R., Jr. (2016), *Engines of Empire: Steamships and the Victorian Imagination*, Stanford: Stanford University Press.
Burke, Timothy (1996), *Lifebuoy Men, Lux Women: Commodification, Consumption and Cleanliness in Modern Zimbabwe*, Durham, NC: Duke University Press.
Burton, Antoinette (1994), *Burdens of History: British feminists, Indian women, and imperial culture*, Chapel Hill: University of North Carolina Press.
Burton, Antoinette (1997), "'Who Needs the Nation?': Interrogating 'British' History," *Journal of Historical Sociology*, 10 (3): 227–48.
Burton, Antoinette (1998), *At the Heart of the Empire: Indians and the Colonial Encounter in Late-Victorian Britain*, Berkeley: University of California Press.
Burton, Antoinette, ed. (2003), *After the Imperial Turn: Thinking with and through the Nation*, Durham, NC: Duke University Press.
Burton, Antoinette (2006), *Archive Stories: Facts, Fictions and the Writing of History*, Durham, NC: Duke University Press.
Burton, Antoinette (2011), "Contesting the Zenana: the mission to make 'lady doctors for India', 1874–85," in Antoinette Burton (ed.), *Empire in Question: reading, writing and teaching British Imperialism*, 151–73, Duke University Press.

Burton, Antoinette (2011), "Imperial Optics: Empire Histories, Interpretive Methods," in *Empire in Question: Reading, Writing and Teaching British Imperialism*, Durham, NC: Duke University Press.
Bush, Barbara (1990), *Slave Women in Caribbean Society: 1650–1838*, Bloomington: Indiana University Press.
Cain, P.J. and A.G. Hopkins (2001), *British Imperialism: 1688–2000*, London: Longman.
Cain, Peter J. and Anthony G. Hopkins (1986), "Gentlemanly Capitalism and British Expansion Overseas. I: The Old Colonial System, 1688–1850," *Economic History Review* 39:4: 501–25.
Cain, Peter J. and Anthony G. Hopkins (1987), "Gentlemanly Capitalism and British Expansion Overseas. II: New Imperialism, 1850–1945," *Economic History Review* 40:1: 1–26.
Calhoun, Craig, ed. (1994), *Social Theory and the Politics of Identity*, London: Blackwell.
Calloway, Colin (1995), *The American Revolution in Indian Country: Crisis and Diversity in Native American Communities*, Cambridge: Cambridge University Press.
Candido, M. (2013), *An African Slaving Port and the Atlantic World: Benguela and its Hinterland*, Cambridge: Cambridge University Press.
Carey, M. (2012), "Climate and History: A Critical Review of Historical Climatology and Climate Change Historiography," *WIREs: Climate Change*, 3 (3): 237.
Carp, Benjamin (2010), *Defiance of the Patriots: The Boston Tea Party and the Making of America*, New Haven: Yale University Press.
Carter, Marina (1994), *Lakshmi's Legacy: The Testimonies of Indian Women in 19th Century Mauritius*, Mauritius: Editions de L'océan Indien.
Carter, Marina (1995), *Servants, Sirdars, and Settlers: Indians in Mauritius 1834–1874*, Oxford: Oxford University Press.
Carter, Marina, ed. (2000), *Across the Kalapani : the Bihari presence in Mauritius*, Port Louis : Centre for Research on Indian Ocean Societies.
Castle, Robert and Jim Hagan (1998), "Settlers and the State: The Creation of an Aboriginal Workforce in Australia," *Aboriginal History*, 22: 24–35.
Center for Contemporary Cultural Studies (1982), *The Empire Strikes Back: Race and Racism in 70s Britain*, London: Hutchinson.
Chakrabarti, P. (2014), *Medicine and Empire: 1600–1960*, Basingstoke: Palgrave Macmillan.
Chakrabarty, Dipesh (2009a), "Aboriginal and Subaltern Histories," in Bain Attwood and Tom Griffiths (eds), *Frontier, Race, Nation: Henry Reynolds and Australian History*, Melbourne: Australian Scholarly Publishing.
Chakrabarty, Dipesh (2009b), "The Climate of History: Four Theses," *Critical Inquiry*, 35 (2): 197–222.
Chakrabarty, Dipesh (2012), "Postcolonial Studies and the Challenge of Climate Change," *New Literary History*, 43 (1): 1–18.
Chakrabarty, Dipesh (2014), "Climate and Capital: On Conjoined Histories," *Critical Inquiry*, 41 (1): 1–23.
Chapman, Herrick and Laura Frader, eds (2004), *Race in France: Interdisciplinary Perspectives on the Politics of Difference*, London: Berghahn.
Chappell, J. and Grove, R.H. (2000), "ENSO: A Brief Overview," in R.H. Grove and J. Chappell (eds), *El Niño: History and Crisis – Studies from the Asia-Pacific Region*, 1–4, Cambridge: White Horse Press.

Chatterjee, Indrani and Richard Eaton, eds (2006), *Slavery & South Asian History*, Bloomington: Indiana University Press.

Chenoweth, M. and D. Divine (2008), "A Document-Based 318-year Record of Tropical Cyclones in the Lesser Antilles, 1690–2007," *Geochemistry Geophysics Geosystems*, 9: Q08013.

Childs, M.D. (2006), *The 1812 Aponte Rebellion in Cuba and the struggle against Atlantic slavery*, Chapel Hill: University of North Carolina Press.

Choate, Mark I. (2014), "New Dynamics and new Imperial Powers, 1875–1905," in Robert Aldrich and Kirsten McKenzie (eds), *The Routledge History of Western Empires*, New York: Routledge.

Christopher, A.J. (1992), "Ethnicity, Community and the Census in Mauritius," *The Geographical Journal* 158 (1): 57–64.

Clancy-Smith, Julia (1994), *Rebel and Saint: Muslim Notables, Populist Protest, Colonial Encounters (Algeria and Tunisia, 1800–1914)*, Berkeley: University of California Press.

Clancy-Smith, Julia, ed. (2001), *North Africa, Islam, and the Medterranean World*, History and Society in the Islamic World, New York: Routledge.

Clancy-Smith, Julia (2012), *Mediterraneans: North Africa and Europe in an Age of Migration, c. 1800–1900*, Berkeley: University of California Press.

Clancy-Smith, Julia and Frances Gouda, eds (1998), *Domesticating the Empire: Race, Gender and Family Life in French and Dutch Colonialism*, Charlottesville: University Press of Virginia.

Clavin, Matthew (2010), *Toussaint Louverture and the American Civil War: The Promise and Peril of a Second Haitian Revolution*, Philadelphia: University of Pennsylvania Press.

Clayton, A. (1988), *France, Soldiers, and Africa*, Washington: Brassey's Defence Publishers.

Clayton, D. (2004), "Imperial Geographies," in J.S. Duncan, N.C. Johnson and R.H. Schein (eds), *A Companion to Cultural Geography*, 449–68, Oxford: Blackwell.

Cleall, Esme (2012), *Missionary Discourses of Difference: negotiating otherness in the British Empire, 1840–1900*, Basingstoke: Palgrave Macmillan.

Clements, Nicholas (2014), *The Black War: Fear, Sex and Resistance in Tasmania*, Brisbane: University of Queensland Press.

Clever, Iris and Willemijn Ruberg (2014), "Beyond Cultural History? The Material Turn, Praxiography, and Body History," *Humanities*, 3: 546–66.

Coen, D.R. (2010), "Climate and Circulation in Imperial Austria," *Journal of Modern History*, 82 (4): 839–75.

Coen, D.R. (2011), "Imperial Climatographies from Tyrol to Turkestan," *Osiris*, 26 (1): 45–65.

Cohn, Bernard (1996), *Colonialism and Its Forms of Knowledge: The British In India*, Princeton: Princeton University Press.

Colley, Linda (1992), *Britons: Forging the Nation, 1707–1837*, New Haven: Yale University Press, 1992.

Comaroff, Jean and John Comaroff (1982), *Ethnography and the Historical Imagination*, Boulder: Westview Press.

Conklin, A.L. (2013), *In the Museum of Man: Race, Anthropology, and Empire in France, 1850–1950*. Ithaca: Cornell University Press.

Connell, R.W. (1995), *Masculinities*, Cambridge: Polity Press.

Conrad, Sebastian (2012), *German Colonialism: A Short History*, Cambridge: Cambridge University Press.
Cooper, Frederick (1980), *From Slaves to Squatters: Plantation Labor and Agriculture in Zanzibar and Coastal Kenya 1890–1925*, New Haven: Yale University Press.
Cooper, Frederick (1992), "Colonizing Time: Work Rhythms and Labor Conflict in Colonial Mombasa," in Nicholas Dirks (ed.), *Colonialism and Culture*, Ann Arbor: University of Michigan Press.
Cooper, Frederick (1994), "Conflict and Connection: Rethinking Colonial African History," *American Historical Review* 99 (5): 1516–45.
Cooper, Frederick (2005), *Colonialism in Question: Theory, Knowledge, History*. Berkeley: University of California Press.
Cooper, Frederick and Ann Laura Stoler, (1997), "Between Metropole and Colony: Rethinking a Research Agenda," in Cooper and Stoler (eds), *Tensions of Empire: Colonial Cultures in a Bourgeois World*, Berkeley: University of California Press.
Copland, Ian (2006), "Christianity as an Arm of Empire: the ambiguous case of India under the Company, c. 1813–1858," *Historical Journal*, 4: 1025–54.
Coquery-Vidrovitch, C. (2003), "Vendre: le mythe économique colonial," in S. Lemaire and P. Blanchard, *Culture Coloniale 1871–1931: La France conquise par son empire*, 163–75, Paris; Éditions Autrement.
Corrigan, Gordon (n.d.), *Sepoys in the Trenches: The Indian Corps on the Western Front, 1914–15*.
Costello, R. (2015), *Black Tommies : British soldiers of African descent in the First World War*, Liverpool: Liverpool University Press.
Crais, Clifton C. and Pamela Scully (2008), *Sara Baartman and the Hottentot Venus: a ghost story and a biography*, Princeton, NJ, Woodstock: Princeton University Press.
Craton, Michael (1982), *Testing the Chains: Resistance to Slavery in the British West Indies*, Ithaca: Cornell University Press.
Crosby, A.W. (1972), *The Columbian Exchange: Biological and Cultural Consequences of 1492*, Westport, CN: Greenwood Press.
Crosby, A.W. (1986), *Ecological Imperialism: The Biological Expansion of Europe, 900–1900*, New York: Cambridge University Press.
Cruikshank, J. (2005), *Do Glaciers Listen? Local Knowledge, Colonial Encounters, and Social Imagination*, Vancouver: UBC Press.
Crutzen, P.J. and E.F. Stoermer (2000), "The 'Anthropocene,'" *IGBP Newsletter*, 41: 17–18.
Cullen, Rose (2012), "Empire, Indian Indentured Labour and the Colony: The Debate over 'Coolie' Labour in New South Wales, 1836–1838," *History Australia*, 9 (1): 84–109.
Cunningham, Hugh (1982), "Class and Leisure in Mid-Victorian England," in Waites, Bennett and Martin (eds), *Popular Culture: Past and Present*, London: Croom Helm.
Cunningham, Hugh (1990), "Leisure and Culture," in F.M.L. Thompson (ed.), *The Cambridge Social History of Britain 1750–1950 vol. 2: The People and their Environment*, Cambridge: Cambridge University Press.
Curthoys, A. (2014), "The Lying Name of 'Government': Empire, Mobility and Political Rights," in J. Carey and J. Lydon, *Indigenous Networks: Mobility, Connections and Exchange*, 75–94, New York: Routledge.
Curtin, P.D. (1989), *Death by Migration: Europe's Encounter with the Tropical World*, New York: Cambridge University Press.

Curtin, P.D. (1998), *Disease and Empire: The Health of European Troops in the Conquest of Africa*, Cambridge: Cambridge University Press.

Cushman, G.T. (2011), "Humboldtian Science, Creole Meteorology and the Discovery of Human-Caused Climate Change in South America," *Osiris*, 26 (1): 19–44.

D'Cruze, Shani (1992), "Approaching the History of Rape and Sexual Violence: notes towards research," *Women's History Review*, 1 (3): 337–97.

Dalrymple, William (2002), *White Mughals: love and betrayal in eighteenth-century India*, London: Harper Collins.

Daniel, Valentine, Henry Bernstein, and Tom Brass, eds (1992), *Special Issue on Plantations, Proletarians and Peasants in Colonial Asia*, London: Frank Cass.

Danziger, Raphael (1977), *Abd al Qadir and the Algerians: Resistance to the French and Internal Consolidation*, New York: Holmes and Meier.

Darwin, John (2009), *The Empire Project: The Rise and Fall of the British World-System, 1830—1970*, Cambridge: Cambridge University Press.

Daughton, J.P. (2008), *An Empire Divided Religion, Republicanism, and the Making of French Colonialism, 1880–1914*, Oxford: Oxford University Press.

Davin, Anna (1978), "Imperialism and Motherhood," *History Workshop*: 9–65.

Davin, Anna (1997), in Ann Stoler and Frederick Cooper, *Tensions of Empire: Colonial Cultures in a Bourgeois World*, Berkeley: University of California Press, 87–151.

Davis, David Brion (1999), *The Problem of Slavery in the Age of Revolution, 1770–1823*, New York: Oxford University Press.

Davis, D.K. (2007), *Resurrecting the Granary of Rome: Environmental History and French Colonial Expansion in North Africa*, Athens, OH: Ohio University Press.

Davis, D.K. (2011), "Imperialism, Orientalism and the Environment in the Middle East," in D.K. Davis and E. Burke III, *Environmental Imaginaries of the Middle East and North Africa*, 1–11, Athens, OH: Ohio University Press.

Davis, M. (2001), *Late Victorian Holocausts: El Niño Famines and the Making of the Third World*, New York: Verso.

De Groot, Joanna (2000), "'Sex' and 'Race': the construction of language and image in the nineteenth century," in Catherine Hall (ed.), *Cultures of Empire, a reader: colonizers in Britain and the empire in the nineteenth and twentieth centuries*, 37–61, Manchester: Manchester University Press.

De Groot, Joanna (2006), "Metropolitan Desires and Colonial Connections: Reflections on Consumption and Empire," in Catherine Hall and Sonya O. Rose (eds), *At Home with the Empire: Metropolitan Culture and the Imperial World*, Cambridge: Cambridge University Press.

De Knecht-Van Eekelen, A. (2001), "The Debate about Acclimatization in the Dutch East Indies (1840–1860)," in N.A. Rupke (ed.), *Medical Geography in Historical Perspective*, 70–85, London: Wellcome Institute Trust for the History of Medicine.

Deacon, Desley, Penny Russell and Angela Woollacott, eds (2010), *Transnational Lives: Biographies of Global Modernity, 1700–Present*, Basingstoke: Palgrave.

Deacon, H. (2000), "The Politics of Medical Geography: Seeking Healthiness at the Cape During the Nineteenth Century," in R. Wrigley and G. Revill (eds), *Pathologies of Travel*, 279–98, Amsterdam: Rodopi.

Delisle, P. (2001), "Un échec relatif : La mission des engagés indiens aux Antilles et à la Réunion (seconde moitié du XIXe siècle)," *Outre-mers*: 189–203.

Demay, A. (2014), *Tourism and Colonization in Indochina, 1898–1939*, Newcastle upon Tyne: Cambridge Scholars Publishing.

Dempsey, M. (2013), "The Symptoms of a Heart of Darkness," *International Journal of Humanities and Social Science*, 3 (7): 327–31.

Derks, Hans (2012), *History of the Opium Problem: The Assault on the East, c. 1600–1950*, Leiden: Brill.

Desai, Ashwin and Goolam Vahed (2015), *The South African Gandhi: Stretcher-Bearer of Empire*, Stanford: Stanford University Press.

Dessalines, Jean-Jacques (1804), "Proclamation." Available online, http://mjp.univ-perp.fr/constit/ht1804.htm [accessed April 15, 2017].

Dickens, Charles and Dutt (1841), "Report of the Committee to Inquire into the Abuses Alleged to Exist in Exporting the Bengal Hill Coolies and Indian Labourers, of Various Classes, to Other Countries, 1839," in *Hill Coolies*, 4–12, London: House of Commons.

Donno, Fabrizio De (2006), "La Razza Ario-Mediterranea: Ideas of Race and Citizenship in Colonial and Fascist Italy, 1885–1941," *Interventions*, 8 (3).

Dorsey, J.C. (2004), "Identity, Rebellion, and Social Justice among Chinese Contract Workers in Nineteenth-Century Cuba," *Latin American Perspectives*, 31 (3): 18–47.

Douglas, K. (2014), "'For the Sake of a Little Grass': A Comparative History of Settler Science and Environmental Limits in South Australia and the Great Plains," in J. Beattie, E. O'Gorman and M. Henry (eds), *Climate, Science and Colonisation: Histories from Australia and New Zealand*, 99–117, Basingstoke: Palgrave Macmillan.

Dowie, M. (2009), *Conservation Refugees: The Hundred-Year Conflict between Global Conservation and Native Peoples*, Cambridge, MA: The MIT Press.

Drayton, R. (2000), *Nature's Government: Science, Imperial Britain, and the 'Improvement' of the World*, New Haven, CT: Yale University Press.

Drescher, S. (2009), *Abolition : a history of slavery and antislavery*, Cambridge: Cambridge University Press.

Dube, F. (2012), "Public Health and Racial Segregation in South Africa: Mahatma Gandhi Debates Colonial Authorities on Public Health Measures 1896–1904," *Journal of the Historical Society of Nigeria*, 21: 21–40.

Dubois, Laurent (2004), *Avengers of the New World: The Story of the Haitian Revolution*, Cambridge, MA: Belknap.

Dubois, Laurent (2007), "The Haitian Revolution and the Sale of Louisiana," *Southern Quarterly* 44 (3): 18–41.

Dubois, Laurent (2012), *Haiti: The Aftershocks of History*, New York: Metropolitan Books.

Dubois, Laurent and John Garrigus (2006), *Slave Revolution in the Caribbean, 1791–1804: A Brief History with Documents*, Boston: Bedford/St. Martin's.

Dubois, Laurent and J.S. Scott (2010), *Origins of the Black Atlantic*, New York: Routledge.

Duncan, J. (1997), "Sites of Representation: Place, Time and the Discourse of the Other," in J.S. Duncan and D. Ley (eds), *Place/Culture/Representation*, 39–56, London: Routledge.

Dunne, Bruce (1994), "French Regulation of Prostitution in Nineteenth-Century Colonial Algeria," *The Arab Studies Journal*, 2 (1), 24–30.

Dussart, Fae (2013), "'To Glut a Menial's Grudge': Domestic servants and the Ilbert Bill controversy of 1883," *Journal of Colonialism and Colonial History*, 14 (1): https://muse.jhu.edu/ [accessed May 14, 2016].

Dwyer, Philip and Lyndall Ryan (2016), "Reflections on Genocide and Settler-Colonial Violence," *History Australia*, 13 (3): 335–50.

Echenberg, M. (2002), "Pestis Redux: The Initial Years of the Third Bubonic Plague Pandemic, 1894–1901," *Journal of World History*, 13 (2): 429–49.

Edwards, P. (2003), "On Home Ground: Settling Land and Domesticating Difference in the 'Non-Settler' Colonies of Burma and Cambodia," *Journal of Colonialism and Colonial History*, 4 (3): doi:10.1353/cch.2004.0002.

Eisenlohr, Patrick (2006), "The Politics of Diaspora and the Morality of Secularism: Muslim Identities and Islamic Authority in Mauritius," *Journal of the Royal Anthropological Institute* 12 (2): 395–412.

Elbourne, Elizabeth (2008), *Blood Ground: colonialism, missions, and the contest for Christianity in the Cape Colony and Britain, 1799–1853*, Montreal: McGill-Queen's University Press.

Ellinghaus, Katherine (2006), *Taking Assimilation to Heart. Marriages of White Women and Indigenous Men in the United States and Australia, 1887–1937*, Lincoln: University of Nebraska Press.

Elliott, J.H. (2006), *Empires of the Atlantic World: Britain and Spain in America, 1492–1830*, New Haven: Yale University Press.

Endfield, G. and S. Randalls (2015), "Climate and Empire," in J. Beattie, E. Melillo and E. O'Gorman (eds), *Eco-Cultural Networks and the British Empire: New Views of Environmental History*, 21–43, New York: Bloomsbury.

Endfield, G.H. (2008), *Climate and Society in Colonial Mexico*, Oxford: Blackwell.

Endfield, G.H. and D.J. Nash (2002a), "Drought, Desiccation and Discourse: Missionary Correspondence and Nineteenth Century Climate Change in Central Southern Africa," *Geographical Journal*, 168 (1): 33–47

Endfield, G.H. and D.J. Nash (2002b), "Missionaries and Morals: Climatic Discourse in Nineteenth-Century Central Southern Africa," *Annals of the Association of American Geographers*, 92 (4): 727–42.

Endfield, G.H. and D.J. Nash (2007), "'A Good Site for Health': Missionaries and the Pathological Geography of Central Southern Africa," *Singapore Journal of Tropical Geography*, 28 (2): 142–57.

Etheridge, Stephen (2012), "Brass bands in the Southern Pennines 1857–1914: The Ethos of Rational Recreation and the Perception of Working Class Respectability," in Baldwin, Ellis, Etheridge, Pye and Laybourn (eds), *Class, Culture and Community: New Perspectives in Nineteenth and Twentieth Century British Labor History*, Newcastle: Cambridge Scholars Publishing.

Fabian, Johannes ([1983] 2000), *Time and the Other: How Anthropology Makes its Object*, New York: Columbia University Press.

Fanon, Frantz (1952), *Black Skin, White Masks*, 1967 translation by Charles Lam Markmann, New York: Grove Press.

Fanon, Frantz (1961), *The Wretched of the Earth*, 1963 translation by Constance Farrington, New York: Grove Weidenfeld.

Featuna'i Liua'ana, Ben (1997), "Dragons in little paradise: Chinese (mis-) fortunes in Samoa, 1900–1950," *Journal of Pacific History*, 32 (1): 29–48.

Feillet, P. (1900), *La politique indigène en Nouvelle Calédonie*, Extrait de 'L'Année Coloniale, Paris: Librairie Charles Tallandier.

Ferguson, James (1999), *Expectations of Modernity: Myths and Meanings of Urban Life in the Zambian Copperbelt*, Berkeley: University of California Press.

Ferrer, Ada (2014), *Freedom's Mirror: Cuba and Haiti in the Age of Revolution*, New York: Cambridge University Press.

Fick, Carolyn (1990), *The Making of Haiti: The Saint Domingue Revolution from Below*, Knoxville: University of Tennessee Press.

Fieldhouse, David (1984), "Can Humpty-Dumpty be put together again? Imperial history in the 1980s," *The Journal of Imperial and Commonwealth History*, 12 (2): 9–23.

Firth, Stewart (1976), "The transformation of the labour trade in German New Guinea, 1899–1914," *Journal of Pacific History*, 11 (1): 51–65.
Fisch, Jörg (2015), *The Right of Self-Determination of Peoples: The Domestication of an Illusion*, trans. Anita Mage, Cambridge: Cambridge University Press.
Fischer, Eugen (1913), *Die Rehebother Bastards und das Bastardisierungsproblem beim Menschen*, Jena: Gustav Fischer.
Fischer, F. (1999), *Alsaciens et Lorrains en Algérie: Histoire d'une migration 1830–1914*, Nice: Jacques Gandini.
Fitzpatrick, Matthew P. (2008), *Liberal Imperialism in Germany: Expansionism and Nationalism, 1848–1884*, New York: Berghahn.
Fitzpatrick, Matthew P. (2015), *Purging the Empire: Mass Expulsions in Germany, 1871–1914*, Oxford: Oxford University Press.
Fleming, J.R. (1998), *Historical Perspectives on Climate Change*, New York: Oxford University Press.
Fleming, J.R. and V. Jankovic (2011), "Revisiting Klima," *Osiris*, 26 (1): 1–15.
Ford, C. (2016), *Natural Interests: The Contest Over Environment in Modern France*, Cambridge, MA: Harvard University Press.
Foucault, Michel (1977), *Discipline and Punish: The Birth of the Prison*, translated by Alan Sheridan, London: Allen Lane.
Foucault, Michel (1990), *The History of Sexuality*, London: Penguin.
Foucault, Michel (2002a), *The Order of Things: An Archaeology of the Human Sciences*, New York, Routledge.
Foucault, Michel (2002b), *The Archaeology of Knowledge*, New York: Routledge.
Frank, Andre Gunder (1998), *ReOrient: The Global Economy in the Asian Age*, Berkeley, University of California Press.
Freund, Bill (1991a), "The Rise and Decline of an Indian Peasantry in Natal," *Journal of Peasant Studies* 18 (2): 263–87.
Freund, Bill (1991b), "Indian Women and the Changing Character of the Working Class Indian Household in Natal 1860–1990," *Journal of Southern African Studies* 17 (3): 414–29.
Frey, Sylvia (1991), *Water from the Rock: Black Resistance in a Revolutionary Age*, Princeton: Princeton University Press.
Gale, G. (2011), *Dying on the vine : how phylloxera transformed wine*, Berkeley: University of California Press.
Gallagher, John and Ronald Robinson (1953), "The Imperialism of Free Trade," *The Economic History Review*, New Series, 6 (1): 1–15.
Garrigus, John (2006), *Before Haiti: Race and Citizenship in French Saint-Domingue*, New York: Palgrave Macmillan.
Geggus, David (1997), "Slavery, War, and Revolution in the Greater Caribbean, 1789–1815," in David Gaspar and David Geggus (eds), *A Turbulent Time: The French Revolution and the Greater Caribbean*, 1–50, Bloomington, IN: Indiana University Press.
Geggus, David (2014), *The Haitian Revolution: A Documentary History*, Indianapolis and Cambridge: Hackett.
Geggus, David and Normal Fiering, eds (2009), *The World of the Haitian Revolution*, Bloomington, IN: Indiana University Press.
Geppert, Alex C.T. (2013), *Fleeting Cities: Imperial Expositions in Fin-de-siècle Europe*, London: Palgrave Macmillan.
Ghachem, Malick (2012), *The Old Regime and the Haitian Revolution*, Cambridge: Cambridge University Press.

Gilman, Sander (1985), *Difference and Pathology. Stereotypes of Sexuality, Race and Madness*, Ithaca: Cornell University Press.

Gilroy, Paul (1993), *The Black Atlantic: Modernity and Double Consciousness*, London: Verso.

Ginio, Ruth (2010), "French Officers, African Officers, and the Violent Image of African Colonial Soldiers," *Historical Reflections*, Vol. 36, no. 2: 59–75.

Glassman, Jonathon (2000), "Sorting out the tribes: The creation of racial identities in colonial Zanzibar's newspaper wars," *Journal of African History* 41: 395–428.

Gobat, Michel (2013), "The Invention of Latin America: A Transnational History of Anti-Imperialism, Democracy, and Race," *American Historical Review* 118 (5): 1345–75.

Gobineau, Joseph Arthur (1983), "Essai sur l'inégalité des races humaines," *Oeuvres*, Vol. 1, Paris: Gallimard.

Golinski, J. (2007), *British Weather and the Climate of Enlightenment*, Chicago: University of Chicago Press.

Gordon, Michelle (2015), "Colonial Violence and Holocaust Studies," *Holocaust Studies*, 21 (4).

Gordon, Robert J. (2009), "Hiding in Full View: The 'Forgotten' Bushman Genocides of Namibia," *Genocide Studies and Prevention*, 4 (1): 29–57.

Gosewinkel, Dieter (2003), *Einbürgern und Ausschließen: Die Nationalisierung der Staatsangehörigkeit vom Deutschen Bund bis zur Bundesrepublik Deutschland*. Göttingen: Vandenhoeck and Ruprecht.

Gott, Richard (2011), *Britain's Empire: Resistance, Repression and Revolt*, London: Verso.

Grandmaison, O.L.C. (2005), *Coloniser Exterminer: Sur la guerre et l'État colonial*, Paris: Fayard.

Green, Nile (2008), "Islam for the Indentured Indian: A Muslim Missionary in Colonial South Africa," *Bulletin of the School of Oriental and African Studies* 71 (3): 529–53.

Greenblatt, S. (2010), *Cultural Mobility: A Manifesto*, New York: Cambridge University Press.

Grieco, Elizabeth (1998), "The Effects of Migration on the Establishment of Networks: Caste Disintegration and Reformation Among the Indians of Fiji," *International Migration Review* 32 (3): 704–36.

Griffiths, T. (2005), "The Roaring Forties," in T. Sherratt, T. Griffiths and L. Robin (eds), *A Change in the Weather: Climate and Culture in Australia*, 152–65, Canberra: NMA Press.

Grimshaw, Patricia (2007), "Faith, missionary life and the family," in Philippa Levine (ed.), *Gender and Empire: The OHBE Companion Series*, 260–81, Oxford: Oxford University Press.

Grosse, P. (2003), "Turning Native? Anthropology, German Colonialism, and the Paradoxes of the 'Acclimatization Question', 1885–1914," in H.G. Penny and M. Bunzl (eds), *Worldly Provincialism: German Anthropology in the Age of Empire*, 179–97, Ann Arbor, MI: University of Michigan Press.

Grove, R.H. (1993), "Conserving Eden: The (European) East India Companies and their Environmental Policies on St. Helena, Mauritius and in Western India, 1660–1854," *Comparative Studies in Society and History*, 35 (2): 318–51.

Grove, R.H. (1995), *Green Imperialism: Colonial Expansion, Tropical Edens and the Origins of Environmentalism, 1600–1860*, Cambridge: Cambridge University Press.

Grove, R.H. (1997), *Ecology, Climate and Empire: Colonialism and Global Environmental History, 1400–1940*, Cambridge: White Horse Press.

Grove, R.H. (1998), "The East India Company, the Raj and the El Niño: The Critical Role Played by Colonial Scientists in Establishing the Mechanisms of Global Climate Teleconnections 1770–1930," in R.H. Grove, V. Damodaran and S. Sangwan (eds), *Nature and the Orient: The Environmental History of South and Southeast Asia*, 301–23, New York: Oxford University Press.

Grove, R.H. (2005), "Revolutionary Weather: The Climatic and Economic Crisis of 1788–1795 and the Discovery of El Niño," in T. Sherratt, T. Griffiths and L. Robin (eds), *A Change in the Weather: Climate and Culture in Australia*, 128–40, Canberra: NMA Press.

Guha, Ranajit, ed. (1997), *A Subaltern Studies Reader, 1986–1995*, Minneapolis, MN: University of Minnesota Press.

Guha, Ranajit (2002), *History at the Limit of World History*, New York: Columbia University Press.

Guiart, J. (1968), "Le cadre social traditionnel et la rébellion de 1878 dans le pays de La Foa, Nouvelle-Calédonie," *Journal de la Société des océanistes*, 97–119.

Ha, Marie-Paule (2013), "The Making of the *Coloniale* Under the Third Republic," in Robert Aldrich and Kirsten Mackenzie (eds), *The Routledge History of Western Empires*, 222–37, London and New York: Routledge 2013.

Ha, Marie-Paule (2014), *French Women and the Empire: The Case of Indochina*, Oxford: Oxford University Press.

Haddad, Mouloud (2010), "Les maîtres de l'Heure. Soufisme et eschatologie en Algérie coloniale (1845–1901), *Revue d'histoire du XIXe siècle* (41): 49–61.

Hagemann, Karen, Gisela Mettele, and Jane Rendall, eds (2010), *Gender, War and Politics: Transatlantic Perspectives, 1775–1830*, Basingstoke: Palgrave Macmillan.

Haggerty, Sheryllynne, Anthony Webster and Nicholas J. White, eds (2008), *The Empire in One City? Liverpool's Inconvenient and Imperial Past*, Manchester: Manchester University Press.

Hall, Catherine (2000), "The Rule of Difference: Gender, Class, and Empire in the Making of the 1832 Reform Act," in Ida Blom, Karen Hagemann, and Catherine Hall (eds), *Gendered Nations, Nationalism and the Gender Order in the Long Nineteenth Century*, Oxford: Berg.

Hall, Catherine (2000), "Introduction: thinking the postcolonial, thinking the empire," in Catherine Hall (ed.), *Cultures of Empire: Colonizers in Britain and the Empire in the Nineteenth and Twentieth Centuries: A Reader*, New York: Routledge.

Hall, Catherine (2002), *Civilising Subjects: Metropole and Colony in the English Imagination, 1830–1867*, Cambridge: Polity; and Chicago: University of Chicago Press.

Hall, Catherine (2004), "Of Gender and Empire: Reflections on the Nineteenth Century," in Phillippa Levine (ed.), *Gender and Empire (The Oxford History of the British Empire, Companion Series)*, Oxford: Oxford University Press.

Hall, Catherine (2007), "Of Gender and Empire: Reflections on the Nineteenth Century," in Phillipa Levine (ed.), *Gender and Empire*, 46–77, Oxford: Oxford University Press.

Hall, Catherine (2014), "Gendering Property, Racing Capital," *History Workshop Journal* 78, (1): 22–38.

Hall, Catherine and Sonya O. Rose (2006), *At Home with the Empire: Metropolitan Culture and the Imperial World*, Cambridge: Cambridge University Press.

Hall, Catherine, Nicholas Draper, Keith McClelland, Katie Donington and Rachel Lang (2014), *Legacies of British Slave-Ownership: Colonial Slavery and the Formation of Victorian Britain*, Cambridge: Cambridge University Press.

Hall, Stuart (1978), *Policing the Crisis*, London: Palgrave.

Hall, Stuart (1996), "Who Needs 'Identity'?" in Stuart Hall and Paul du Gay (eds), *Questions of Cultural Identity*, London: Sage.

Hall, Stuart (1997), *Race: The Floating Signifier*. Directed by Sut Jhally. The transcript can be found at http://www.mediaed.org/transcripts/Stuart-Hall-Race-the-Floating-Signifier-Transcript.pdf [accessed January 25, 2017].

Hämäläinen, Pekka (2008), *The Comanche Empire*, New Haven: Yale University Press.

Harding, R.E. (2003), *A Refuge in Thunder: Candomblé and Alternative Spaces of Blackness*, Bloomington: Indiana University Press.

Hardy, R.D. and B.L. Nuse (2016), "Global Sea-Level Rise: Weighing Country Responsibility and Risk," *Climatic Change*, 137 (3–4): 333–45.

Harlow, Barbara and Mike Carter, eds (1999), *Imperialism and Colonialism: A Documentary Sourcebook*, Oxford: Blackwell.

Harries, Patrick (1987), "Plantations, Passes and Proletarians: Labor and the Colonial State in Nineteenth Century Natal," *Journal of Southern African Studies* 13 (3): 372–99.

Harrison, M. (1996), "'The Tender Frame of Man': Disease, Climate and Racial Difference in India and the West Indies, 1760–1860," *Bulletin of the History of Medicine*, 70 (1): 68–93.

Harrison, M. (1999), *Climates and Constitutions: Health, Race, Environment and British Imperialism in India, 1600–1850*, Oxford: Oxford University Press.

Harrison, M. (2000), "Differences of Degree: Representations of India in British Medical Topography, 1820–c.1870," *Medical History Supplement*, 44 (20): 51–69.

Harrison, M. (2001), "Medicine and Orientalism: Perspectives on Europe's Encounter with Indian Medical Systems," in B. Pati and M. Harrison (eds), *Health, Medicine and Empire: Perspectives on Colonial India*, 37–87, Hyderabad: Orient Longman.

Haslam, E. (2012), "Redemption, Colonialism and International Criminal Law: The Nineteenth Century Slave-Trading Trials of Samo and Peters," in D. Kirby, *Past Law, Present Histories*, 7–22, Australian National University E Press.

Hay, S. (1989), "The Making of a Late-Victorian Hindu: M. K. Gandhi in London, 1888–1891," *Victorian Studies*, 33 (1): 75–98.

Hendrickson, H., ed. (1996), *Clothing and Difference: Embodied Identities in Colonial and Post-Colonial Africa*. Durham, NC: Duke University Press.

Herndon, Ruth Wallis (2002), "Women as Symbols of Disorder in Early Rhode Island," in Tamara Hunt and Micheline Lessard (eds), *Women and the Colonial Gaze*, 79–91, Basingstoke: Palgrave.

Heuer, J. (2009), "The One-Drop Rule in Reverse? Interracial Marriages in Napoleonic and Restoration France," *Law and History Review*, 27 (3): 515–48.

Heymann, M. (2010), "The evolution of climate ideas and knowledge," *WIREs: Climate Change*, 1 (4): 581–97.

Hilhorst, D. and G. Bankoff (2004), "Mapping Vulnerability," in G. Bankoff, G. Frerks and D. Hilhorst (eds), *Mapping Vulnerability: Disasters, Development and People*, 1–9, London: Earthscan.

Hill, John (1999), *British Cinema in the 1980s: issues and themes*, Oxford: Clarendon Press.

Hobsbawm, Eric (1989), *The Age of Empire 1875–1914*, New York: Vintage.

Hobson, J.H. (1902), *Imperialism: A Study*, London: James Nisbet and Co.

Hochschild, Adam (1999), *King Leopold's Ghost: A Story of Greed, Terror and Heroism in Colonial Africa*, Boston: Houghton Mifflin.

Hoffenberg, Peter J. (2001), *An Empire on Display: English, Indian and Australian Exhibitions from the Crystal Palace to the Great War*, Berkeley: University of California Press.

Hollup, Oddyar (1994), "The Disintegration of Caste and Changing Concepts of Indian Ethnic Identity in Mauritius," *Ethnology* 33 (4): 297–316.

Hopkins, Ruth (2015), Tweet, May 20, 2015. Available online, https://twitter.com/RuthHHopkins/status/601081779831721984 [accessed May 11, 2017].

Howe, Stephen, (2010), "Introduction: New Imperial Histories," in Stephen Howe (ed.), *The New Imperial Histories Reader*, London and New York: Routledge.

Howell, P. (2009), *Geographies of Regulation: Policing Prostitution in Nineteenth-Century Britain and the Empire*, Cambridge: Cambridge University Press.

Howkins, Alan (1981), "The Taming of Whitsun," in S. Yeo and E. Yeo (eds), *Popular Culture and Class Conflict*, Brighton: Harvester.

Hughes, L. (2006), *Moving the Maasai: A Colonial Misadventure*, Basingstoke and New York: Palgrave Macmillan.

Hulme, M. (2011), "Reducing the Future to Climate: A Story of Climate Determinism and Reductionism," *Osiris*, 26: 245–66.

Hunt, Doug (2007), "Hunting the Blackbirder: Ross Lewin and the Royal Navy," *Journal of Pacific History*, 42 (1): 37–53.

Hunt, Tamara (2002), "Introduction: The Colonial Gaze," in Tamara Hunt and Micheline Lessard (eds), *Women and the Colonial Gaze*, 1–17, Basingstoke: Palgrave.

Hurgobin, Y. (2016), "Making Medical Ideologies: Indentured Labor in Mauritius," in A. Winterbottom and F. Tesfaye (eds), *Histories of Medicine and Healing in the Indian Ocean World*, vol. 2, 1–26, Basingstoke: Palgrave Macmillan.

Hussain, N. (2003), *The jurisprudence of emergency : colonialism and the rule of law*, Ann Arbor: University of Michigan Press.

Hyam, Ronald (1988), "Imperialism and Sexual Exploitation: a reply," *Journal of Imperial and Commonwealth History* 17 (1): 90–8.

Hyam, Ronald (1990), *Empire and Sexuality: The British Experience*. Manchester: Manchester University Press.

Hyslop, Jonathan (1999), "The Imperial Working Class makes itself 'White': White Laborism in Britain, Australia and South Africa Before the First World War," *The Journal of Historical Sociology* 12 (4): 398–421.

Hyslop, Jonathan (2011), "An 'Eventful' History of Hind Swaraj: Gandhi between the Battle of Sushima and the Union of South Africa," *Public Culture* 23 (2): 299–319.

Iyob, Ruth (2000), "Madamismo and Beyond: The Construction of Eritrean Women," *Nineteenth Century Contexts*, 22 (2).

Jackson, Anna and Amin Jaffer, eds. (2009), *Maharaja: The Splendour of India's Royal Courts*, London: V&A Publishing.

Jacobs, Margaret D. (2009), *White Mother to a Dark Race: Settler Colonialism, Maternalism, and the Removal of Indigenous Children in the American West and Australia, 1880–1940*, Lincoln, University of Nebraska Press.

Jaffer, Amin, ed. (2013), *Beyond Extravagance: A Royal Collection of Gems and Jewels*, New York: Assouline Publishing, 2013.

James, C.L.R. (1938; 2nd edn 1963), *The Black Jacobins: Toussaint Louverture and the San Domingo Revolution*, New York: Vintage.

Jankovic, V. (2000), *Reading the Skies*, Chicago: University of Chicago Press.

Jasanoff, Maya (2011), *Liberty's Exiles: American Loyalists in the Revolutionary World*, New York: Alfred Knopf.

Jayawardena, Chandra (1980), "Culture and Ethnicity in Guyana and Fiji," *Man* 15 (3): 430–50.

Jefferess, David (2008), *Postcolonial Resistance: Culture, Liberation, and Transformation*, Toronto and Buffalo: University of Toronto Press.

Jefferson, Thomas (1809), Letter to James Madison, April 27, 1809. Available online, https://www.loc.gov/exhibits/jefferson/149.html [accessed May 11, 2017].

Jennings, E.T. (2006), *Curing the Colonizers: Hydrotherapy, Climatology, and French Colonial Spas*, Durham, NC: Duke University Press.

Jennings, E.T. (2011), *Imperial Heights: Dalat and the Making and Undoing of French Indochina*, Berkeley, CA: University of California Press.

Jennings, E.T. (2014), "Hill Stations, Spas, Clubs, Safaris and Colonial Life," in K. McKenzie and R. Aldrich (eds), *The Routledge History of Western Empires*, 824–60, Abingdon: Routledge.

Johnson, S. (2011), *Climate and Catastrophe in Cuba and the Atlantic World in the Age of Revolution*, Chapel Hill, NC: University of North Carolina Press.

Johnson, S.E. (2012), *The Fear of French Negroes: Transcolonial Collaboration in the Revolutionary Americas*, Berkeley: University of California Press.

Jones, Robin D. (2007), *Interiors of Empire: Objects, Space and Identity within the Indian Subcontinent, c. 1800–1947*, Manchester: Manchester University Press.

Kale, Madhavi (1998), *Fragments of Empire: Capital, Anti-slavery, and Indian Indentured Labor Migration to the British Caribbean*, Philadelphia: University of Pennsylvania Press.

Kalifa, D. (2009), *Biribi: Les bagnes coloniaux de l'armée française*, Paris: Perrin.

Kaplan, Martha and John Kelly (1994), "Rethinking Resistance: Dialogics of 'Disaffection' in Colonial Fiji," *American Ethnologist* 21 (1): 123–51.

Kappeler, Andreas (2001), *The Russian Empire: A Multi-Ethnic History*, New York: Routledge.

Kaps, M.H.S.K., ed. (2017), *Merchants and Trade Networks in the Atlantic and Medterranean 1550–1800 Connectors of Commercial Maritime Systems*, New York: Routledge.

Karabell, Zachary (2003), *Parting the Desert: The Creation of the Suez Canal*, London: John Murray.

Kateb, Kamel (2001), *Européens, 'indigènes' et juifs en Algérie (1830–1962). Représentations et réalités des populations*, Paris: Presses universitaires de France.

Kelly, John (1988), "From Holi to Diwali in Fiji: An Essay on Ritual and History," *Man* 23 (1): 40–55.

Kelly, John (1992), "Fiji Indians and 'Commoditization of Labor,'" *American Ethnologist* 19 (1): 97–120.

Kelso, C. and C. Vogel (2007), "The Climate of Namaqualand in the Nineteenth Century," *Climatic Change*, 83 (3): 357–80.

Kennedy, D. (1996), *The Magic Mountains: Hill Stations and the British Raj*, Berkeley, CA: University of California Press.

Kenny, J. (1995), "Climate, Race and Imperial Authority: The Symbolic Landscape of the British Hill Station in India," *Annals of the Association of American Geographers*, 85 (4): 694–714.

Kent, Susan Kingsley (1993), *Making Peace: The Reconstruction of Gender in Interwar Britain*, Princeton: Princeton University Press.

Kent, Susan Kingsley (2009), *Aftershocks: The Politics of Trauma in Britain, 1918–1931*, Basingstoke: Palgrave Macmillan.
Kerber, Linda (1980), *Women of the Republic: Intellect and Ideology in Revolutionary America*, Chapel Hill: University of North Carolina Press.
Kerr, I.J. (2007), *Engines of Change: The Railroads that Made India*, Westport, CT: Praeger.
Klein, M. (1998), *Slavery and Colonial Rule in French West Africa*, Cambridge: Cambridge University Press.
Kleingeld, Pauline (2007), "Kant's Second Thoughts on Race," *Philosophical Quarterly*, 57 (229): 573–92.
Klose, F. (2016), "Enforcing Abolition: the Entanglement of Civil Society Action, Humanitarian Norm-Setting, and Military Intervention," in F. Klose, *The Emergence of Humanitarian Intervention: Ideas and Practice from the Nineteenth Century to the Present*, 91–120, Cambridge: Cambridge University Press.
Kolsky, Elizabeth (2010), "The Rule of Colonial Indifference," *The Journal of Asian Studies*, 69 (4): 1093–111.
Kramer, Paul (2006), "Race-Making and Colonial Violence in the US Empire: The Philippine-American War as Race War," *Diplomatic History*, 30 (2).
Krebs, Paula M. (2004), *Gender, Race, and the Writing of Empire: Public Discourse and the Boer War*, Cambridge: Cambridge University Press.
Kurlansky, Mark (1998), *Cod: A Biography of the Fish That Changed the World*, London: Jonathan Cape.
Kwass, M. (2014), *Contraband: Louis Mandrin and the Making of a Global Underground*, Cambridge, MA, Harvard University Press.
Lahiri, S. (2000), *Anglo-Indian Encounters, Race and Identity 1880–1930*, London: Cass.
Laidlaw, Zoë (2012), "Breaking Britannia's Bounds? Law, Settlers, and Space in Britain's Imperial Historiography," *The Historical Journal* 55 (3): 807–30.
Lake, Marilyn (1999), *Getting Equal: the history of Australian feminism*, St. Leonards, NSW: Allen & Unwin.
Lake, Marilyn and Henry Reynolds (2008), *Drawing the Global Colour Line: White Men's Countries and the International Challenge of Racial Equality*, Cambridge: Cambridge University Press.
Lal, Brij (1980), "Approaches to the Study of Indian Indentured Emigration with Special Reference to Fiji," *The Journal of Pacific History* 15 (1): 52–70.
Lal, Brij (1983), *Girmitiyas: The Origins of the Fiji Indians*, Canberra: Fiji Institute of Applied Studies.
Lal, Brij (2011), "New Homelands: Hindu Communities in Mauritius, Guyana, Trinidad, South Africa, Fiji and East Africa," *The Journal of Pacific History* 46 (3): 405–6.
Lambert, David and Alan Lester, eds (2006), *Colonial Lives Across the British Empire: Imperial Careering in the Long Nineteenth Century*, Cambridge: Cambridge University Press.
Larrimore, Mark (2008), "Antinomies of Race: Diversity and Destiny in Kant," *Patterns of Prejudice*, 42 (4–5).
Lawrence, Bonita (2003), "Gender Race and the Regulation of Native Identity in Canada and the United States: An Overview," *Hypatia*, 18 (2).
Laxman, S. (1997), *Cotton and Famine in Berar 1850–1900*, New Delhi: Manohar.
Lazarus Moritz ([1880] 2008), "What Does National Mean," in Marcel Stoetzler, *The State, the Nation and the Jews. Liberalism and the Antisemitism Dispute in Bismarck's Germany*, Lincoln: University of Nebraska Press.

Le Goff, Jacques (1980), *Time, Work, and Culture in the Middle Ages*, Chicago: University of Chicago Press.
Legassick, M. (2006), "From prisoners to exhibits: representations of Bushmen of the Northern Cape 1880–1900," in A.E. Coombes, *Rethinking Settler Colonialism*, Manchester: Manchester University Press.
Lehning, James R. (2013), *European Colonialism since 1700*, Cambridge: Cambridge University Press.
Lenin, V.I. (1939 [1917]), *Imperialism, the Highest Stage of Capitalism*, New York: International Publishers.
Lester, Alan (2012), "Humanism, Race and the Colonial Frontier," *Transactions of the Institute of British Geographers*, 37: 132–48.
Lester, Alan (2013), "Spatial concepts and the historical geographies of British colonisation," in Andrew S. Thompson (ed.), *Writing Imperial Histories*, Manchester: Manchester University Press.
Lester, Alan and Dussart, Fae (2015), *Colonization and the origins of humanitarian governance: protecting Aborigines across the nineteenth-century British empire*, Cambridge: Cambridge University Press.
Levine, P. (2003), *Prostitution, Race, and Politics: Policing Venereal Disease in the British Empire*, New York and London: Routledge.
Levine, Philippa (2006a), "Sexuality," *At Home with the Empire: metropolitan culture and the Imperial world*, 122–43, Cambridge: Cambridge University Press.
Levine, Phillippa (2006b), "Sexuality and Empire," in Catherine Hall and Sonya Rose (eds), *At Home with the Empire: Metropolitan Culture and the Imperial World*, Cambridge: Cambridge University Press.
Lewis, S.L. and M.A. Maslin (2015), "Defining the Anthropocene," *Nature*, 519 (7542): 171–80.
Lind, J. (1768), *Essay on the Diseases Incidental to Europeans in Hot Climates*, London: T. Becket and P.A. De Hondt.
Linebaugh, P. and M. Rediker (2007), *The many-headed Hydra : sailors, slaves, commoners, and the hidden history of the revolutionary Atlantic*, London [u.a.]: Verso.
List, Friedrich (1971), *Le systèm naturel d' économie politique* in A. Sommer (ed.), *Friedrich List. Schriften / Reden / Briefe*, Aalen: Scientia Verlag.
Livingstone, D.N. (2002), "Race, Space and Moral Climatology: Notes Towards a Genealogy," *Journal of Historical Geography*, 28 (2): 159–80.
Lombroso, Cesare (1876), *L'uomo deliquente: Studiato in rapporto alla antropologia, alla medicina legale ed alle discipline carcerarie*, Milan: Ulrico Hoepli.
Look Lai, Walton (2004), *Indentured Labor, Caribbean Sugar: Chinese and Indian Migrants to the British West Indies 1838–1918*, Baltimore: Johns Hopkins University Press.
Look Lai, W. (2009), "Asian Diasporas and Tropical Migration in the Age of Empire: A Comparative Overview," *Journal of Chinese Overseas*, 5 (1): 28–54.
Loomba, Ania (2007), "Periodization, Race and Global Contact," *Journal of Medieval and Early Modern Studies* 37 (3): 595–620.
Loy-Wilson, Sophie (2017), "Coolie Alibis: Seizing Gold from Chinese Miners in New South Wales," *International Labor and Working Class History* 91: 28–45.
Lunn, Joe (2009), "Remembering the Tirailleurs Sénégalais and the Great War: Oral History as a Methodology of Inclusion in French Colonial Studies," *French Colonial History*, Vol. 10: 125–50.

Luttikhuis, Bart (2013), "Beyond Race: Constructions of 'Europeanness' in Late-Colonial Legal Practice in the Dutch East Indies," *European Review of History*, 20 (4).

Lyons, M. (1992), *The colonial disease : a social history of sleeping sickness in northern Zaire, 1900–1940*, Cambridge: Cambridge University Press.

Machiels, Christine (2008), "Dealing with the Issue of Prostitution; Mobilizing Feminisms in France, Switzerland and Belgium (1875–1920)," *Women's History Review*, 17 (2): 195–205.

MacKenzie, John (1987), "The Imperial Pioneer and Hunter and the British Masculine Stereotype in Late Victorian and Edwardian Times," in J.A. Mangan and James Walvin, eds, *Manliness and Morality: Middle-Class Masculinity in Britain and America, 1800–1940*, New York, 1987.

MacKenzie, John (1995), *Orientalism: History, Theory and the Arts*, Manchester: Manchester University Press.

MacKenzie, John (2008), "'Comfort' and Conviction: A Response to Bernard Porter," *Journal of Imperial and Commonwealth History* 36 (4): 659–68.

Madley, B. (2004), "Patterns of Frontier Genocide 1803–1910: The Aboriginal Tasmanians, the Yuki of California, and the Herero of Namibia," *Journal of Genocide Research*, 6 (2): 167–92.

Madley, Benjamin (2016), *An American Genocide: The United States and the California Indian Catastrophe, 1846–1873*, New Haven: Yale University Press.

Magee, Gary and Andrew Thompson (2000), *Empire and Globalisation: Networks of People, Goods and Capital in the British World, c. 1850–1914*, Cambridge: Cambridge University Press.

Mahoney, Michael (2012), *The Other Zulus: The Spread of Zulu Ethnicity in Colonial South Africa*, Durham: Duke University Press.

Mahony, M. (2016), "For an Empire of 'All Types of Climate': Meteorology as an Imperial Science," *Journal of Historical Geography*, 51 (Jan): 29–39.

Malm, A. (2016), "Who Lit this Fire? Approaching the History of the Fossil Economy," *Critical Historical Studies*, 3 (2): 215–48.

Mani, Lata (1998), *Contentious Traditions, the Debate on Sati in Colonial India*, Berkeley: University of California Press.

Manktelow, Emily J. (2014), "The Rise and Demise of Missionary Wives," *Journal of Women's History* 26, (1): 135–59.

Mann, Gregory (2000), "What Was the Indigénat? The 'Empire of Law' in French West Africa," *Journal of African History*, 50: 331–53.

Martin, J.R. (1839), *Official Report of the Medical Topography and Climate of Calcutta: With Brief Notices of its Prevalent Diseases, Endemic and Epidemic*, Calcutta: G.H. Huttmann.

Martin, Phyllis (1995), *Leisure and Society in Colonial Brazzaville*, Cambridge: Cambridge University Press.

Martinez, J.S. (2012), *The slave trade and the origins of international human rights law*, Oxford: Oxford University Press.

Marx, Karl and Friedrich Engels ([1848] 1971), *The Communist Manifesto*, Harmondsworth: Penguin.

Matera, Marc, Misty L. Bastian, and Susan Kingsley Kent (2012), *The Women's War of 1929: Gender and Violence in Colonial Nigeria*, Basingstoke: Palgrave Macmillan.

Mathur, Saloni (2007), *India by Design: Colonial History and Cultural Display*, Berkeley: University of California Press.

Mawani, Renisa (2009), *Colonial Proximities: Crossracial Encounters and Juridical Truths in British Columbia, 1871–1921*, Vancouver: University of British Columbia Press.

Mawson, Stephanie (2011), "'The Workingman's Paradise', White Supremacy and Utopianism: The New Australia Movement and Working Class Racism," *Labor History* 101: 91–104.

McCarthy, Angela and T.M. Devine (2017), *Tea and Empire: James Taylor in Victorian Ceylon*, Manchester: Manchester University Press.

McClintock, Anne (1995), *Imperial Leather: Race, Gender and Sexuality in the Colonial Contest*, London: Routledge.

McCulloch, Jock (2000), *Black Peril, White Virtue: Sexual Crime in Southern Rhodesia, 1902–1935*, Bloomington: Indiana University Press.

McDougall, James (2017), *A History of Algeria*, Cambridge: Cambridge University Press.

McEwan, I. (2010), *Solar*, London: Jonathan Cape.

McKenzie, Kirsten (2007), "'My voice is sold, & I must be a Slave': Abolition, Industrialisation and the Yorkshire Election of 1807," *History Workshop Journal* 64: 48–73.

McKenzie, Kirsten (2015), "Imperial History by the Book: A Roundtable on John Darwin's *The Empire Project*." Comment: "A Field Divided," *Journal of British Studies* 54: 983–7.

McKenzie, Kirsten (2016), *Imperial Underworld: An escaped convict and the transformation of the British colonial order*, Cambridge: Cambridge University Press.

McNeill, J.R. (2010), *Mosquito Empires: Ecology and War in the Greater Caribbean, 1620–1914*, New York and Cambridge: Cambridge University Press.

Meadows, R.D. (2000), "Engineering Exile: Social Networks and the French Atlantic Community, 1789–1809," *French Historical Studies*, 23 (1): 67.

Megarrity, Lyndon (2006), "'White Queensland': The Queensland Government's Ideological Position on the Use of Pacific Island Labourers in the Sugar Sector 1880–1901," *Australian Journal of Politics and History*, 52 (1): 1–12.

Meredith, Martin (2008), *Diamonds, Gold, and War: The British, The Boers, and the Making of South Africa*, New York: Public Affairs.

Mertel, Kurt C.M. (2014), "Historicism and Critique in Herder's *Another Philosophy of History*: Some Hermeneutic Reflection," *European Journal of Philosophy*, 24 (2).

Mesnard, Éric, Catherine Coquery-Vidrovitch and Ibrahima Thioub, eds (2013), *Être Esclave: Afrique Amériques, XVe-XIXe Siècle*, Paris: La Découverte.

Mesthrie, Uma (2009), "The Passenger Indian as worker: Indian Immigrants in Cape Town in the Early Twentieth Century," *African Studies* 68 (1): 111–34.

Midgley, Claire (1992), *Women against Slavery: The British Campaigns, 1780–1870*, New York: Routledge.

Midgley, Clare (2007), *Feminism and Empire: women activists in imperial Britain, 1790–1860*, Oxford: Routledge.

Mikkelsen, Jon, ed. (2012), *Kant and the Concept of Race*, New York: SUNY Press.

Mill, James (1817), *A History of India*, London.

Miller, Michael B. (1981), *The Bon Marché: Bourgeois Culture and the Department Store, 1869–1920*, Princeton: Princeton University Press.

Mintz, S.W. and R. Price (1992), *The birth of African-American culture : an anthropological perspective*, Boston: Beacon Press.

Mishra, Pankaj (2012), *From the Ruins of Empire: The Revolt Against the West and the Remaking of Asia*, London: Allen Lane.
Mohanty, Chandra Talpade (1984), "Under Western Eyes: feminist scholarship and colonial discourses," *Boundary*, 2: 333–58.
Mohanty, Chandra Talpade (1984), "Under Western Eyes: Feminist Scholarship and Colonial Discourses," *boundary 2* 12/13 (3–1): 333–58.
Monnais, L. (2013), "Rails, Roads and Mosquito Foes: The State Quinine Service in French Indochina," in Robert Peckham and David M. Pomfret, *Imperial Contagions: Medicine, Hygiene, and Cultures of Planning in Asia* Hong Kong: Hong Kong University Press.
Montgomery, Max (2017), "Colonial Legacy of Gender Inequality: Christian Missionaries in German East Africa," *Politics and Society*, 45 (2): 225–68.
Moreton-Robinson, Aileen (2015), *The White Possessive: Property, Power, and Indigenous Sovereignty*, Minneapolis: University of Minnesota Press.
Morgan, Jennifer (2004), *Laboring Women: Reproduction and Gender in New World Slavery*, Philadelphia: University of Pennsylvania Press.
Morgan, Jennifer (2005), "Male Travellers, Female Bodies, and the Gendering of Racial Ideology, 1500–1770," in Tony Ballantyne and Antoinette Burton (eds), *Bodies in Contact: Rethinking Colonial Encounters in World History*, 54–67, Durham: Duke University Press.
Morgan, Kenneth (2007), *Slavery and the British Empire: From Africa to America*, Oxford: Oxford University Press.
Morgan, R.A. (2015), "Salubrity and the Survival of the Swan River Colony: Health, Climate and Settlement in Colonial Western Australia," in A. Varnava (ed.), *Imperial Expectations and Realities: El Dorados, Utopias and Dystopias*, 89–104, Manchester: Manchester University Press.
Mortensen, Reid (2000), "Slaving in Australian Courts: Blackbirding Cases, 1869–1871," *Journal of South Pacific Law*, 4, 2000, https://www.usp.ac.fj/index.php?id=13200.
Morton, Giles (1999), *Nathaniel's Nutmeg: How One Man's Courage Changed the Course of History*, London: Hodder and Stoughton.
Morton, Phyllis M. (1995), *Leisure and Society in Colonial Brazzaville*, Cambridge: Cambridge University Press.
Moxham, Roy (2009), *A Brief History of Tea: The Extraordinary Story of the World's Favourite Drink*, London: Constable & Robinson.
Moyd, M.R. (2014), *Violent Intermediaries: African Soldiers, Conquest and Everyday Colonialism in German East Africa*, Athens, Ohio: Ohio University Press.
Muckle, A. (2010), "Troublesome Chiefs and Disorderly Subjects: The 'Indigénat' and the internment of Kanak in New Caledonia (1887–1928)," *French Colonial History*, 11: 131–60.
Muckle, Adrian (2010), "Troublesome Chiefs and Disorderly Subjects: The Indigénat and the Internment of Kanak in New Caledonia (1887–1928)," *French Colonial History*, 11: 131–60.
Munro, Doug (1995), "The Labor Trade in Melanesians to Queensland: An Historiographic Essay," *Journal of Social History*, 28 (3): 609–27.
Nandy, Ashis (1988), *The intimate enemy: loss and recovery of self under colonialism*, New Delhi; New York: Oxford University Press, 1988.
Nanni, Giordano (2012), *The Colonisation of Time: Ritual, Routine and Resistance in the British Empire*, Manchester: Manchester University Press.

Nash, D.J. and G.C.D. Adamson (2014), "Recent Advances in the Historical Climatology of the Tropics and Subtropics," *Bulletin of the American Meteorological Society*, 95 (1): 131–46.

Nash, D.J. and G.H. Endfield (2002), "A 19th Century Climate Chronology for the Kalahari Region of Central Southern Africa Derived from Missionary Correspondence," *International Journal of Climatology*, 22 (7): 821–41.

Nash, D.J. and S.W. Grab (2010), "'A Sky of Brass and Burning Winds': Documentary Evidence of Rainfall Variability in the Kingdom of Lesotho, Southern Africa, 1824–1900," *Climatic Change*, 101 (3–4): 617–53.

Nash, D.J., K. Pribyl, J. Klein, G.H. Endfield, D.R. Kniveton and G.C.D. Adamson (2015), "Tropical Cyclone Activity over Madagascar during the Late Nineteenth Century," *International Journal of Climatology*, 35 (11): 3249–61.

Nash, D.J., K. Pribyl, J. Klein, R. Neukom, G.H. Endfield, G.C.D. Adamson and D.R. Kniveton (2016), "Seasonal Rainfall Variability in Southeast Africa during the Nineteenth Century Reconstructed from Documentary Sources," *Climatic Change*, 134 (4): 605–19.

Nasson, Bill (2011), *The War for South Africa: The Anglo-Boer War, 1899–1902*, New York: History Publishing Group.

Neill, D.J. (2012), *Networks in Tropical Medicine: Internationalism, Colonialism, and the Rise of a Medical Specialty*, Stanford: Stanford University Press.

Nelson, Keith L. (1970), "The 'Black Horror on the Rhine': Race as a Factor in Post-World War I diplomacy," *Journal of Modern History* 42: 606–27.

Newton, Gail (2004), *Picture Paradise: Asia-Pacific Photography, 1840s–1940s*, Canberra: National Gallery of Australia.

Newton, Gail, ed. (2008), *Garden of the East: Photography in Indonesia, 1850s–1940*, Canberra: National Gallery of Australia, Canberra.

Ngai, Mae M. (2017), "Trouble on the Rand: The Chinese Question in South Africa and the Apogee of White Settlerism," *International Labor and Working Class History* (91): 59–78.

Nicolay, W. (1840), "Correspondence respecting the employment of Indian labourers in the Mauritius," in *Mauritius: Of Despatch from Sir William Nicolay*, 7–9, London: House of Commons.

Norindr, Panivong (1996), *Phantasmatic Indochina: French Colonial Ideology in Architecture, Film and Literature*, Durham, NC: Duke University Press.

Northeast Iowa Tourism Association (2012), "Historic Tour of Scenic Elkader." Available online: http://www.visitiowa.org/business/historic-tour-of-scenic-elkader.html [accessed January 15, 2017].

Northrup, David (1995), *Indentured Labor in the Age of Imperialism 1834–1922*, Cambridge: Cambridge University Press.

Northrup, David (2003), "Free and Unfree Labor Migration, 1600–1900: An Introduction," *Journal of World History* 14 (2): 125–30.

Nott, Josiah (1843), "The Mulatto a Hybrid – Possible Extermination of the Two Races if the Whites and Blacks Are Allowed to Intermarry," *The American Journal of the Medical Sciences*, 6 (11).

Nott, Josiah (1856), "Appendix," in Arthur Gobineau, *The Moral and Intellectual Diversity of Races*, trans. H. Hotz, 461–512, Philadelphia: JB Lippincott.

O'Neill, Helen (2013), *David Jones' 175 Years*, Sydney: NewSouth Publishing.

Ogle, Vanessa (2015), *The Global Transformation of Time 1870–1950*, Cambridge: Harvard University Press.

O'Malley, P. (1994), "Gentle Genocide: Government of Aboriginal Peoples in Central Australia," *Social Justice/Global Options*, 21 (4): 46–65.
Osborne, M.A. (2000), "Acclimatizing the World: A History of the Paradigmatic Colonial Science," *Osiris*, 15: 135–51.
Ostler, Jeffrey (2004), *The Plains Sioux and U.S. Colonialism from Lewis and Clark to Wounded Knee*, Cambridge: Cambridge University Press.
Padayachee, Vishnu and Robert Morrell (1991), "Indian Merchants and Dukkawallahs in the Natal Economy, c.1875–1914," *Journal of Southern African Studies* 17 (1): 71–102.
Paisley, F. (2000), *Loving protection?: Australian feminism and Aboriginal women's rights, 1919–1939*, Carlton: Melbourne University Press.
Palladino, P. and Michael Worboys, M. (1993), "Science and Imperialism," *Isis*, 84 (1): 91–102.
Palsetia, Jesse S. (2015), *Jamsetjee Jejeebhoy of Bombay: Partnership and Public Culture in Empire*, New Delhi: Oxford University Press.
Pape, John (1990), "Black and White: The 'Perils of Sex' in Colonial Zimbabwe," *Journal of Southern African Studies*, 16 (4): 699–720.
Paquette, Gabriel (2013), *Imperial Portugal in the Age of Atlantic Revolutions: The Luso-Brazilian World, c. 1770–1850*, Cambridge: Cambridge University Press.
Parenti, C. (2011), *Tropic of Chaos: Climate Change and the New Geography of Violence*, New York: Nation Books.
Parés, L.N. (2013), *The Formation of Candomblé: Vodun History and Ritual in Brazil*, Chapel Hill: University of North Carolina Press.
Park, Yoon (2009), *A Matter of Honour: Being Chinese in South Africa*, Auckland Park: Jacana.
Paton, Diana (2004), *No Bond but the Law: Punishment, Race and Gender in Jamaican State Formation 1780–1870*, Durham: Duke University Press.
Patterson Smith, James (1994), "The Liberals, Race and Political Reform in the British West Indies," *Journal of Negro History*, 79 (2).
Paxton, Nancy (1999), *Writing under the Raj: gender, raced and rape in the British colonial imagination, 1830–1947*, New Brunswick: Rutgers University Press.
Peabody, Sue and Keila Grinberg (2007), *Slavery, Freedom, and the Law in the Atlantic World: A Brief History with Documents*, Boston: Bedford/St. Martin's.
Peckham, R. (2013), "Matshed Laboratory: Colonies, Cultures, and Bacteriology," in R. Peckham and D. M. Pomfret, *Imperial Contagions: Medicine, Hygiene, and Cultures of Planning in Asia*, 123–47, Hong Kong: Hong Kong University Press.
Peckham, R. and D.M. Pomfret, eds (2013), *Imperial Contagions: Medicine, Hygiene, and Cultures of Planning in Asia*, Hong Kong: Hong Kong University Press.
Pérez, L.A. (2001), *Winds of Change: Hurricanes and the Transformation of Nineteenth Century Cuba*, Chapel Hill, NC: University of North Carolina Press.
Perry, Adele (2001), *On the Edge of Empire: Gender, Race, and the Making of British Columbia, 1849–1871*, Toronto: University of Toronto Press.
Phillips, Richard (2006), *Sex, Politics and Empire*, Manchester: Manchester University Press.
Phillips, Richard (2007), "Histories of Sexuality and Imperialism: What's the Use," *History Workshop Journal*, 63: 136–53.
Pilbeam, Pamela M. (2014), *Saint-Simonians in Nineteenth-Century France: From Free Love to Algeria*, London: Palgrave Macmillan.

Pitts, J. (2006), *A Turn to Empire: The Rise of Imperial Liberalism in Britain and France*, Princeton: Princeton University Press.

Ploetz, Alfred (1904), "Die Begriffe Rasse und Gesellschaft und die davon abgeleiteten Diziplinen," *Archiv für Rassen- und Gesellschafts-Biologie einschliesslich Rassen- und Gesellschafts-Hygiene*, 1 (1).

Poliakov, Léon (1982), "Racism from the Enlightenment to the Age of Imperialism," in R. Ross (ed.), *Racism and Colonialism*, The Hague: Martinus Nijhoff.

Pols, H. (2012), "Notes from Batavia, the Europeans' Graveyard: The Nineteenth Century Debate on Acclimatization in the Dutch East Indies," *Journal of the History of Medicine and Allied Sciences*, 67 (1): 120–48.

Poovey, Mary (1988), *Uneven Developments: The Ideological Work of Gender in Mid-Victorian England*, Chicago: University of Chicago Press.

Popkin, Jeremy (2011), *You Are All Free: The Haitian Revolution and the Abolition of Slavery*, New York and Cambridge: Cambridge Univeristy Press.

Popkin, Jeremy (2012), *A Concise History of the Haitian Revolution*, Malden, MA: Wiley-Blackwell.

Porter, Andrew N. (2004), *Religion Versus Empire: British protestant missionaries and overseas expansion, 1700–1914*, Manchester: Manchester University Press.

Porter, Bernard (1975), *The Lion's Share: A Short History of British Imperialism, 1850–1983*, London: Routledge.

Porter, Bernard (2004), *The Absent-Minded Imperialists: Empire, Society and Culture in Britain*, Oxford: Oxford University Press.

Porter, Bernard (2008), "Further Thoughts on Imperial Absent-Mindedness," *Journal of Imperial and Commonwealth History* 36 (1), 101–7.

Prakash, Gyan, ed. (1992), *The World of the Rural Labourer in Colonial India*, Delhi: Oxford University Press.

Prasad, Ritika (2015), *Tracks of Change: Railways and Everyday Life in Colonial India*, Cambridge: Cambridge University Press.

Price, R. (1983), *First-time : the historical vision of an Afro-American people*, Baltimore: Johns Hopkins University Press.

Price, R. (2008), *Making Empire: Colonial Encounters and the Creation of Imperial Rule in Nineteenth-Century Africa*, New York: Cambridge University Press.

Protschky, S. (2011), *Images of the Tropics: Environment and Visual Culture in Colonial Indonesia*, Leiden: KITLV Press.

Quarles, Benjamin (1969), *Black Abolitionists*, New York: Oxford University Press.

Ramamurthy, Anand (2003), *Imperial Persuaders: Images of Africa and Asia in British Advertising*, Manchester: Manchester University Press, 2003.

Rand, Gavin and Kim A. Wagner (2012), "Recruiting the 'Martial Races': Identities and Military Service in Colonial India," *Patterns of Prejudice*, Vol. 46, Nos. 3–4: 232–54.

Rand, Jacki (2008), *Kiowa Humanity and the Invasion of the State*, Lincoln, NE: University of Nebraska Press.

Rangan, H., J. Carney and T. Denham (2012), "Environmental History of Botanical Exchanges in the Indian Ocean World," *Environment and History*, 18 (3): 311–42.

Ranger, Terence (1975), *Dance and Society in Eastern Africa 1890–1970: The Beni Ngoma*, Berkeley: University of California Press.

Ranger, Terence (1991), "Missionaries, Migrants and the Manyika: The Invention of Ethnicity in Zimbabwe" in Leroy Vail (ed.), *The Creation of Tribalism in Southern Africa*, Berkeley: University of California Press.

Ranger, Terence O. (1968a), "Connexions between 'Primary Resistance' Movements and Modern Mass Nationalism in East and Central Africa. Part I," *Journal of African History* 9 (4): 437–53.

Ranger, Terence O. (1968b), "Connexions between 'Primary Resistance' Movements and Modern Mass Nationalism in East and Central Africa. Part II," *Journal of African History* 9 (4): 631–41.

Ranger, Terence and Eric Hobsbawm, eds (1983), *The Invention of Tradition*, Cambridge: Cambridge University Press.

Rappaport, Erika (2017), *The Thirst for Empire: How Tea Shaped the Modern World*, Princeton: Princeton University Press.

Ratcliff, J. (2016), "Travancore's Magnetic Crusade: Geomagnetism and the Geography of Scientific Production in a Princely State," *British Journal for the History of Science*, 49 (3): 325–52.

Raven, James (2002), *Judging New Wealth: Popular Publishing and Responses to Commerce in England, 1750 – 1800*, Oxford: Clarendon Press.

Ray, Carina (2013), "Interracial Sex and the Making of Empire," in Ato Quayson and Girish Daswani (eds), *A Companion to Diaspora and Transnationalism*, 190–211, London: Blackwell.

Ray, Carina (2015), *Crossing the Color Line: Race, Sex and the Contested Politics of Colonialism in Ghana*, Athens: Ohio University Press.

Rediker, M. (2007), *The Slave Ship: A Human History*, New York: Penguin Books.

Reid, Richard J. (2007), "Revisiting Primitive War: Perceptions of Violence and Race in History," *War and Society*, 26:2, 1–25.

Renan, Ernst ([1882] 1990), "What is a Nation?" in Homi Bhabha (ed.), *Nation and Narration*, 8–22, New York: Routledge.

Reynolds, H. (2006), *The Other Side of the Frontier: Aboriginal Resistance to the European Invasion of Australia*, University of New South Wales Press.

Reynolds, Henry and Marilyn Lake (2008a), *Drawing the Global Colour Line: White Men's Countries and the International Challenge of Racial Equality*, Cambridge: Cambridge University Press.

Reynolds, Henry and Marilyn Lake (2008b), *Drawing the Global Colour Line: White Men's Countries and the Question of Racial Equality*, Cambridge: Cambridge University Press.

Ritz-Deutch, Ute (2015), "Germans and Indians in Brazil: The Transatlantic Construction of Ethnic Identity in the Discourse of Indian Protection," in Anke Finger, Gabi Kathöfer and Christoph Larkosh, *KulturConfusão – On German-Brazilian Interculturalities*, Berlin: De Gruyter.

Robert, Hannah (2001), "Disciplining the Female Aboriginal Body: inter-racial sex and the pretence of separation," *Australian Feminist Studies*, 16 (34): 69–81.

Robinson, David (2000), *Paths of Accommodation: Muslim Societies and French Colonial Authorities in Senegal and Mauritania, 1880–1920*, Athens, OH: Ohio University Press.

Robinson, Roland and John Gallagher (1953), "The Imperialism of Free Trade," *Economic History Review* 2nd Series VI: 1–15.

Rodet, M. (2014), "Le Sous-Lieutenant Mansouka (c. 1860–1920): Un parcours d'esclave affranchi entre rebellion et allégance au temps de la conquête coloniale française en Afrique," in O. Leservoisier and S. Travelsi, *Résistances et mémoires des esclavages: espaces arabo-musulmans et transatlantiques*, Paris: Karthala.

Rodney, W. (1981), *A History of the Guyanese Working People*, Baltimore: The Johns Hopkins University Press.

Roediger, David (1991), *The Wages of Whiteness: Race and the Making of the American Working Class*, New York: Verso.

Rogers, Rebecca (2011), "Teaching morality and religion in nineteenth-century colonial Algeria: Gender and the civilising mission," *History of Education*, 40 (6): 741–59.

Rogers, Thomas James and Stephen Bain (2016), "Genocide and frontier violence in Australia," *Journal of Genocide Studies*, 18 (1): 83–100.

Ross, Robert (1979), "Oppression, Sexuality and Slavery At the Cape of Good Hope," *Historical Reflections / Réflexions Historiques*, 6 (2): 421–33.

Rowse, Tim, (2014), "Indigenous Heterogeneity," *Australian Historical Studies*, 45 (3): 297–310.

Roy, Tirthankar (2008), "Sardars, Jobbers, Kanganies: The Labor Contractor and Indian Economic History," *Modern Asian Studies* 42 (5): 971–98.

Royal Commission on the Sanitary State of the Army in India (1863), *Report of the Commissioners Appointed to Inquire into the Sanitary State of the Army in India*, London: Eyre and Spottiswoode.

Rushdie, Salman (1992), "Outside the Whale," in *Imaginary Homelands: Essays and Criticism, 1981–1991*, London: Penguin.

Russell, Dave (2013), "The Making of Modern Leisure: The British Experience 1850–1960," in Tony Blackshaw (ed.), *Routledge Handbook of Leisure Studies*, London: Routledge.

Saada, Emmanuelle (2011), "The Republic and the Indigènes," in Edward Berenson, Vincent Duclert, and Christophe Prochasson, *The French Republic: History, Values, Debates*, Ithaca, Cornell University Press.

Said, Edward (1978), *Orientalism*, London: Routledge.

Said, Edward (1993), *Culture and Imperialism*, New York: Knopf.

Said, Edward (1994), *Culture and Imperialism*, London: Vintage.

Said, Edward (2003), *Orientalism*, London: Penguin.

Saldanha, Arun (2006), "Reontologising Race: The Machinic Geography of Phenotype," *Environment and Planning D, Society and Space*, 24 (1).

Salesa, Damon Ieremia (2011), *Racial Crossings; Race, Intermarriage, and the Victorian British Empire*, Oxford: Oxford University Press.

Sanchez, J.-L. (2013), *A perpetuité: relégués au bagne de Guyane*, Paris: Vendémiaire.

Sarkin, J. (2011), *Germany's Genocide of the Herero: Kaiser Wilhelm II, His General, His Settlers, His Soldiers*, Suffolk: UCT Press/James Curry.

Saunders, Kay, ed. (1984), *Indentured Labor in the British Empire 1834–1920*, London: Croom Helm.

Schomburgk, R.H. (1848), *The History of Barbados*, London: Longman, Brown, Green and Longmans.

Schröder, Iris (1995), "Welfare, women's questions and gender politics. Social policy ideas of the women's movement in the German Empire 1871–1914," *Geschichte und Gesellschaft*, 21 (3): 368–90.

Scott, James (1985), *Weapons of the Weak: Everyday Forms of Peasant Resistance*, New Haven: Yale University Press.

Scott, R.J. and J. Hébrard (2012), *Freedom Papers: An Atlantic Odyssey in the Age of Emancipation*, Cambridge, MA: Harvard University Press.

Scully, Pamela (1995), "Rape, Race, and Colonial Culture. The Sexual Politics of Identity in the Nineteenth century Cape Colony, South Africa," *American Historical Review*, 100 (2): 335–59.

Seddon, D. (2000), "Unfinished business: Slavery in Saharan Africa," *Slavery & Abolition*, 21 (2): 208–36.

Sen, I. (2010), "Memsahibs and Health in Colonial Medical Writings, *c.* 1840 to *c.* 1930," *South Asia Research*, 30 (3): 253–74.

Sen, S. (2011), "The Asiatic Society and the Sciences in India, 1784–1947," in U. Das Gupta (ed.), *Science and Modern India: An Institutional History, c. 1784–1947*, 27–68, New Delhi, Pearson Longman.

Sepinwall, Alyssa, ed. (2012), *Haitian History: New Perspectives*, New York: Routledge.

Sessions, Jennifer (2011), *By Sword and Plow: France and the Conquest of Algeria*, Ithaca: Cornell University Press.

Sharma, Jayeeta (2009), "'Lazy' Natives, Coolie Labour, and the Assam Tea Industry," *Modern Asian Studies*, 43 (6): 1287–324.

Sheftall, Mark David (2009), *Altered Memories of the Great War. Divergent Narratives of Britain, Australia, New Zealand and Canada*, London: I.B. Tauris.

Shepherd, Verene (2002), *Maharani's Misery: Narratives of a Passage from India to the Caribbean*, Barbados: University of the West Indies Press.

Shlomowitz, Ralph (2005), "Keith Windschuttle's Contribution to Australian History: An Evaluation," *Australian Economic History Review*, 45 (3).

Showers, K.B. (2005), *Imperial Gullies: Soil Erosion and Conservation in Lesotho*, Athens, OH: Ohio University Press.

Showers, K.B. (2010), "Prehistory of Southern African Forestry: From Vegetable Garden to Tree Plantation," *Environment and History*, 16 (3): 295–322.

Sicard, C. (1998), *La Kabylie en Feu: Algérie 1871*, Paris: Éditions Georges SUD.

Silverman, Deborah (2011), "Art Nouveau, Art of Darkness: African Lineages of Belgian Modernism," *West 86th*, 18:2 (2011): 139–81.

Sinha, Mrinalini (1995), *Colonial Masculinity: The "Manly Englishman" and the "Effeminate Bengali" in the Late Nineteenth Century*, Manchester: Manchester University Press.

Sivasundaram, Sujit (2013), *Islanded: Britain, Sri Lanka & the Bounds of an Indian Ocean Colony*, Chicago: University of Chicago Press.

Skeie, Karina Hestad (1999), "Building God's Kingdom. The Importance of the House to Nineteenth Century Norwegian Missionaries in Madagascar," in Karen Middleton (ed.), *Ancestors, Power and History in Madagascar*, 71–103, Brill: London.

Slocum, John W. (1998), "Who, and When, Were the Inorodtsy? The Evolution of the Category of 'Aliens' in Imperial Russia," *Russian Review*, 57 (2): 173–90.

Smith, Adam (2012 [1776]), *The Wealth of Nations*, London: Wordsworth Editions.

Smith, Alison (2016), *Artist and Empire: Facing Britain's Imperial Past*, London: Tate.

Smith, S.M. (2015), "Seasoning and Abolition: Humoural Medicine in the Eighteenth-Century British Atlantic," *Slavery and Abolition*, 36 (4): 684–703.

Smith, W.D. (1980), "Friedrich Ratzel and the Origins of Lebensraum," *German Studies Review*, 3 (1): 51–68.

Soloway, Richard A. (1990), *Demography and Degeneration: Eugenics and the Declining Birth Rate in Twentieth-Century Britain*, Chapel Hill, NC: University of North Carolina Press.

Speedy, Karin (2015), "The Sutton Case: The First Franco-Australian Foray into Blackbirding," *Journal of Pacific History*, 50 (3): 344–64.

Spieler, M.F. (2009), "The Legal Structure of Colonial Rule During the French Revolution," *The William and Mary Quarterly*, 66 (2): 362–408.

Spieler, M.F. (2012), *Empire and underworld : captivity in French Guiana*, Cambridge, MS: Harvard University Press.

Spivak, Gayatri Chakravorty (1988), "Can the Subaltern Speak?" in Cary Nelson and Lawrence Grossberg (eds), *Marxism and the Interpretation of Culture*, 271–313, Basingstoke: Macmillan.

Stanley, Brian (1990), *The Bible and the Flag: Protestant missions and British imperialism in the nineteenth and twentieth centuries*, Leicester: Apollo.

Steel, Frances (2014), "Lines Across the Sea: Trans-Pacific passenger shipping in the age of steam," in Robert Aldrich and Kirsten McKenzie (eds), *The Routledge History of Western Empires*, New York: Routledge.

Steinmetz, George (2007), *The Devil's Handwriting. Precoloniality and the German Colonial State in Qingdao, Samoa, and Southwest Africa*, Chicago: University of Chicago Press.

Stibbe, M., ed. (2009), *Captivity, forced labour and forced migration in Europe during the First World War*, London: Routledge.

Stoler, Ann Laura A.L. (1989), "Making Empire Respectable: The Politics of Race and Sexual Morality in 20th Century Colonial Cultures," *American Ethnologist*, 16 (4): 634–60.

Stoler, Ann Laura Ann (1995a), *Capitalism and Confrontation in Sumatra's Plantation Belt 1870–1979*, Ann Arbor: University of Michigan Press.

Stoler, Ann Laura (1995b), *Race and the Education of Desire: Foucault's* History of Sexuality *and the Colonial Order of Things*, Durham, NC, Duke University Press.

Stoler, Ann Laura (2002), *Carnal Knowledge and Imperial Power: race and the intimate in colonial rule*, Durham and London: Duke University Press.

Stoler, Ann Laura (2016), *Duress: Imperial Durabilities in Our Times*, Durham, NC: Duke University Press.

Stovall, T. (1998), "The Color Line behind the Lines: Racial Violence in France during the Great War," *The American Historical Review*, 103 (3): 737–69.

Streets, Heather (2004), *Martial Races: The Military, Race and Masculinity in British Imperial Culture, 1857–1914*, Manchester: Manchester University Press.

Strobel, Margaret (1991), *European Women and the second British Empire*, Indiana: Indiana University Press.

Sweet, J.H. (2003), *Recreating Africa: Culture, Kinship, and Religion in the African-Portuguese World, 1441–1770*, Chapel Hill: University of North Carolina Press.

Sweets, John (1986), *Choices in Vichy France: The French Under Nazi Occupation*, Oxford: Oxford University Press.

Tabili, Laura (1996), "Women 'of a very low type': Crossing Racial Boundaries in Imperial Britain," in Laura Frader and Sonya Rose (eds), *Gender and Class in Modern Europe*, Ithaca: Cornell University Press.

Tabili, Laura (2003), "Race is a Relationship, and Not a Thing," *Journal of Social History* 37 (1): 125–30.

Tabili, Laura (2006), "A homogenous society? Britain's internal 'others', 1800 – present," in Hall, Catherine and Sonya O. Rose, *At Home with the Empire: Metropolitan Culture and the Imperial World*, Cambridge: Cambridge University Press.

Taraud, C. (2003), *La prostitution colonial: Algérie, Tunisie, Maroc 1830–1962*, Payot.

Taraud, C. (2015), "Le réglementarisme colonal au Maghreb de 1830 à 1962: une biopolitique de genre, de classe et de race?" in M. Spensky, *Le contrôle du corps des femmes dans les Empires* coloniaux, 137–55, Paris: Karthala.

Thampi, Madhavi (1999), "Indian Soldiers, Policemen and Watchmen in China in the Nineteenth and Early Twentieth Centuries," *China Report*, 35 (4).

Thompson, Andrew S. (2005), *The Empire Strikes Back? The Impact of Imperialism on Britain from the Mid-Nineteenth Century*, New York: Pearson Longman.

Thompson, Andrew S. (2013), "Introduction," in Andrew S. Thompson (ed.), *Writing Imperial Histories*, Manchester: Manchester University Press.

Thompson, Christina A. (1997), "A Dangerous People Whose Only Occupation is War: Maori and Pakeha in 19th-Century New Zealand," *The Journal of Pacific History*, 32:1, 109–19.

Thompson, E.P. ([1963] 1968), *The Making of the English Working Class*, New York: Vintage.

Thompson, E.P. (1967), "Time, Work-Discipline and Industrial Capitalism," *Past and Present* 38: 59–97.

Thompson, E.P. (1974), "Patrician Society, Plebeian Culture," *Journal of Social History* 7 (4).

Thompson, J. Malcolm (1990), "Colonial Policy and the Family of Black Troops in French West Africa, 1817–1904," *International Journal of African Historical Studies*, 23 (3): 423–53.

Thoral, M-C. (2012), "Colonial Medical Encounters in the Nineteenth Century: The French Campaigns in Egypt, Saint Domingue and Algeria," *Social History of Medicine*, 25 (3): 608–24.

Thornton, John (1993), "'I Am the Subject of the King of Congo': African Political Ideology and the Haitian Revolution," *Journal of World History* 4 (2): 181–214.

Thornton, John (1998), *Africa and Africans in the Making of the Atlantic World, 1400–1800*, 2nd edn, Cambridge: Cambridge University Press.

Tignor, R.L. (1976), *The Colonial Transformation of Kenya: The Kamba, Kikuyu and Maasai from 1900 to 1939*, Princeton: Princeton University Press.

Tindley, Annie and Andrew Wodehouse (2016), *Design, Technology and Communication in the British Empire, 1830–1914*, London: Palgrave Macmillan.

Tinker, Hugh (1974), *A New System of Slavery: The Export of Indian Labor Overseas 1830–1920*, London: Oxford University Press.

Tissié, P.-A. (2005), *Les aliénés voyageurs: le cas Albert, avec une introduction de Serge Nicolas*, Paris: L'Harmattan.

Toth, S.A. (2006), *Beyond Papillon : the French overseas penal colonies, 1854–1952*, Lincoln: University of Nebraska Press.

Trentmann, Frank (2016), *Empire of Things: How We Became a World of Consumers, from the Fifteenth Century to the Twenty-first*, London: Allen Lane.

Triner, Gail D. (2005), "Race, With or Without Color? Reconciling Brazilian Historiography," *History Compass*, 3.

Trnka, Susanna (2008), *State of Suffering: Political Violence and Community Survival in Fiji*, Ithaca: Cornell University Press.

Trouillot, Michel-Rolph (1995), *Silencing the Past: Power and the Production of History*, Boston: Beacon Press.

Vahed, Goolam (1999), "Control and Repression: The Plight of Indian Hawkers and Flower Sellers in Durban, 1910–1948," *The International Journal of African Historical Studies* 32 (1): 19–48.

Vahed, Goolam (2001), "Mosques, Mawlanas and Muharram: Indian Islam in Colonial Natal, 1860–1910," *Journal of Religion in Africa* 31 (3): 305–35.

Vahed, Goolam (2002), "Constructions of Community and Identity Among Indians in Colonial Natal, 1860–1910: The Role of the Muharram Festival," *The Journal of African History* 43 (1): 77–93.

Vahed, Goolam (2005), "Passengers, Partnerships, and Promissory Notes: Gujarati Traders in Colonial Natal, 1870–1920," *The International Journal of African Historical Studies* 38 (3): 449–79.

Vahed, Goolam (2006), "'Unhappily Torn by Dissensions and Litigations': Durban's 'Memon' Mosque, 1880–1930," *Journal of Religion in Africa* 36 (1): 23–49.

Vahed, Goolam and Ashwin Desai (2010), *Inside Indian Indenture: A South African Story 1860–1914*, Cape Town: HSRC Press.

Vail, Leroy (1991), "*Ethnicity in Southern African History*," in Leroy Vail (ed.), *The Creation of Tribalism in Southern Africa*, Berkeley: University of California Press.

Valenčius, C.B. (2001), "Histories of Medical Geography," in N.A. Rupke (ed.), *Medical Geography in Historical Perspective*, 3–30, London: Wellcome Institute Trust for the History of Medicine.

van Onselen, Charles (1976), *Chibaro: African Mine Labour in Southern Rhodesia 1900–1933*, London: Pluto Press.

van Onselen, Charles ([1982] 2001), *New Babylon and New Nineveh: Everyday Life on the Witwatersrand, 1886–1914*, Witwatersrand: Jonathan Ball.

Vann, Michael G. (2003), "The Good, the Bad, and the Ugly: Variation and Difference in French Racism in Colonial *Indochine*," in Tyler Stovall and Sue Peabody (eds), *The Color of Liberty: The History of Race in France*, Durham: Duke University Press.

Vansina, Jan (1985), *Oral Tradition as History*, Oxford: James Currey.

Veracini, Lorenzo (2010), *Settler Colonialism: A Theoretical Overview*, Houndsmills: Palgrave Macmillan.

Verhandlungen des Reichstages (VdR) Vol. 285, 1912.

Visana, V. (2016), "Vernacular Liberalism, Capitalism, and Anti-Imperialism in the Political Thought of Dadbhai Naoroji," *The Historical Journal* 59 (3): 775–97.

Visram, R. (1986), *Ayahs, Lascars, and Princes: Indians in Britain 1700–1947*, London: Pluto Press.

Voeltz, Richard (1996), "The British empire, sexuality, feminism and Ronald Hyam," *European Review of History*, 3 (1), 41–4.

von Humboldt, A. (1836), "On the Advancement of the Knowledge of Terrestrial Magnetism by the Establishment of Magnetic Stations and Corresponding Observations," *London and Edinburgh Philosophical Magazine*, 9: 42–53.

von Humboldt, A. (1845), *Cosmos: A Survey of the General Physical History of the Universe*, Part 1, (trans. Augustin Pritchard), New York: Harper & Brothers.

Wakeman, Frederic Jr. (1966), *Strangers at the Gate: Social Disorder in South China, 1839–1861*, Berkeley: University of California Press.

Walker, Francesca (2012), "'Descendants of a Warrior Race': the Maori Contingent, New Zealand Pioneer Battalion, and Martial Race Myth, 1914–1919," *War and Society*, 31:1, 1–21.

Walther, Daniel J. (2002), *Creating German Abroad: Cultural Policies and Settler Identities in Namibia*. Athens: Ohio University Press.

Walvin, James (1997), *Fruits of Empire: Exotic Produce and British Taste, 1660–1800*, London: Palgrave Macmillan.

Ward, Stuart (2013), "The MacKenziean moment in retrospect (or how a hundred volumes bloomed)," in Andrew S. Thompson (ed.), *Writing Imperial History*, Manchester: Manchester University Press.

Ware, Vron (1992), *Beyond the Pale: white women, racism and history*, London: Verso.

Warren, J.F. (2015), "Philippine Typhoons, Sources and the Historian," *Water History*, 7 (2): 213–31.

Weaver, John (2003), *The Great Land Rush and the Making of the Modern World, 1650–1900*, Montreal and Kingston: McGill-Queen's University Press.

Weindling, Paul (2010), "German Eugenics and the Wider World: Beyond the Racial State," in Alison Bashford and Philippa Levine, *The Oxford Handbook of the History of Eugenics*, Oxford: Oxford University Press.

Weiner, M. (2009), *An Empire on Trial: Race, Murder and Justice under British Rule, 1870–1935*. New York, Cambridge University Press.

Wesseling, H.L. (2004), *The European Colonial Empires, 1815–1919*, New York: Routledge.

Whitaker, Jan (2011), *The Department Store: History – Design – Display*, London: Thames & Hudson.

White, Ashli (2010), *Encountering Revolution: Haiti and the Making of the Early Republic*, Baltimore: Johns Hopkins University Press.

White, Deborah Gray (1999), *Ar'n't I A Woman? Female Slaves in the Plantation South*, revised edn, New York: W.W. Norton.

White, Owen (1999), *Children of the French Empire: Miscegenation and Colonial Society in French West Africa 1895–1960*, Oxford: Clarendon Press.

Wickramasinghe, Nira (2003), *Dressing the Colonial Body*, New Delhi: Orient Longman.

Wickramasinghe, Nira (2014), *Metallic Modern: Everyday Machines in Colonial Sri Lanka*, New York: Berghahn Books.

Wigger, Iris (2009), "The Interconnections of Discrimination," *European Societies*, 11:4: 553–82.

Wildenthal, Lora (2001), *German Women for Empire, 1884–1945*, Durham: Duke University Press.

Wilder, G. (2005), *The French imperial nation-state : negritude & colonial humanism between the two world wars*, Chicago: University of Chicago Press.

Williams, R. (2014), *On Culture & Society: Essential Writings*, London: Sage.

Williamson, F. (2015), "Weathering the Empire: Meteorological Research in the Early British Straits Settlements," *British Journal for the History of Science*, 48 (3): 475–92.

Wilson, Kathleen (2007), "Empire, Gender and Modernity in the Eighteenth Century," in Phillipa Levine, (ed.), *Gender and Empire*, Oxford: Oxford University Press.

Windschuttle, Keith (1994), *The killing of history: how a discipline is being murdered by literary critics and social theorists*, Paddington, N.S.W.: Macleay.

Winegard, Timothy C. (2012), *Indigenous Peoples of the British Dominions and the First World War*, Cambridge: Cambridge University Press.

Wolfe, Patrick (1999), *Settler Colonialism and the Transformation of Anthropology The Politics and Poetics of an Ethnographic Event*, New York and London: Cassell.

Wolfe, Patrick (2001), "Land, Labor, and Difference: Elementary Structures of Race," *American Historical Review*, 106 (3).

Wolfe, Patrick (2002), "Race and Racialisation: Some Thoughts," *Postcolonial Studies*, 5 (1).

Wolfe, Patrick (2006), "Settler Colonialism and the Elimination of the Native," *Journal of Genocide Research*, 8 (4): 387–409.

Woollacott, Angela (2008), "Gender and Sexuality," in Deryck M. Schreuder and Stuart Ward (eds), *Australia's Empire: The OHBE Companion Series*, 312–36: Oxford: Oxford University Press.

Worden, Nigel (1992), "Adjusting to Emancipation: Freed Slaves and Farmers in the Mid-Nineteenth Century South-Western Cape," in Wilmot G. James and Mary

Simons, *Class, Caste and Color: A Social History of the South African Western Cape*, New Brunswick: Transaction Publishers.

Wright, Ashley (2013), *Opium and Empire in Southeast Asia: Regulating Consumption in British Burma*, London: Palgrave Macmillan.

Yee, Jennifer (2001), "'L'Indochine androgyne': Androgyny in turn-of-the-century French writing on Indochina," *Textual Practice*, 15 (2): 269–82.

Yee, Shirley (1992), *Black Women Abolitionists: A Study in Activism, 1828–1860*, Knoxville: University of Tennessee Press.

Zeleza, Paul Tiyambe and Cassandra Rachel Veney, eds (2003), *Leisure in Urban Africa*, Trenton, NJ: Africa World Press.

Zimmerer, Jürgen (2002), *Deutsche Herrschaft über Afrikaner. Staatlicher Machtanspruch und Wirklichkeit im kolonialen Namibia*. Hamburg: Lit Verlag.

Zimmerman, Andrew (2003), "Adventures in the Skin Trade: German Anthropology and Colonial Corporeality," in H. Glenn Penny and Matti Bunzl (eds), *Worldly Provincialism: German Anthropology in the Age of Empire*, 156–78, Ann Arbor: University of Michigan Press.

Zimmerman, Andrew (2010), *Alabama in Africa: Booker T Washington, the German Empire and the Globalization of the New South*, Princeton: Princeton University Press.

Zola, Emile (2008 [1883[), *The Ladies' Paradise*, Oxford: Oxford University Press.

NOTES ON CONTRIBUTORS

Robert Aldrich is Professor of European History at the University of Sydney. Among his recent publications are *Vestiges of the Colonial Empire in France: Monuments, Museums and Colonial Memories* (2005; updated French edition, 2011), *Cultural Encounters and Homoeroticism in Sri Lanka: Sex and Serendipity* (2014), and *Banished Potentates: Dethroning and Exiling Indigenous Monarchs under British and French Colonial Rule, 1815–1955* (2018). He is the editor, with Kirsten McKenzie, of *The Routledge History of Western Empires* (2014), and with Cindy McCreery, of *Crowns and Colonies: European Monarchies and Overseas Empires* (2016), and *Royals on Tour: Politics, Pageantry and Colonialism* (2018).

Utathya Chattopadhyaya is a doctoral candidate at the Department of History at the University of Illinois, Urbana-Champaign. He is the author of "Talking History: E.P. Thompson, C.L.R. James and the Afterlives of Internationalism," *Historical Reflections/Reflexions Historiques* 2015, and a contributor to the forthcoming *Animalia: An Anti-Imperial Bestiary for Our Times* eds Antoinette Burton and Renisa Mawani. In 2017, he was awarded the Thomas and Barbara Metcalf Junior Research Fellowship in Indian History by the American Institute of Indian Studies for his dissertation on intoxication and imperialism in colonial India and the Indian Ocean.

Esme Cleall is a lecturer in the History of the British Empire at the University of Sheffield, UK. Her first book was *Missionary Discourses of Difference: Negotiating Otherness in the British Empire, c. 1840–1900* which was published with Palgrave Macmilllan in 2012. She is now working on the history of disability on which she has published several articles and is working on a monograph.

Matthew P. Fitzpatrick is an Associate Professor in International History at Flinders University, Adelaide. He is the author of *Purging the Empire: Mass Expulsions in Germany, 1871–1914* (2015) and *Liberal Imperialism in Germany: Expansionism and Nationalism, 1848–1884* (2008). He was the 2014 winner of the Chester Penn Higby Prize and has been a Humboldt fellow at the Westphalian Wilhelms University in Münster, Germany.

Susan Kingsley Kent is Arts and Sciences Professor of Distinction in the Department of History at the University of Colorado, Boulder. She is the author of a number of books, including *Sex and Suffrage in Britain, 1860–1914*; *Making Peace: The Reconstruction of Gender in Interwar Britain*; *Gender and Power in Britain, 1640–1990*; *Aftershocks: Politics and Trauma in Britain, 1918–1931*; *Africans and Britons in the Age of Empire* (with Myles Osborne); *A New History of Britain since 1688: Four Nations and an Empire*; and *The Global 1930s* (with Marc Matera). She is currently writing a book entitled *Horse Power: Equines and Empires in Native North America since 1493*.

Kirsten McKenzie is Professor of History at the Department of History, University of Sydney, Australia. She is the author of *Scandal in the Colonies: Sydney and Cape Town 1820–1850* (2004), *A Swindler's Progress: Nobles and Convicts in the Age of Liberty* (2009), and *Imperial Underworld: An Escaped Convict and the Transformation of the British Colonial Order* (2016). Her current work on imperial commissions of inquiry is funded by the collaborative Australian Research Council project, "Inquiring into empire: remaking the British world after 1815."

Ruth A. Morgan is a Senior Research Fellow in the School of Philosophical, Historical and International Studies at Monash University. She has published widely on the climate and water histories of Australia and the British Empire, including her award-winning book, *Running Out? Water in Western Australia* (2015). She has also co-edited volumes of *Studies in Western Australian History* (2013); *History of Meteorology* (2015); *Rachel Carson Center Perspectives* (2017); and *International Review of Environmental History* (2018). Her current book project, on water scarcity in the British Indian Ocean world, has been generously supported by the Australian Research Council and the Alexander von Humboldt Foundation.

Jennifer E. Sessions is Associate Professor of History at the University of Iowa. She is the author of *By Sword and Plow: France and the Conquest of Algeria* (2011), which received the 2012 Mary Alice and Philip Boucher Prize from the French Colonial Historical Society. She is currently at work on a book about an uprising in the Algerian colonial village of Margueritte in 1901 and the public debate about French settler colonialism that it sparked.

Miranda Spieler is Associate Professor of History at the American University of Paris. She is the author of *Empire and Underworld: Captivity in French Guiana* (2012), winner of the George H. Mosse Prize and the J. Russell Major Prize from the American Historical Association. Her work explores the mobility of law in European empires and the relationship between law and imperial violence. Articles and book chapters include "The Vanishing Slaves of Paris," "Slave Flight, Slave Torture, and the State," "Abolition and Reenslavement in the Caribbean," and "The Structure of Colonial Rule During the French Revolution French Guiana."

INDEX

Aborigines (Aust.) 22, 122, 142, 145, 186, 191, 193
acclimatization 73–4, 78–9
advertizing 7, 47, 55, 57, 60, 61, 62–3, 64, 65
Afghanistan 8, 23
Afrikaners 31–2, 92
al-Qadir, Abd 151–3, 170–1
Alaska 81
alcohol 44, 47, 49, 50, 58, 62, 64, 92, 96, 99, 102
Alec-Tweedie, Mrs. 38
Algeria 8, 54, 79, 80, 120, 121, 122, 125, 136, 151, 169–71, 173
Amaru, Túpac 159
Annam 23
architecture 1, 17, 52, 54–5, 62
archives 6, 12, 15, 16, 72, 89
Armenians 52
art 1–2, 6, 11, 17, 51, 65–6
Arya Samaj 95, 96
Assam 43, 186
Australia 37, 63, 70, 80–1, 84, 91–2, 104, 111, 116, 122–3, 148, 186, 187, 191, 193; colonization 4, 6, 22, 49, 118, 121, 169
Austro-Hungian empire 5, 72

Baartman, Sara
Baden-Powell, Robert 33
Bangladesh 84

Banks, Joseph 6–7, 78
Barbados 168
Bartlett, John 139
Batavia 54, 75
Belgian empire 4, 23, 148
Benin 23
Bentham, Jeremy 121
Berer 22
Bhumihars 26
bicycles 44, 47, 103
"blackbirding" 184, 186
Blumenbach, Johann 178
Bólivar, Simón 159, 163
Bombay 53, 69, 72, 78
Bonnal, Henri 30
Bosch, Willem 75
bourgeois culture 43–4, 47, 56, 59, 60, 99
Boy Scouts 33, 102
Brazil 6, 116, 157, 167, 186, 192
Britain 3, 14, 21, 30, 92, 145, 148; empire 3, 18, 21, 22, 23, 49, 75, 77, 90, 93, 98, 116, 118, 122, 128–9, 132, 136, 149–50, 154, 162, 195
British Columbia 22, 99
British Guiana 93, 118
Buchan, John 44
bureaucracy 6, 15, 101, 115
Burma 22, 76, 118
Butler, Josephine 147–8

Calcutta 69, 78
Callwell, Charles 27–8
Canada 3, 22, 84, 92, 111, 148, 168, 169, 195
Cape Colony 76, 134, 139, 144, 186
Cape Town 54, 78
capitalism 5, 9–10, 47, 50–1, 87, 102, 184
Caribbean islands 3, 4, 14, 18, 72, 74, 93, 141, 155–6
cars 44, 47, 60
Central African Republic 23
Ceylon 43, 46, 58, 62
Chad 23
Charles X (Fr.) 170
children 13, 31, 32, 40, 76–7, 142; indigenous 26, 121, 132, 137, 171, 176; mixed-race 122, 125, 141, 144–6, 160, 187, 188–9
Chile 167
China 7, 52, 53, 58, 62, 93; diaspora 52, 91–2, 117–18, 186
chocolate 44, 50, 62
Christianity 9, 49, 50, 61, 131, 136, 140, 164, 194
civilizing mission 8–9, 14, 22, 49, 50, 136, 153
Classicism 21, 23–4, 28–9
climate 67–85; change 79–82; determinism 67–8, 73–4, 75–6, 77, 79, 84; disasters 81–2, 84; measurement 67, 68, 69–72; morality 74, 75
clothing 1, 21, 22, 43, 49, 50, 56, 58–9, 61, 62, 65–6, 73, 88, 103, 104
coffee 44, 50, 62, 160, 166
Comanche 169
concentration camps 31, 32, 112, 127
Congo 23, 46, 51, 103–4, 123, 127, 193
Cook, James 6, 7, 26
Cook, Thomas 47
coolies 45, 93, 182, 184, 185, 186, 189
cricket 44, 103
Cuba 82, 114, 157, 168

Dadas, Albert 120–1
Dahomey 28–9
dancing 26, 28, 89, 99, 104–5, 106, 171
Darjeeling 43
Darwin, Charles 26
Darwinism 24, 30–1, 178
David Jones 55–7

decolonization 3, 16, 153
deforestation 79–80, 123, 127
Demerara 168
department stores 54–7, 61, 64
Dessalines, Jean-Jacques 165–6
Dillon, John 32
disease 7–8, 23, 24, 35, 52, 73, 74, 76, 79, 84, 90, 94, 95, 112, 115, 126–9, 160, 165, 169; sexual 128–9, 146–7
displacement 6, 110, 121–3, 183
dispossession 2, 4, 90, 151–2, 168, 169, 183, 193
Dom Pedro I (Sp.) 157
Dominican Republic 167
Douglass, Frederick 164

East India Company (British) 4, 9, 26, 50, 51, 69, 80, 156
East India Company (Dutch) 51
East Indies 44, 54, 74, 75, 117, 132, 140, 175, 183
Egypt 20–1, 23
Eiffel, Gustave 54–5
Elkader 151–3
Equiano, Oloudah 164
Eritrea 189, 192
exhibitions 44, 54, 55, 57, 65
exploration 4, 6–7, 114, 133
Eyre, Edward 9, 193

Falkland Islands 17
families 15, 43–4, 58–9, 77, 99, 100, 101, 103, 132, 137–8, 142, 148, 160, 188
Fanon, Frantz 12
Federal Republic of Central America 167
femininity 22, 37, 38–9
feminism 11, 37, 122, 146–9, 50
Ferdinand VII (Sp.) 156
Ferry, Jules 50
Fiji 93, 95, 96–7, 139
Fischer, Eugen 178–80
football 102–4
Forbes, Frederick 28
Ford, Ford Madox 39
Foucault, Michel 10, 12, 110, 129, 132, 182
France 3, 20–1, 30, 112, 145, 148, 156, 161; empire 3, 4, 22–3, 39, 48–9, 50, 75–6, 78–9, 93, 114, 117, 119–20, 132, 136, 140–1, 149, 154, 161, 162–3, 164–6, 170–1, 194–5

Franco-Prussian War 4
French Guiana 119–20
French Revolution 3, 20, 161

Gabon 23
Gandhi, Mohandas 64, 96
Gaugin, Paul 65–6
gender 2, 12, 20, 38–9, 41, 47, 88, 90, 98–9, 131, 132, 136–8, 140, 142, 187
genocide 6, 121–3, 169, 172, 176, 180, 183–4, 190–1
George III (U.K.) 155
Germany 30, 39–40, 145, 148; empire 4, 5, 9–10, 23, 49, 50, 117, 149
Ghana 99
Glasgow 54, 58
Gobineau, Arthur de 178
Gold Coast 22
Gordon, Charles 192
governance (imperial) 22, 23, 87, 88, 112–13, 126–7, 146–7, 181, 193–5
Goyder, George 80–1
gramaphones 60, 64–5, 66
Great War 3, 4–5, 19, 34–41
Grenada 155
Guadaloupe 76
Guinea 23
Gurkhas 27

Hahl, Albert 189
Haiti 3, 114–15, 128, 159–60, 166, 78
Hann, Julius 71–2
Hegel, Georg 177–8
Heihachirō, Tōgō 7
Herder, Johann 177
Herero 185
Hidalgo, Miguel 158
Hobsbawm, Eric 87
Hobson, John 9–10, 47, 50–1
Holtby, Winifred 38
Hong Kong 22, 128
honor 20, 21, 24, 101
humanitarianism 9, 116, 122
Humboldt, Alexander von 70–1, 80
Hume, David 177

identity 1–2, 11, 12, 13, 14, 18, 19–20, 36–7, 88–98; gender 38–9, 98–101; labor 89–101; religion 96–7

imperialism: cultural 11–18; ecological 68, 78; economic 2, 8, 9–10, 47, 48–51, 64, 87; etymology 9; historiography 2, 9–18, 110; morality 50–1, 64–5, 73, 129, 132
India 4, 19, 22, 26–7, 62, 78, 93, 123–4, 132, 137, 139, 143–4, 192; diaspora 52, 76, 77, 93–4, 95, 117, 126; rebellion (1857) 26–7, 111, 124, 143, 189
Indian Corps 34
Indians (Canada) 35
Indochina 19, 23, 50, 76, 127, 133
Ireland 103
Isandlwana 8
Islam 27, 46, 64, 96, 170–1
Italian empire 4, 22–3, 50
Ivory Coast 23

Ja Ja, King (Opopo) 52
Jamaica 9, 14, 35, 43, 168, 193
Janse, Sara 139
Japan 4, 7, 145; empire 22, 23, 30, 50, 92
Java 74
Jefferson, Thomas 168
Jejeebhoy, Jamsetjee 52–3, 60
Jews 52, 92, 170, 194
jingoism 9, 13, 17

Kaingang 192
Kamara, Kande 36
Kanakas 182, 186–7
Kant, Immanuel 176–7
Kenya 23, 35, 62, 127, 169
Kermorgant, Alexandre 76
Khoisan 127, 139
Kiowa 171
Kipling, Rudyard 44, 124
Kirkpatrick, James 139
Kitchener, Herbert 32
Korea 7

labor 2, 5, 15, 87–107, 112, 184–7; bonded 6, 160; class 87, 88; convict 6, 16, 89, 93–4, 117, 125, 185; female 100–1; history 87–8, 90; indentured 6, 65, 89, 92, 93–6, 99–100, 106, 117, 128, 166, 184; indigenous 184, 185–7; *see also* slavery
Lane, William 92–3

Langlois, Hippolyte 24–5
lascars 97–8, 126
Lazarus, Moritz 180
leisure 102–3, 104–5
Leopold II (Belg.) 51
Lesotho 72
Lesseps, Ferdinand de 49
Lind, James 73–4
Lindequist, Friedrich von 188
Lipton, Thomas 62
List, Friedrich 184
literature 6, 11, 44, 109, 129, 133, 143
Livingstone, Thomas 49
Lombroso, Cesare 180
London Missionary Society 138–9
Louis XVI (Fr.) 162
Louverture, Toussaint 164–5

Maasai 122
Macao 82
Macaya 162
MacKenzie, John (historian) 16–17
Mackenzie, John (missionary) 136
Madagascar 6, 23, 72, 76, 137, 139
Madras 69, 70, 78
Maitee, Hari Mohan 148
Malaya 46, 139
Mali 23
Mamluks 21
Manchuria 7
Mandinka 24
Mangin, Charles 30, 39
Manilla 54
Māori 9, 22, 26, 35, 148
marriage 98, 131, 132, 137, 139, 142, 144, 146, 148, 149, 176; interracial 96, 100, 115, 139–40, 188
Marseille 54
Marx, Karl 184
masculinity 92, 103, 133, 140–1, 148; military 20–2, 23–4, 30–1, 33, 36, 39, 41
mass media 9, 60, 88
Maurice, Frederick 33
Mauritania 23
Mauritius 43, 62, 77, 78, 93, 95, 96, 100, 102, 118
medicine 7–8, 23, 52, 58, 73, 77–8, 79, 126–9

Melbourne 54, 121
mental illness 10, 36, 39, 120–1
Meskawaki 151–2
Messines 34
métis 13, 144
Mexico 72, 82, 158, 166–7
Michelin 47
migration 5–6, 91, 96, 121, 168–9
Mill, James 131–2
miscegenation 92, 145–6, 178, 180, 187, 188
missionaries 8, 51, 61, 72, 76, 81, 99, 104, 136–9, 171, 186, 188
mobility 15–16, 39, 46, 73, 79, 88, 106, 109–30; labor 89, 90, 91, 93, 98
Morant Bay rebellion 9, 193
Morel, E.D. 40–1
Morocco 170, 171
Mueller, Ferdinand von 80
Mueller, Hermann 40

Namibia 122
Napoleon I (Fr.) 165, 167
Napoleon III (Fr.) 49, 119
Napoleonic Wars 3, 20–2, 156
Natal 22, 43, 72, 93, 95–6, 100–1, 106
nationalism 4, 7, 36, 92, 151, 168, 180; post-colonial 46, 65, 97, 98, 99, 103, 124, 126, 148, 153
Nauru 48
Nelson, Horatio 21
Netherlands 74–5; empire 4, 13, 49, 74, 132
New Caledonia 48, 119–20, 123
New Guinea 186, 189
New Hebrides 48
"new imperialism" 4–5, 8, 22, 30, 66
New Zealand 8, 22, 26, 37, 49, 76, 81, 116, 137, 148, 188–9, 195
New Zealand Wars 9, 182
Nigeria 22, 23

Ogé, Vincent 161
opium 44, 47, 52, 58, 62
Opium Wars 7, 58
Orientalism 11–12, 46, 78, 133, 143
Ottoman empire 5, 169–70
Oudh 22

Papua 139
Paraquay 92
Penang 94, 118, 128
Peru 155, 159
Philippines 72, 79, 82, 191
Phnon Phen 55
photography 9, 60–1
pianos 60
Picon, Gaëtan 64
Pitt, William 24
Ploetz, Alfred 180–1
Polverel, Étienne 163
Polynesia 133, 134–6, 137
Portuguese empire 3, 4, 120, 132, 136, 154, 157
Prince, Mary 164
prostitution 44, 47, 65, 112, 128, 131, 140, 146, 148, 188
Puerto Rico 157
Punjab 22

Quakers 90, 163–4
quarantine 112, 127, 128, 129
Queensland 43, 181, 183, 186–7, 191
quinine 23, 127

race 4, 22, 58, 88, 90, 157, 175–96; biological 9, 115, 121–2, 127, 177, 178–80, 181, 194, 195; defining 176–7, 180–4, 196; degeneracy 8, 33, 145, 178, 180; gendered 22, 133, 134–6, 187; infantilization 22, 41; "martial" 8, 24–30, 36, 41; morality 98–9; segregation 75–6, 91, 95–6, 99, 127, 128, 140, 143, 160–1, 187; supremacy 35, 178
racism 11, 40, 61, 91–2, 98, 99, 115, 139–40, 160–1, 177–8, 182, 184, 195
railways 7, 23, 66, 101, 103–4, 109, 111, 123–6, 127
Raimond, Julien 161
Rajputs 26
Ratzel, Friedrich 121–2
Réunion Island 76, 118
Read, James 139
religion 88, 90, 96–7, 102, 154; indigenous 160, 162, 171
resistance 7, 8, 9, 13, 19, 68, 79, 143, 151–73; armed 151, 153, 154; indigenous 169, 171–2; labor 87, 91–2, 95, 98, 105, 106, 153, 159, 160
Rhodesia 23, 104–5, 143
Rosebery, Lord 30
Royal Navy (U.K.) 21–2, 111, 116
Royal Society (U.K.) 71
rubber 5, 44, 46–7, 127, 193
Russia 4, 194
Russo-Japanese War 7

Said, Edward 11–12, 13
Saigon 54, 76, 82
Saint-Domingue 78, 114, 115, 156, 159, 160–2, 164–6, 173
Saint Helena 69, 80
Saint-Simonians 49
Samoa 176, 186, 188, 189
San 110, 185
sati 132, 149
Sauk 151–2
savagery 7, 22, 24, 27–9, 30, 36, 39, 40–1, 123, 134
Schmelen, Johann 139
Schoelcher, Victor 166
Schomburgk, Robert 77
Scotland 24
Senegal 23, 123
settler colonialism 5–6, 111, 153, 168–9, 173, 183–4, 191
Seven Years War 24
sewing machines 58–9, 64–5
sex/sexuality 10, 13, 131–50, 128–9, 131, 134–6; female 99, 133–4; indigenous 28, 131, 132, 133, 136–7, 187; interracial 131, 132, 138–40, 141–2, 149–50, 187–9; same-sex 131, 133, 146
Sierra Leone 22, 74, 111, 116, 117
Sikhs 26, 27
Sind 22
Singapore 65, 69, 94, 118, 128
Singer, Isaac 58–9
Singh, Rajinder 60
Sioux 169
slave trade 6, 24, 65, 93, 110–12, 114–15, 116, 164
slavery 6, 49, 77, 89, 90, 99, 110–11, 115, 141–2, 160, 184; abolition 9, 17–18, 90, 111, 142, 162–4, 166–7
Smith, Adam 49

soap 43, 54, 61, 123
soldiers: American 21; British 21–2, 32, 34, 74, 76, 142, 146, 156, 193; Canadian 34; citizen 20–2, 33; female 28–9, 38; French 21, 34, 64, 120; German 34; masculinity 23–4, 33, 36, 39, 41; non-European 8, 19, 21, 24–30, 34–6, 39–41, 123, 162, 189, 192–3; patrician 21, 26; Senegalese 24, 35, 36, 40, 41, 117; settler 31–2, 34–7; volunteer 21–2, 34–5
Solf, Wilhelm 175–6
Solomon Islands 139
Somaliland 23
Somerville, Mary 38
Sonthonax, Léger 163
South Africa 22, 31, 92, 96, 111, 127, 169
South African (Boer) War 9–10, 31–2, 92
South Australia 148
Southwest Africa 169, 180, 183, 185, 188, 189
Soyza, Susew de 58, 59–60
Spanish empire 3, 4, 74, 115, 132, 154, 155, 156–7, 162–3, 191
Spivak, Gayatri 12, 13
statistics 67, 70–1
steam 5, 66, 84, 109, 111, 112, 129, 130; ships 5, 7, 23, 46, 47, 123, 126, 127
Sudan 23
Suez Canal 5, 46, 49–50
sugar 4, 43, 58, 62, 93, 114, 160, 164
Sumatra 46
Switzerland 148

Tanganyika 140, 169
Tasmania 182, 191
tea 43, 44, 57, 61–3, 156
technologies of power 10, 12, 89
technology 2, 10, 23, 46, 49, 58, 65
telegraph 5, 23, 49, 69, 123
Tenasserim 94
Thompson, E.P. 88
time 88–9, 101–6, 109; morality 102
tobacco 44, 49, 58, 62, 101
Tocqueville, Alexis de 122
Togoland 35
Tokyo 82
Tonkin 23
Toucouleurs 24
tourism 6–7, 60, 61, 126

trade 6, 7, 43–66, 176; class 43–4, 48, 50, 52; free 7, 87; intercolonial 45–6, 47, 49, 62–4
transport 5, 23, 46, 52, 54, 65
Transvaal 22, 92
travelers 6, 46, 47, 60
Truth, Sojourner 164
Tunisia 23, 76

Uganda 23, 127
un-Nissa, Khair 139
United States 3, 4, 30, 92, 167, 168; empire 9–10, 22–3, 30, 49, 93, 159, 168, 175, 183, 191; independence 20, 82, 114, 152, 155, 156
Uruguay 157, 167

Van de Kemp, Johannes 139
Venezuela 79–80, 157–8, 159, 166
Verne, Jules 109
Victoria, Queen (U.K.) 22, 56
Vietnam 23, 47, 63, 84
violence 1, 101, 141, 142, 153, 170; frontier 4, 183, 191, 193; racial 99, 121, 122; sexual 40–1, 99–100, 102, 140, 141, 142–4, 146, 150, 189
Voltaire 177
Vuitton, Louis 61

war 19–41; class 20, 37; climate 82; prisoners 31–2; racial 190–3; women 31–2, 37–8, 40–1
weaponry 7, 9, 23
Western Australia 191
whales/whaling 43, 48, 62
whiteness 90–93, 112
Wimmer, Michael 139
women 75–6, 93, 99, 128, 131–2, 136, 137–8, 145, 156, 164; European 139, 140, 142–3, 148; non-European 139, 142, 145, 148–9, 171; slave 141–2, 160

Xokleng 192

Ypres 34, 36
Yukon 81

Zola, Emile 55
Zulu 8, 72, 105–6